Rethinking the Cuban Revolution Nationally and Regionally: Politics, Culture and Identity

The *Bulletin of Latin American Research* Book Series

The *Bulletin of Latin American Research* publishes original research of current interest on Latin America, the Caribbean, inter-American relations and the Latin American Diaspora from all academic disciplines within the social sciences, history and cultural studies. The BLAR/SLAS book series was launched in 2008 with the aim of publishing research monographs and edited collections that compliment the wide scope of the Bulletin itself. It is published and distributed in association with Wiley-Blackwell. We aim to make the series the home of some of the most exciting, innovatory work currently being undertaken on Latin America and we welcome outlines or manuscripts of interdisciplinary, single-authored, jointly-authored or edited volumes. If you would like to discuss a possible submission to the series, please contact the editors at blar@liverpool.ac.uk

Rethinking the Cuban Revolution Nationally and Regionally: Politics, Culture and Identity

EDITED BY
PAR KUMARASWAMI

This edition first published 2012
Editorial Organisation © 2012 Society for Latin American Studies, text © 2012 The Authors

Blackwell Publishing was acquired by John Wiley & Sons in February 2007. Blackwell's publishing program has been merged with Wiley's global Scientific, Technical and Medical business to form Wiley-Blackwell.

Registered Office
John Wiley & Sons Ltd, The Atrium, Southern Gate, Chichester, West Sussex, PO19 8SQ, United Kingdom

Editorial Offices
350 Main Street, Malden, MA 02148-5020, USA
9600 Garsington Road, Oxford, OX4 2DQ, UK
The Atrium, Southern Gate, Chichester, West Sussex, PO19 8SQ, UK

For details of our global editorial offices, for customer services, and for information about how to apply for permission to reuse the copyright material in this book please see our website at www.wiley.com/wiley-blackwell.

The right of Par Kumaraswami to be identified as the author of the editorial material in this work has been asserted in accordance with the UK Copyright, Designs and Patents Act 1988.

Wiley also publishes its books in a variety of electronic formats. Some content that appears in print may not be available in electronic books.

Designations used by companies to distinguish their products are often claimed as trademarks. All brand names and product names used in this book are trade names, service marks, trademarks or registered trademarks of their respective owners. The publisher is not associated with any product or vendor mentioned in this book. This publication is designed to provide accurate and authoritative information in regard to the subject matter covered. It is sold on the understanding that the publisher is not engaged in rendering professional services. If professional advice or other expert assistance is required, the services of a competent professional should be sought.

Library of Congress Cataloging-in-Publication Data
Rethinking the Cuban Revolution nationally and regionally : politics, culture and identity / edited by Par Kumaraswami.
     p. cm. – (The bulletin of Latin American research book series)
  Includes bibliographical references.
  ISBN 978-1-4443-6154-4 (pbk.)
1. Cuba – History – Revolution, 1959 – Influence. 2. Cuba – History – Revolution, 1959 – Social aspects. 3. Cuba – Politics and government – 1959–1990. 4. Cuba – Politics and government – 1990-
5. Cuba – Social conditions – 1959- 6. Cuba – Foreign relations. 7. Political culture – Cuba. I. Kumaraswami, Par.
  F1788.R424 2012
  972.9106'4 – dc23

              2011045539

A catalogue record for this book is available from the British Library.

This book is published in the following electronic formats: Wiley Online Library 978-1-4443-6154-4

Set in 10 on 13pt and Palatino
by Laserwords Private Limited, Chennai, India
Printed and bound in the United Kingdom by Page Brothers, Norwich

Contents

Introduction: Towards an Integrated Understanding of the Cuban Revolution

PAR KUMARASWAMI

University of Manchester, UK

The 50th anniversary of the Cuban Revolution proved to be not only a time for celebration or regret, but, more significantly, for reflection, reassessment and reform. Indications of continued political and socio-economic change in the context of a new relationship with the new US administration, and the strengthening of the 'pink tide' in Latin America, all emphasised the fact that the Revolution was at a crucial stage in its trajectory.

As many scholars of Cuba – both on and off the island – recognise, the unexpected survival of the Revolution cannot be attributed solely to political or economic factors; the vision or pragmatism of the political leadership (or, even, of an individual leader) and the success of economic policies, although these are certainly central elements in the overall picture, only go some way to explaining how the Revolution has survived through adaptation, debate and reinvention. Intrinsic to these processes over 50 years has been the constantly changing articulation of values and identity through social, political, cultural and economic life, and at individual and collective levels. Indeed, one of the unique aspects of the Revolution, at least for its first 30 years, was the way in which individual and personal visions of the Revolution could be incorporated effectively into national or public versions of *cubanidad*, or that national narratives of *cubanía revolucionaria* could be personalised meaningfully at an individual level. Vital to these mechanisms of integration and unification were factors such as mass social and political participation and cultural expression.

Indeed, as many of the contributors to this book have observed, policy and practice in revolutionary Cuba has long been a blend of pragmatism and idealism, initially harnessing the power of mobilisation, inventiveness and subjective commitment – in many areas of socio-cultural, political and economic activity life – when objective conditions were particularly unfavourable; and, from the 1970s onwards, creating an institutional framework in which the aim – if not always the reality – was an integrated approach to policy and practice through the creation of multi-dimensional organisational structures to facilitate the development of coherent solutions. The term 'integral' was even formalised in revolutionary discourse, and applied to development models incorporating health, education, housing and social policy.

The economic crisis of 1990 and the subsequent Special Period, however, gravely threatened to undermine this national unity, by creating economic, social and cultural divisions against the backdrop of weakened state structures. Although the Revolution survived this period, many consider that it did so at great cost to the core values and policies that had been developed over the preceding 30 years. With significant emigration, a growing crisis of faith in the revolutionary project, family and social fragmentation and increasing reliance on remittances from abroad, the question of how the integrity of the nation itself should be defined became increasingly present in debates of the early 1990s. The notion of a Cuban *diaspora*, for long the centre of many Cuban Americans' visions of the nation, was recognised through controversial but vital dialogues and encounters between Cubans living on and off the island. And, in the twenty-first century, the impact of new technologies in creating new transnational communities invited us to consider the relevance of a territorial understanding of nation.

Indeed, some of the key questions that Cuban scholars are asking include: at what cost did the Revolution survive? How have the pragmatic responses of the 1990s and 2000s irreversibly affected the ideological and social coherence that had existed until 1989? To what extent is a national project of revolution relevant to the twenty-first century? How precisely have individual and collective values and identities been transformed by constant reinvention? What effect has the economic liberalisation of the early 1990s had for Cuba's self-image and national identity?

This book therefore brings together an multi-disciplinary range of contributions to the topic of culture, politics and identity in revolutionary Cuba, underpinned by three organising principles: (i) to offer new perspectives on the complex and changing landscape over 50 years, thus rethinking both the continuities as well as the ruptures caused by the Special Period; (ii) additionally, and with the benefit of hindsight, to reassess in close detail the first 30 years of revolutionary change, thus re-evaluating the foundations which were subsequently affected by the crisis; (iii) to understand and reassess Cuba in the context of wider geopolitical, ideological and cultural regional contexts, whether they be pan-Latin American or Caribbean, and across real or imagined boundaries.

Across the contributions, attention is paid to new ways of examining questions of cultural and political identity, using theoretical frameworks and methodologies that can shed light on hitherto neglected areas of understanding, and reveal new directions in Cuban Studies. Most importantly, each of the chapters underlines the need for theoretical approaches to Cuba to be grounded in empirical methods and an understanding of the historical trajectory of the Revolution, as both rupture and continuity. Artaraz and Kirk examine Cuba's internationalist work in education and health, two areas which receive significant media and academic attention but which are often presented in overly simplistic – and idealistic – terms which lack a more profound understanding of the types of capital or prestige that are at play: Artaraz explores the recent revitalisation of Cuba's educational models for literacy through the Alianza Bolivariana para los Pueblos de Nuestra América (ALBA) network and the complex and dynamic mixture of motivations and objectives that lies behind Cuba's internal and external vision for education; and Kirk investigates the impact and implications of efficiency measures introduced under the leadership of Raúl Castro for Cuba's medical internationalism programmes. Ludlam deals with the always-controversial question of human rights in Cuba, and, along with a historical overview of this vexed and problematic question, offers a perspective which underlines how the question is always a relational and dynamic one. Other contributors take a more historical path: Kapcia assumes the unenviable task of assessing and defining Cuba's present political moment through an examination of the Revolution's continuities and ruptures over fifty years, whilst others focus on specific identity groups and discourses: Antón Carrillo traces a history of the relationship between constructions of ideas of race and nation in the Cuban press over the same period, whilst Luke traces the under-researched area of youth as a social category, and the risks of creating extreme and polarised expectations of this social group which exclude the majority of young people in contemporary Cuba. Finally, the question of cultural production is also approached through two very different perspectives: Casamayor-Cisneros undertakes the detailed textual analysis of the novels of three of Cuba's 'new' literary talents and argues for their grouping as postmodernist novels which reflect the void – rather than crisis – of values for young writers and intellectuals in twenty-first-century Cuba; whilst Kumaraswami questions the textual and contextual assumptions, and reveals some of the difficulties, that have accompanied the formation of canons of Cuban literature.

Given the broad-ranging and multi-disciplinary shape of this collection, the decision not to order the chapters (other than alphabetically) is an intentional one – based on a method that seeks to integrate rather than divide – to encourage the possibility of new connections between areas of Cuban life through new and productive contradictions and tensions. Indeed, this spirit reflects that of the many years of intellectual dialogue between scholars gathered under the auspices of the Cuba Research Forum (University of Nottingham/Universidad de La Habana), and, specifically, at its two international conferences celebrated in July and September of 2009. By thus combining the respective specialisms and disciplines of experienced Cubanists with newer scholars, both in Cuba and internationally, it constitutes an innovative contribution to contemporary debates about the Revolution in both national and regional contexts.

2

Ideas of Race, Ethnicity and National Identity in the Discourse of the Press During The Cuban Revolution

ELVIRA ANTÓN CARRILLO

University of Roehampton, UK

During the first half of the twentieth century, the discourse of the most influential newspapers, such as *Diario de la Marina*, affirmed that the racial problem did not exist in Cuba. Ever since the beginning of the Republic, José Martí's proposition of 'Cuban, more than black, more than white' was socially accepted, as was the 'racial brotherhood' founded during the wars of independence (1868–1878 and 1895–1898), and the equality proclaimed in the 1902 Constitution. Thus, in the understanding of the elites, the question had been resolved. Nevertheless, discrimination still existed at the beginning of 1959. Forty years later, Fidel Castro admitted that racial discrimination had still not been fully eradicated:

> We believed at the beginning that when we established the fullest equality before the law and complete intolerance for any demonstration of sexual discrimination in the case of women, or racial discrimination in the case of ethnic minorities, these phenomena would vanish from our society. It was some time before we discovered that marginality and racial discrimination with it are not something that one gets rid of with a law or even with ten laws, and we have not managed to eliminate them completely, even in 40 years. (Castro, 2000).

Following Appelbaum, Macpherson and Rosemblat's idea (2003: 2), that in post-independence Latin America, 'national identities have been constructed in racial terms and that definitions of race have been shaped by the process of nation building', this chapter presents an analysis of the discourse of the Cuban elites[1] on race and otherness, or what Wade (2000) calls the process

---

1   I am referring here to the elites that van Dijk (1993) called symbolic elites, whose power lies in the control of knowledge, beliefs and social discourses, which is to say, ideological power.

of racialisation. It deals with discourse in the press and, more specifically, in opinion articles from certain key periods in the Cuban Revolution, as well as the idea of national identity these articles espoused.

The analysis of some discursive strategies, constitutive of the genre of opinion pieces – specifically the argumentation and strategies of mitigation and emphasis, both lexical as well as semantic, in the polarisation of groups of 'us' vs. 'them' – unveils how newspapers justified and legitimised the idea of national identity they supported. At the same time, this chapter explores the uses made of the terms 'race' and 'ethnicity', considering not only the way in which they constitute groups, but also, and more especially, the political interests with which they are constituted (Fenton and May, 2002:3).

To this end, different media and periods are examined here. First of all, for 1959, the first year of the Revolution, the conservative and Catholic *Diario de la Marina*,[2] as well as *Revolución*,[3] the official mouthpiece of the 26th of July Movement are examined. For the other periods, the analysis focuses on articles from the newspaper *Granma*,[4] the official organ of the Committee of the Cuban Communist Party. These further periods are: 1975–1976, when the system was already consolidated and the Constitution of 1976 passed; and the end of the twentieth century. The final part investigates the terms 'race' and 'ethnic group', as well as the idea of nation and political goals with this end, as used in certain academic publications, given the almost absolute silence on this issue in newspapers.

The analysis begins with the theoretical assumption that the concepts of race, ethnicity and nation are not stable categories, and have no fixed definitions, but are instead socially shared concepts whose meanings are interwoven and can often be interchangeable. In fact, their definitions have gradually transmuted over time and with various different social and historical processes.

Through their definitions of national identity, the Cuban elites during the twentieth century sought, by means of different political and cultural options, a homogenising formula that would impose itself over the social and cultural heterogeneity of Cuban society, and that would be understood as a necessary condition for the realisation of the nation. In other words, a way to assimilate the black population within an idea of nation as defended by the

---

2   Published in Havana from 1832 until 12 May 1960, and continuing in exile in Miami from 31 December 1960 until 6 May 1961. It is the oldest newspaper published in Cuba and with the largest circulation.

3   Published in Havana from 1959 to 1965 when it disappeared as such to form part of Granma.

4   Published in Havana. Created in 1965 from the merger of *Revolución* and *Noticias de Hoy*.

elites, and which initially, in the nineteenth century and part of the twentieth, was defined as white and Latin, and later, from the 1930s onwards, as *mestiza*. To achieve this goal, their recommendation was whitening, a physical assimilation: on one hand, through a significant bias towards white and especially Spanish immigration, as well as a ban on the immigration of persons of African origin; on the other hand, a cultural whitening or assimilation, fundamentally by means of education and the rejection of certain customs. The theories and beliefs on race at that time were used as arguments to legitimise these proposals. From the 1920s, the definition of national identity as *mestiza* began to be created, yet always in an endeavour to find a homogenising form that would accept part of African culture, though softened and whitened, as national, always mixed with the Hispanic culture and on the terms dictated by the latter. The concept of race was no longer used as an argument, giving way to that of culture, which similarly evaluated and imposed a hierarchy on the cultures of the different groups, and maintained group differentiation and the domination of one of the groups – as demonstrated in studies carried out from different disciplines: art, Moore (1997); history, De la Fuente (2001); literature, Duno Gottberg (2003), Leclerq (2004), Arnedo-Gómez (2006); press, Antón-Carrillo (2006).

The identitarian discourse of the elites in other Latin American republics was very similar to that of Cuba during the second half of the nineteenth century and the early years of the twentieth century. The intention of whitening society through immigration from the Iberian Peninsula was common, albeit in different degrees, to many Latin American countries such as Brazil, Venezuela, Argentina and Colombia. However, from the 1920s onwards, in countries such as Mexico and Peru, a greater importance was lent to the ideology of *indigenismo*, the glorification of the Indian ancestry of the nation while, in many cases, at the same time positing the ideology of *mestizaje*, even though both were intended to modernise, integrate and educate the indigenous population for citizenship (Graham, 1997; Wade, 1997; de la Cadena, 2000; Appelbaum et al., 2003). After the Second World War, the use of the term 'race' was gradually abandoned, though the same cannot be said for racial thinking, and the term 'ethnicity' was viewed as more acceptable. Many Latin American countries tended to use the terms 'ethnicity' or 'ethnic relations' for the study of Indians and 'racism', and 'race relations' for the study of blacks. However, as Wade (1997) argues, the difference is not so clear and both have aspects of ethnic and racial categorisations.

1959: Racism Discredited

In Cuba in 1959, discrimination continued to exist. Some sectors of the work force, such as banks and offices, remained closed off to the black population, who were also denied admission to luxury hotels, beaches and restaurants, and there was even segregation in parks, and so on. The Constitution of 1940, which banned discrimination, had not achieved its aims.

While the issues of race and discrimination were not central to the political programme of the 26 July Movement, Fidel Castro, urged all Cubans to elim- inate discrimination in a 'new homeland' but did not put forward any law to eliminate discrimination. Instead he proposed to achieve this aim via a public campaign (Castro, 1959) in this way accepting, as de la Fuente (2001) argues, the traditional division between public and private life. Castro declared that discrimination was anti-Cuban and counter-revolutionary, claiming that Revolution and racism were incompatible. Racism was a national disgrace that ought to be eliminated. However, he laid the bulk of the emphasis on employment, an area that could be legislated. On the other hand, programmes were implemented to make up for the dearth of legislation with regards to discrimination on various fronts: educating the people, a policy of gradual integration in public and recreational establishments, and the organisation of programmes to create opportunities for the poorer segments of the popula- tion, among which a large part of the black population was to be found (de la Fuente, 2001).

During this year of 1959, the issue of race was not raised in editorials in *Diario de la Marina*, nor in *Revolución*, and there are only two opinion articles in *Diario de la Marina* and three from *Revolución* in which it was raised. In point of fact, the scant coverage lent to the issue is constant in opinion articles and leaders in the mainstream press throughout the whole of the twentieth century, with the exception of the months of the so-called 'Guerrita del 12' (Antón Carrillo, 2006).

In the articles in *Revolución*, the term 'race' is used with the meaning of 'nation': 'que haya una sola raza: la cubana, de hermanos, sin reservas ni complejos' ('that there should be one single race: the Cuban race, of brothers, without provisos or complexes') (Fernández López, 1959). This in fact is a common use, especially during the first 30 years of the century, and reveals the semantic proximity between the two terms, while at once legitimising, from a biological perspective, this type of social organisation, presenting it as 'natural'. At the same time in the discourse of these articles, however, the term is used with the meaning of a set of ideas that serves to justify the domination of one group over another and to justify the creation and maintenance of social classes in the case of capitalism, as well as of colonialism and imperialism, in this way bringing the meaning of the term 'race' closer to that of 'class'. Race is, in the discourse of Despestre (the author of the article), a mystification, which is to say, a fake invented for those goals (Despestre, 1959). In the same article he defines racism as the 'expresión de la dominación económica de las capas dirigentes de Occidente sobre los pueblos negros' (expression of the economic domination of Western ruling classes over black peoples) (Despestre, 1959), an expression that, he says, can don various guises: 'unas veces agresivas, otras insidiosas, sutiles, paternalistas otras veces' (sometime aggressive, other time insidious, subtle, and yet other times paternalistic) (Despestre, 1959).

Though the strategy of polarisation via the groups 'us' vs. 'them' is not predominant, the discourse of these articles from *Revolución* speaks from the point of view of an 'us' that clearly defines itself as anti-racist, and that advocates measures aimed at doing away with prejudice and discrimination. Nonetheless, the articles did not consider it necessary to promulgate laws that would punish the agent of racism, or that would regulate racial integration, because, 'en un régimen como el nuestro no se transforman por decreto, sino mediante la educación y el empleo adecuados, la permanente sugerencia, el suave acontecer que no irrite ni compulse, sino que predisponga y convenza' (in a regime like ours, one does not transform by decree, but through appropriate education and employment, permanent suggestion, a non-aggressive intervention that neither irritates nor coerces, but rather predisposes and convinces) (Vázquez Candela, 1959). In this discourse, discrimination is considered the consequence of prejudice and this is understood to belong to the territory of the personal or private.

Following more or less the same line is the *Diario de la Marina*, which, in the only two articles it dedicates to the issue of race, restricts itself to considering the concept of discrimination. Indeed, these articles were published after Fidel Castro's decision not to legislate specifically on the racial question and they support and legitimise[5] the position adopted by him: 'El doctor Castro, por tanto, acierta cuando aboga por que los hombres de su patria se miren recíprocamente como hermanos, pero acierta en igual medida cuando se plantea y hace público que ello más que una empresa de la legislación estatal es una obra de la educación y de la cultura' (As such, Doctor Castro is right when he advocates for men of their homeland to look upon each other as brothers, but he is equally right when he considers and declares that, more than the jurisdiction of state legislation, this is a task for education and for culture) (García Pons, 1959). Furthermore, the newspaper believes that it is 'cosa de claridad espiritual, de luz interior que ha de hacerse siempre pecho adentro' (a matter of spiritual clarity, of inner light that must always be carried out internally) (García Pons, 1959), and, from its Catholic ideology, the newspaper even defines discrimination as a sin because it goes against the ways of God (Barbeito, 1959). In fact, the journalists of *Diario de la Marina* believe that discrimination does not exist, nor did it ever exist during the Republic, because of the brotherhood of all Cubans and the equality proclaimed in the Constitution.

---

5 Legitimisation is understood as the search for normative approval for an institutional action.

The leaders of the 26 July Movement had taken on the task of putting an end to discrimination from various angles, and this goal was mirrored in the three articles from *Revolución*: to educate the people in the mechanisms of racism and in its pointlessness, in other words, to legitimise the process by which it was intended to end this discrimination, and to create true national integration without the need to legislate. At the same time, the articles recall and propagate the steps taken by the Revolution, and its successes, in the achievement of said integration. One of the articles shows the functioning of racist ideology to be owing to economic and class domination, and lays bare the stupidity of the behaviour of the agent of racism (Despestre, 1959). The other two articles address the successes of the Revolution in its fight against discrimination. The article titled 'Reforma psicológica' (Psychological Reform) (Vázquez Candela, 1959) explores the change that needed to take place in people's minds so that prejudice and discrimination would disappear, offering as an example one of the Revolution's successes: a black commanding officer had presided over the coronation of a beauty queen – something that happened for the very first time and without causing an outcry. The beauty queen was, as was always the case, still white, but the author does not find this fact worth questioning or that the canon of beauty continued to be that of a white woman. Likewise, the third article, entitled 'Hermano negro' (Black Brother) (Fernández López, 1959) also announced another success: the construction of the new Vidal Park in Santa Clara, in which there was no longer the old division, the 'cantero-jardín' or flowerbed-garden, which maintained separate spaces for the white and black population. It puts the discourse into the mouth of a black child, directly tugging at the heartstrings through the voice of innocence. It shows a nation united by the feeling of brotherhood: 'ser hijos iguales de una Patria que es con todos y para el bien de todos' (to be the equal children of a Homeland that is with everyone and for the good of everyone) (Fernández López, 1959).

The structure of ideological value put forward by *Revolución* lays the emphasis on the values possessed by the group itself (the 'other', then, being previous governments and those who fought against the 26 July Movement), as the promoters of anti-discriminatory and anti-racist measures that will lead towards achieving a nation united in racial brotherhood. The supporters of this Humanist Revolution can attain the meaning of the human and the universal, possess humility as a virtue of the spirit, and maintain justice as the basis for their relationships. Their most important defining social values will be anti-racism and social justice, which differentiate them from the Christian values of brotherhood and charity as defended by the discourse of the articles in the *Diario de la Marina*.

The ultimate aim of the articles of both newspapers is to maintain the unity of the nation, given that the racial separations at its heart could prove to create a risk of social dissolution (in the discourse of *Diario de la Marina*), though still maintaining a certain superiority or hegemony (or the possibility that this can take place) of the white group by means of the lack of legislation in certain areas promoting integration.

1975–1976: Racism Resolved

In 1962 the 'racial' problem, in other words the problem of discrimination, was declared to have been resolved. Many of the campaigns and programmes that the government had organised were beginning to bear fruit, especially in areas such as education and health, eliminating what had been the foundation of institutional discrimination in the Republic (segregation, a high rate of illiteracy, etc. among the population of African origins). Perhaps in the belief that it had already been resolved, the articles on the issue in *Granma* are very few in number and even fewer are those that address the situation specifically in Cuba.

In general, those articles that do exist use the terms 'race', 'national minority', 'national majority', 'racism', 'segregation' and 'discrimination' from the viewpoint of class, basically addressing the phenomenon from a Marxist economic approach, and therefore concluding that, in essence, racism is a phenomenon of economic exploitation. According to this argument, the capitalist system, given its very make-up, and to perpetuate its own existence, creates and reproduces racism, and will never find a valid solution to the situations it generates; therefore, it concludes, 'sólo el socialismo, solo el comunismo, sólo la sociedad sin explotados ni explotadores, sólo la sociedad sin clases puede resolver el problema del hombre, de las minorías y de las mayorías nacionales' (only socialism, only communism, only a society without exploited or exploiters, only a classless society can resolve the problems of man, of national minorities and majorities) (*Granma*, 1976a). It offers the example of the Soviet state that has incorporated a number of nations in its state: a multinational state. Yet, according to the discourse of *Granma*, the United States will never find a solution to the problem of minorities and majorities, because its system needs them to survive and 'por eso no habrá solución en el capitalismo para puertorriqueños, latinos, chicanos. No habrá solución para la población negra de Estados Unidos, como tampoco habrá solución para su población blanca' (that's why there will be no solution in capitalism for Puerto Ricans, Latinos, Chicanos. There will be no solution for the black population of the United States, just as there will be no solution for its white population) (*Granma*, 1976a). The newspaper uses the terms 'minoría' o 'mayoría nacional' (national minority or majority), similarly to the way the Soviet Union explained its creation of the multinational state (Brubaker, [1996] 2003), to refer to groups that share certain cultural and physical features that differentiate them from the rest of the population, or from other groups that would constitute the national majority. The articles from *Granma* mention the following groups: Puerto Ricans, Latinos, Chicanos, Indians and Blacks. *Granma* supposes that the Soviet Union had resolved the problem of discrimination and segregation, unlike the United States, by means of integrating these groups into the state. The term 'national' refers to the state and, thus, national minorities would therefore be groups that were not integrated into the state, and that did not have the same rights, as they were subject to segregation and discrimination. In the discourse of *Granma*, however, the creation of these groups is not so much cultural and/or racial, as economic and class based. Examples of those groups are included to support the central thesis that the formation or maintenance of those groups in the capitalist system, as well as their discrimination and segregation as cheap labour, are necessary for the survival of the system. Therefore, the ideas of state, nation, ethnic group, race and class are all mixed together in these groups, known as 'national minorities and majorities'.

From a total of 16 articles (some with a specific author, others not), 13 deal with the issue of racism in the United States, examining examples of situations of discrimination and segregation to which 'national minorities' are relegated: Chicanos, Blacks, Indians, as well as violent repression and institutional racism 'con capucha y sin capucha' ('with and without hood') (Díaz, 1976). There is silence, however, with regard to Cuba, with only three articles mentioning the island. This silence can only contribute towards confirming the solution to the conflict, a solution that is underscored by means of showing how the problem affects the other, and the violence and injustice that the problem generates.

The strategy of polarisation in groups is at the core of the discourse of these articles, whose goal is to underline a statement that is silenced, perhaps because it is general knowledge: 'we' (Cuba, the Revolution, socialism) are not racist and in our society this situation has already been resolved. This goal is achieved by means of highlighting and describing acts by 'them' (the United States, capitalism), the racists. In other words, 'we' are to be understood as the mirror image created by the polarisation of groups, as the opposite to what 'they' are. The emphasis on the negative aspects of 'them' enhances the opposite aspects in 'us' without the need to make them explicit.

The examples of 'their' racism and violent repression also function as what van Dijk calls models,[6] both mental and experience models, as well as event

---

6   From van Dijk's socio-cognitive viewpoint (1998), models represent individual models through which human beings understand our environs and interpret

and context (van Dijk, 1998), especially for the black population, who are reminded of the situation of discrimination and segregation in which they found themselves before the Revolution, thus underscoring the success of the changes it has brought about.

They also serve the purpose of supporting and legitimising some political decisions taken by the Revolutionary government, for instance, the Cuban participation in wars and missions in Africa, at that time in full swing. This foreign policy demonstrates the stance of the Revolutionary govern-ment as a champion of the international fight against racism, as well as the recognition of brotherhood between countries that share common roots, in other words, the recognition of its Africanness. At the same time, and more generally speaking, it legitimises the socialist model, representing it as a system of values morally superior to the capitalist system represented by the United States.

The values represented by 'their' system, in other words, capitalism, are: injustice, racism, discrimination, segregation, exploitation. Meanwhile, 'our' system would be, in contradistinction to the other, a model of social justice, anti-racism, equality, integration and freedom. The values of 'their' society are social division, ambition and greed, disdain, repression, cruelty, conflict; while 'ours' is characterised by the opposite: social unity, solidarity and altruism, cooperation and harmony.

As regards the idea of Cuban national identity, the only article found, by Manuel Moreno Fraginals and entitled 'Manuel de Angola', claims that national identity has reached 'al hondo proceso de integración cultural cubano' (the deep process of Cuban cultural integration) (Moreno Fraginals, 1976), a process that has taken place through 'raíces y pueblos que a veces parecen lejanos [con los que] se ha ido formando un contenido nacional cubano' (roots and peoples that sometimes seem far removed but [with which] a Cuban national content has been formed) (Moreno Fraginals, 1976). This is, it says, a process that has taken place by means of transculturation that 'no opera por agresión sino por síntesis, creando formas nuevas dis-tintas de sus elementos componentes' (does not operate by aggression but by synthesis, creating new different forms from its component elements) (Moreno Fraginals, 1976). Moreno Fraginals explains the creation of *cuban-idad* or national identity by means of the theory of 'transculturation', which Fernando Ortiz coined in *Contrapunteo del tabaco y el azúcar* (1940), using the

---

events and discourses; and can be divided into four models: i) mental model or model: subjective representation of an episode; ii) experience model: represents personal participation in or observation of episodes in our own lives; iii) event model: interprets events or situations referred to by the discourse; and iv) context model: represents events in the media.

metaphor of *ajiaco*, the components standing in for the different human and cultural elements that coexist on the island, and which 'a rebullir y disolverse en el caldo de Cuba y a diferir la consolidación de una definitiva y básica homogenidad nacional' (are mixed and dissolved in the stock of Cuba and distinguish the consolidation of a definitive and basic national homogeneity) (Ortiz, [1949]1991: 30). The theory presented in the Moreno Fraginal's article from *Granma*, on the integration of the Cuban nation, has been the official theory of the Revolution, propagated, among other channels, in books published on the question of national identity, for instance, Walterio Carbonell's *Cómo surgió la cultura nacional* (1961), Nancy Morejón's *Nación y mestizaje en Nicolás Guillén* (1982) and *Fundación de la imagen* (1988), and Pedro Serviat's *El problema negro en Cuba y su solución definitiva* (1986).

The nation, through accepting all these elements into its heart, would then become an integrated nation, without majorities or minorities, which, in Moreno Fraginals's (1976) discourse, accepts both its African as well as its European origins, and represents both. As he says, unlike the preceding bourgeois governments whose concept of culture was limited to the European, and for which African culture was a non-culture, the Revolution accepts both, and represents the two equally. Therein lies the 'nationalisation' of the culture of African origin as an integrating solution, a homogenisation that was the goal of the elites, and which they had sought by means of various strategies ever since the idea of the Cuban nation was conceived. The Revolution is here presented as the final solution. In the discourse of *Granma* it is a solution that does not create majorities or minorities; on the contrary, it is a solution that integrates, because its system does not require the segregation or discrimination that are proper to capitalism.

Nonetheless, and on the one hand, as many researchers have pointed out, this union and 'transculturation' of different elements did not produce a situation of equality for both sides; rather it took place in a context of hegemonic inequality. More than union, what there was, in fact, was a cultural clash and domination, what academics such as Moore (1997), Arnedo (2001) and others have considered a 'whitening' of the culture of African origins. The theory of transculturation held out the possibility that all citizens, without race or class divisions, would feel themselves a formative part of the nation, but, as Leclercq (2004) claims, the Revolution went much further: it vindicated the African origin of the Cuban nation and diluted it in a more inclusive, more integrating idea, in the national body, thus converting the culture of African origin into Cuban. In the words of Nancy Morejón, 'un cubano, aunque pareciese un yoruba o un gallego, responde al carácter primero de su nacionalidad, forjada, como se sabe en las luchas independentistas [...] nos caracterizamos por habernos propuesto una nación homogénea en su heterogeneidad, caracterizada por un fin político (la Revolución Cubana encabezada por Fidel Castro), más allá de cualquier cándida controversia sólo cultural o racial' (a Cuban, though he might appear to be a Yoruba or a Gallego, responds to the primary character of his nationhood, forged, as is known, in the struggles for independence [. . .] we are characterised by having proposed a nation that is homogeneous in its heterogeneity, characterised by a political goal [the Cuban Revolution led by Fidel Castro], over and above any naïve cultural or racial controversy) (Morejón, 1988:189–190).

Like other previous or possible conceptions of national identity, this one is also a social construct, a myth or an imaginative creation and, also like previous versions, its goal is to offer the idea of a homogeneous nation. As Brubaker states, 'ethnicity could be understood as a potentially serious *impediment* to nation-building and national integration' ([1996] 2003: 81, italics in the original). The Revolution has managed to dissolve the 'ethnic' in the concept of the 'national', ensuring that only the latter category would be taken in account in defining identity. Furthermore, in the case of the Revolution, as Morejón maintains, the goal of this homogeneous nation goes far beyond an innocent discussion on culture or race, and is in fact the very political project of the Revolution. In this project, according to Caño Secade (1996), the integrating and homogenising strategy has underscored unity as a fundamental way of preserving victory, especially in the light of the pressure from the United States from the first moments of the Revolution.

On the other hand, and as some authors, including Duno Gottberg and Leclercq have argued, there was continuing evidence of a polarity in Cuban culture between a popular or 'folklore' culture and another 'high' or 'hege-monic' culture that corresponded to two different 'racial' groups, a polarity in which one of these cultures imposed its rule. According to Wade, 'like any meanings, national meanings are defined relationally, both with respect to other nations and to forms within the nation that are defined as inferior. So appropriation implies a parallel process of differentiation' (Wade, 2000: 8). The differentiation between 'popular' and 'high' in Cuban culture meant the creation of a scale of values. From this viewpoint, from the hegemonic group, the Revolution has seen a folklorisation of the culture of African origins while, as García Canclini (1990) has pointed out in relation to Latin America and indigenous cultures, its study and conservation has been entrusted to ethnologists, museologists and folklorists whose goals are to rescue, conserve and study traditions. This folklorisation enumerates, exalts, exhibits and theatricalises popular Cuban culture without making reference to everyday practices or without situating this culture in the here and now of social relationships and tensions. The Revolution, in Leclercq's opinion, exoticises this culture, decontextualises it and thus freezes it in the past (Leclercq, 2004).

Moreover, the Revolution institutionalises this classification, appropriating and institutionalising the culture of African origins, that is, shifting it into the domain of state institutions such as the Instituto Nacional de Etnología y Folklore (National Institute of Ethnology and Folklore), the Conjunto Folklórico Nacional (National Folklore Group), the Museo de Etnología (Museum of Ethnology), and so on, while at the same time sustaining cultural institutions that respond to the idea of high culture, for instance the Ballet Nacional (National Ballet).

This is a process of classification that is not helpful in putting an end to the cultural values of the past, or prejudices towards blacks, given that, according to Wade's theory, in the process of 'appropriation and resignification [. . .] certain dominant values tend to pervade' (Wade, 2000: 10). In the same sense, Caño Secade (1996) has claimed that the process of integration has not ended the scale of values existing prior to the Revolution, in other words with the subordination of the culture of African origins, and that the weight lent to the homogenising focus has enabled the continuation and reproduction of racial prejudices and stereotypes.

End of the Twentieth Century, Beginning of the Twenty-first

If, in the 1970s the space given by the press to the issue was scant, at the end of the twentieth century the silence was complete. After the declaration of the final solution to the problem in 1962, the racial question began to be silenced, not only in the press, but also in all other cultural and social fields. On one hand, perhaps the most obvious reason is that, if something does not exist there is no reason to talk about it. On the other, it was, as de la Fuente (2001) has already underscored, believed to be separatory, divisionary of the nation throughout the whole of the twentieth century, and has seemed even more important during the Revolution, given that unity was defined as key to survival. After it was declared resolved, it became a taboo subject, and bringing it up for debate was considered unpatriotic, thus further hampering any revision of the issue for a certain period of time.

At the current moment, there is a wider acceptance of the existence of discrimination in Cuban society. The silence is now not so all-pervasive and, though the question is not discussed in newspapers, one can detect the first signs of a revision of the issue and an attempt to rectify certain stances, which are being dealt with in some periodical publications. In 1996, the racial question was addressed in various articles in the magazine *Temas* and in a book by Jesús Guanche, *Componentes étnicos de la nación cubana* (1996a). In 2002, numbers 24–25 of the magazine *Caminos (Revista Cubana de Pensamiento Socioteológico)* were dedicated to race and racism, and were followed by two anthologies ('Otra vez raza y racismo' 2008 and Pérez and Lueiro, 2009), which repeated some of the articles already published. In *Catauro*, no. 6 (2002) there were two articles, one by Rafael Hernández and the other by Esteban Morales Domínguez. Issue no. 45 of *Temas* dealt with the question again in 2006 in the article 'Raza y desigualdad en la Cuba actual' (Espina Prieto and Rodríguez Ruiz, 2006) and, in 2007, the publication of the book by Morales Domínguez, *Desafíos de la problemática racial en Cuba,* analysed the issue, as did a brief summary of the ideas by Morales Domínguez in *Temas* no. 56 (2008).

All of the above books and articles accept that discrimination has not disappeared completely, because of the force of the inheritance of colonisation and of previous governments, and that the intervening time has not been sufficient for its total eradication. It is also explained as a consequence of the so-called Special Period and of certain socio-economic policies that were necessary to adopt in order to respond to the crisis, such as dollarisation, development and the economic dependency on tourism. Generally speaking, greater proximity to economic policies closer to capitalism gives rise to new situations of discrimination, especially in the economic sectors known as *emergentes* (emerging). This is the case, for instance, in the tourism sector, in which the majority of jobs involving direct contact with tourists are occupied by the white population, and where the black population is over-represented in the jobs not requiring direct contact. There is also a greater proportion of the black population in prisons, non-executive or non-professional jobs, and among those with the poorest living conditions, which is generally explained as a structural socio-cultural inheritance from the past and the reconstruction of this inheritance during the crisis (and the competitive spaces created to manage it) (Espina Prieto and Rodríguez Ruiz, 2006).

Both Guanche, in his article 'Etnicidad y racialidad en la Cuba actual' (1996b: 56) and in his book *Componentes étnicos de la nación cubana* (1996a: 136) and Morales Domínguez in *Desafíos de la problemática racial en Cuba* (2007: 324) define Cuba as a 'nación uniétnica y multirracial' (uni-ethnic and multiracial nation). The ethnic and racial composition in this definition should, as Guanche says, be distinguished. In his opinion the *etnos* 'constituye uno de los tipos más antiguos y estables de organización social, que está condicionado por el modo de pensar y actuar de las personas en sociedad' (constitutes one of the oldest and most stable forms of social organisation, and is conditioned by the way of thinking and acting of the people in society) (1996a: 4); while race 'abarca las características físicas (biológicas) del ser humano y sus mecanismos hereditarios de transmisión' (embraces the physical (biological) features of the human being and their hereditary mechanisms of transmission) (1996a: 4). In short, he adds, the difference between race and ethnic group 'es la diferencia e interacción entre natura y cultura' (is the difference and interaction between nature and culture) (1996a: 4).

Guanche defines what he calls 'etnos-nación' as a social body constituted by a set of shared features, among which he includes language, culture (with local and regional variations) and a self-awareness of belonging that, he says, outlines the profile of *nacionalidad cubana* (Cuban nationhood) (Guanche, 1996a: 127). Thus, the Cuban *ethnos*-nation is 'el resultado histórico-cultural y poblacional de los conglomerados multiétnicos hispánico, africano, chino y antillano principalmente, que se fusionaron de manera compleja y disímil desde el s.XVI, hasta crear una entidad étnica nueva' (the historic-cultural and populational result of the Hispanic, African, Chinese and West Indian multiethnic conglomerates, fused together in a complex and dissimilar fashion ever since the sixteenth century until a new ethnic entity was created) (Guanche, 1996a: 135); this *ethnos*-nation forms the majority from the second half of the nineteenth century, when, because of the wars of independence, a 'national ethnic self-awareness' was created; and from 1959 onwards the Cuban *ethnos* accounted for up to 98 percent of the population.

Meanwhile, 'ethnic group' is defined as a 'pequeña parte de un etnos que reside en el territorio habitado principalmente por uno o más etnos mayores, que constituyen un organismo etnosocial estable con aparato gubernamental o estatal' (small part of an ethnos that resides in the territory mainly inhabited by one or more larger ethnos, that constitute a stable ethno-social body with a governmental or state system) (Guanche, 1996a: 5); and 'ethnic minority' is defined as an 'etnos cuya totalidad o casi totalidad vive en su territorio de pertenencia históricamente determinado, junto con uno o más etnos cuantitativamente mayores dentro del contexto de un gobierno o estado' (ethnos whose totality or quasi-totality lives in its territory of historically-determined belonging, together with one or more quantitatively larger ethnos within the context of a government or state) (Guanche, 1996a: 5). For this reason, he believes that Cuba does not possess ethnic groups or ethnic minorities, except for a few small groups that do not account for more than 1 per cent of the population, made up of some families of Spaniards, Haitians, Jamaicans, and so on. A hypothetical ethnic minority could be formed, according to Guanche, by the descendents of the island's aboriginal population, although after many generations they are now Cubans as a result of the mix that has taken place (Guanche, 1996).

Guanche uses the term 'ethnicity' with the meaning of, or as a synonym for, nation, cultural identity, national identity or nationhood, nationality, state and country of origin. Ethnicity, in Guanche's definition, does not comprise groups within the nation-state, because it is a core constitutive part of it. The original 'multi-ethnicity' became a single ethnicity when the ethnos-nation-state was formed with the independence of Cuba, when it was organised politically as a republic, as a state with its own government. It would respond to what Kapcia refers to as *'cubanía* as the political belief in *cubanidad'*

(2000: 22). Ethnicity and national identity are, in Guanche's definition, mainly political markers that relate to the state, a definition of terms that enables the continuity of the proposal of national identity posed by the Revolution. The ideology upheld responds to a nationalist logic: non-differentiation as a strategic factor in all national discourse, a reluctance to accept the existence of minorities, thanks to the use of terms that nationalise the differences.

Though Guanche says it is a question of nature and biology – or colour in the discourse of Morales Domínguez (2007) – race is also understood to possess a socio-cultural and class connotation, a conceptual hangover derived from racism. In the case of Cuba, these authors maintain, this connotation is owing to the colonial inheritance that, though resolved by the Revolution on an institutional level, has lingered on at a deeper and more complex level, and is reproduced and multiplied, bearing an influence on forms of behaviour and feelings. Race, Guanche claims, is strictly biological, but can prove deceptive by virtue of the socio-cultural and class connotation that racism and racial prejudices add to the strictly biological, what Guanche calls, following Fernando Ortiz's book title 'el hábil engaño de las razas' (the skilful deceptiveness of races) (Guanche, 1996b: 53). For Guanche and Morales, race seems to be mainly a question of 'epithelium' or colour, and a statistical category, a unit of social accounting, hence their definition of Cuba as a multiracial nation.

Nonetheless, this division between *culture* and *nature*, which seems to be clear-cut in Guanche's definition, may not be so patent after all. The idea of *nature* (or biology), which would describe the racial in this definition, is subject to historical and geographical variations, as also happens with the idea of *culture*, and, as a consequence, *pace* Wade (2002), they lend themselves to strategic manipulation by political interest groups.

Likewise, these definitions do not take into account that racial and ethnic categorisations have been based on criteria that are both cultural and biological. The idea of race has been defined by different markers, such as civilisation, honour, education, forms of behaviour, as well as by physical questions. This can be seen, for instance, in the analysis of the discourse of the Cuban press during the twentieth century (Antón Carrillo, 2006). During the first part of the century, the term 'race' was used to refer to human groups who shared physical, biological or natural features, a set of features that carry with them certain moral, social and cultural attributes. During this same period, the term was also used as a synonym of culture and civilisation, for example, 'the Latin race' or 'the Anglo-Saxon race'. In the 1930s we find the mixture of nature and culture still colouring the use of the term 'race' in the Cuban press, though at this time the reference is not so much to biology, or to blood, but to 'spirit' and 'personality' as synonyms of culture; thus, for instance, the unions of persons of different races were called 'transfusiones espirituales' ('spiritual transfusions') (*El Mundo*, 1939), transmitting the idea of mixed blood (nature) and culture. During the Revolution, as shown in the newspaper articles analysed here, the term 'race' is mainly understood as class, and therefore resolved, given that class has been eradicated in the socialist system. However, this politico-economic focus overlooks the politico-cultural dimension of identity, which will enable the persistence of previous stereotypes, and also the values of the culturally dominant group.

At the same time, and as Crow (2010) maintains, the values associated with different phenotypes or physical features are always cultural, which means that racial variations are always to be found underpinning categories of a cultural order. In practice, racial and ethnic identifications overlap (Wade, 1997). Both of them divide individuals and groups according to positive or negative values. This can be seen in the survival and reproduction of stereotypes of the black population in Cuba, despite egalitarian legislation (Caño Secade, 1996; Sawyer, 2006).

Prejudice, as well as the creation and reproduction of stereotypes, is therefore not a question that belongs to and remains within the private sphere of the individual, as claimed in the discourse of *Diario de la Marina* and *Revolución* in 1959. Rather it forms part of the public domain and therefore it is also reproduced socially. As a result, the elites, through their discourses, as well as the control of the means of production of public opinion and education, as shown by van Dijk (1993), play a crucial role in the creation, maintenance and reproduction of stereotypes, prejudice and discrimination. And, as argued by Crow (2010), the state has an absolutely key role in the dissemination of images of different racial or ethnic groups, in schools, museums, mass media, and so on, and, as a consequence, in the reproduction of prejudice, beliefs and discrimination.

Some studies of recent Cuban periodical publications advocate the need for changes in the definition of cultural identity, considering it to be excessively homogeneous and influential in perpetuating norms and aesthetic conventions of the historically dominant culture. They state the need to bear in mind the socio-cultural diversity of the Cuban nation (Caño Secade, 1996; Hernández, 2002; Morales Domínguez, 2007, 2008) and recommend social policies that strengthen the identity values of the black population, as well as the recognition of its contribution to cultural and social life, through education and schools, that would reflect the existing cultural diversity. These studies also coincide in the fact that the recognition of diversity ought to be based on equality and also, and above all, without transforming the acceptance of this difference into the possibility of exclusion or separation (Hernández, 2002). In the words of Caño Secade, they should enhance these values but be always watchful to prevent them from leading to 'valores reaccionarios, desintegradores en relación con el resto de los grupos raciales' (reactionary, dis-integrating values with regards the rest of the racial groups) (1996: 63). In short, the treatment of the racial question and its acceptance should not influence the unity of the nation, nor should it become a question that divides, a fear that persisted throughout the whole of the last century and has become even more urgent during the Revolution.

While during the first part of the twentieth-century discourses on race were very similar in Cuba and most other Latin American countries, the second part of the century differed considerably; this is even truer in the final decades of the last century and the beginning of this one. During the 1980s and 1990s, postmodernist ideas dominated thinking on race and ethnicity. They helped change the definitions of identity, internationally as well as in Latin America. As Wade (1997) shows, identity is now defined as a process under constant renegotiation instead of an arrival point, and the idea of a core defining essence has given way to the idea of multiple identities, with the central focus on the politics of culture.

During the 1980s and 1990s, and in most Latin American countries, black, and Indian social movements spread and intensified. Some states reacted to those movements by passing new legislation that recognises multiculturality or special rights for ethnic groups. There seems to be an official acceptance of multiculturality as 'a postmodern nationalism that defines the nation in terms of its multiculturality, rather than an ideally homogeneous culture' (Wade, 1997: 105). De la Cadena sees the 1945 official agreement between the Peruvian and Bolivian states as the precursor of the present multiculturalism, imagining the nation as 'coordination among dissimilar groups – rather than the sum of homogeneous units' (2005: 275), where 'unity within diversity was the slogan' (de la Cadena, 2005: 275). These are the cases of countries such as Nicaragua, Bolivia, Peru, Brazil, Colombia, who redefined their nations as 'pluriethnic and multicultural'. But as Wade argues (1997, 2000), these new definitions need to be examined because, just like previous definitions, they clearly serve political purposes. In many cases the definitions have come from the state, with the goal of legitimising political strategies such as coping with protest or, alternatively, of being seen by the outside world as a postmodern and democratic country. Heterogeneity now has a new legitimacy, but always within the nation as wholeness.

Acknowledgements

The author would like to thank Lambe and Nieto for their translation of this chapter.

3

Cuba's Internationalism Revisited: Exporting Literacy, ALBA, and a New Paradigm for South–South Collaboration

KEPA ARTARAZ

University of Brighton, UK

> Cuba's achievements in social development are impressive given the size of its gross domestic product per capita [...] it does demonstrate how much nations can do with the resources they have if they focus on the right priorities – health, education, and literacy. (Annan, 2000: 2)

Cuba continually confounds those observers and critics whose positions are based on orthodox views, informed by a Cold War prism that historically portrayed the island as a Soviet satellite. It confounds them because the Cuban Revolution has developed in ways that have often followed a very Cuban path, based on an endogenous ideology. A critical element of this must be found in the moral content of the Cuban leaders' ideological demand to fundamentally transform society immediately after the triumph of the Revolution in 1959, in a way that was not sustainable by the logic of the socio-economic order at the time. The provision of free and universal education and healthcare to Cubans became the pillars on which this radical transformation would take place; they were some of the benefits to be enjoyed by the majority, not the few. These elements, necessary for the fulfilment of Cuba's ideological potential, could in turn reinforce the feeling of 'belonging' in the population, strengthening the social fabric in a hitherto dislocated society and recreating Cuban national identity along newly radicalised positions. Inevitably, Cuba's 'true' national birth had to be accompanied by a 'socialist' one if it was to fulfil the moral promise of its ideology.

A second element of this ideology has to be found in the zeal with which the Revolution tried early on to export both the revolutionary method of transition to socialism and the social benefits that it was delivering at home. 'Internationalism' took expression in the form of practical and moral support for liberation struggles around the world, indeed in a belief that the 'Cuban revolutionary method' could be replicated in countries where the objective conditions of exploitation were present, unleashing a wave of calls for revolutionary struggles during the Tricontinental conference of 1966 in Havana. Having gathered leaders from the so-called Third World, the conference became one of a number of Cuban-led initiatives to make common cause with the poor peoples of the global South and, to quote Guevara, create 'one, two, three, many Vietnams' (Castro, 1967b).

The strategy of exporting the Revolution never really worked, however, and the death of Guevara himself in the Bolivian jungle symbolised a transition in the following decade to a more orthodox type of military intervention – backed by the Soviet Union – that allowed Cuba to punch above its weight on the international stage. This type of 'internationalism' would itself fall prey to the new post-Cold War realities. However, military support for liberation struggles has always been accompanied by a clearer expression of internationalism in the form of humanitarian missions and exchanges of solidarity with countries around the world (Harris, 2009). This has been a permanent feature of the Cuban Revolution and has not been affected in principle, even during the harshest of economic times in the 1990s (Kirk and Erisman, 2009).

The scale of Cuba's internationalist cooperation is breathtaking. Data from Kirk and Erisman (2009), the most reliable and updated compilation of data from multiple sources, refers to this as consisting of more than 35,000 staff operating in over 70 countries around the world. Cuban health personnel operate as closely by as Haiti – without whom the country would just not have a health service infrastructure – and as far away as East Timor, with a particularly strong presence in the Latin American and Caribbean region and in poor countries of southern Africa. Not only this, the Escuela Latinoamericana de Medicina (ELAM; Latin American School of Medicine) trains thousands of young people from those countries entirely free of charge (Van Gelder, 2007).

Data for Cuba's contribution to literacy and education abroad is also hard to come by, although we know that it is not as labour intensive as health internationalism, with support for nation-wide literacy campaigns normally provided by a few hundred advisers at most. Cuba's contribution to literacy campaigns around the world consists mainly of having produced a tried and tested audiovisual method called 'Yo sí puedo' (Yes, I can) that can easily be adapted to specific cultural and language requirements. The scale of success in terms of outcomes is no less impressive, however. After a strong presence in Nicaragua's literacy campaign in the 1980s, Cuba's export of literacy campaigns and techniques around the world has seen a marked increase since the creation in 2004 of the Alianza Bolivariana para los Pueblos de Nuestra América (ALBA) and is now present in 26 countries around the world, including in the city of Seville in Spain (Shabbir, 2009). Having taught literacy to over 1.5 million people in Venezuela alone by 2005 and another million in Bolivia by the end of 2008, it is not surprising that the ALBA region is itself the biggest beneficiary. Currently five Latin American countries have been declared free of illiteracy by UNESCO: Cuba, Venezuela, Bolivia, Nicaragua and Ecuador.

The set of explanations that could help us understand the reasons why a small poor country such as Cuba would engage in this level of international cooperation is, however, less impressive. As Kirk and Erisman (2009) argue, the ideologically motivated arguments from the right are unconvincing, either because they subsume Cuba's international role to the decisions taken by a single man (Castro) and present this as part of the messianic nature of the man, or because they look for self-serving reasons for action as a way of increasing international weight to Cuba. The argument that exporting international cooperation, in the form of doctors and teachers, contributes to Cuba's access to hard currency and foreign earnings has some merit (in cases such as that of Qatar or South Africa), but there are many more cases in which Cuba's humanitarian and cooperative support comes free of charge and with no strings attached, even to countries such as Colombia and Peru that can hardly be said to be Cuba's allies in the region. A similar argument about Cuba's independence of action in relation to military interventions abroad has been made by Leogrande (1982), arguing that the island's support for regimes ranging from Algeria, Ghana or Angola to Nicaragua has not been dependent on their adoption of Marxist–Leninist politics.

Two serious perspectives that can help us understand Cuba's internationalist endeavours come from Feinsilver (1993, 2003) and Joseph Nye (2004). The first has explored the question of medical internationalism in terms of the symbolic capital that this cooperation abroad delivers for the island, symbolic capital that can be exchanged for ad hoc instances of diplomatic capital. The second is a perspective that emphasises the international status and 'soft' power that Cuba is able to exert in the global stage, especially in the poor South and among neighbouring and Latin American countries, where Cuba has more recently concentrated its efforts. The support that Cuba receives from poor countries against regular US-sponsored anti-Cuba resolutions at the UN Human Rights Commission in Geneva could be seen a direct result of this medical diplomacy. Equally, we could see a payoff for the island's alternative diplomacy in the overwhelming decision by Latin American countries in 2009 to reverse the 1962 US-inspired suspension of Cuba from the Organisation of American States (OAS) (Brice, 2009). So, according to this view, Cuba would have exchanged attempts to effect 'hard' power through the export of revolutions for the opportunity to exercise soft power by exporting doctors (Clemons, 2009).

The explanation of Cuba's internationalism in terms of the position that it affords the island in the global battle of ideas and by means of effecting 'soft' power is convincing enough, but it does not seem to offer a complete understanding of the reasons why the Revolution has engaged in this practice over its five decades of existence. One particular limitation of this set of explanations is that, without exception, they consider Cuba's actions at the level of international relations and as a particular form of diplomacy. This chapter agrees broadly with Kirk and Erisman in their argument that, notwithstanding the symbolic and real diplomatic benefits that Cuba is able to derive from the numerous internationalist missions in which it engages, the primary reason for them has to be found in an ideological commitment that seeks to replicate and share its domestic achievements in well-being through meeting basic human needs with the poor around the world (2009).

This chapter explores Cuba's involvement in internationalist cooperation. It does so with reference to the country's support for literacy campaigns abroad, a relatively neglected aspect of Cuba's internationalism in the literature that, like Cuba, has concentrated its efforts on making sense of medical internationalism. The chapter examines Cuba's 1961 literacy campaign, explaining this in the context of revolutionary ideology in the 1960s, the broad outcomes of such campaign, and the ideological sources of influence that can explain the role of adult education in Cuba. The chapter then jumps forward to Bolivia's literacy campaign (2006–2008) as part of Cuba's latest ALBA-sponsored internationalist mission, exploring the key policy objective of this mission and its unexpected outcomes. A key argument in this exposition is that ALBA represents a new institutional framework that permits Cuba to contribute effectively towards the creation of a new form of regionalism (Katz, 2006), with strong social policy delivery powers (Briceño Ruiz, 2007) made possible by exchanges of solidarity that may come to symbolise the future of South–South relations.

Cuba in the 1960s: A Radical Transformation of Society

In the 1960s, Cuba's radical social transformation called upon the ethical content of an ideology that put man at the centre and demanded international recognition for it. Although a clear symbolic capital was (and is still) extracted from Cuba's advances in welfare and equality, these have proved themselves to nevertheless be only too real. Cuba's undisputed advances in health and education have, throughout the decades, provided a model of development and embodied the aspirations of millions fighting for national liberation and independence in the Third World.

An almost obsessive concern about the health of the population was, from day one, one of the pillars on which this transformation was to be built. The universalisation of medical services had already taken place three years into the revolutionary process, giving priority to the neediest areas of rural Cuba. By 1969, any remaining vestiges of past, semi-private, forms of health provision had been totally eradicated. However, what astonished international observers was the boldness of some of the vertical intervention programmes of mass vaccination and sanitation that reached 100 per cent of the population and eradicated diseases at a single stroke. All this, it must be said, was driven by the remainder of a highly politicised medical profession (about half of which had left Cuba since 1959), whose current Hippocratic Oath includes a commitment to work for the benefit of humanity and rejects individual private profit.

Similar in effect was the great emphasis given to education by the revolutionary leadership. The problem of illiteracy had already been identified by Castro as one of the great obstacles to the development of pre-revolutionary Cuba as early as 1953 when, during his trial for the failed attack on the Moncada Barracks, he made an impassionate speech immortalised as 'History will Absolve Me' (Castro, 1960b). After the triumph of the rebellion, it was clear that education was to become the second pillar on which the new society would be built. The beginnings of the Cuban literacy campaign have to be seen in the announcement made by Castro to the world during his speech to the UN on 20 September 1960, that the Cuban state would eradicate illiteracy within a year (Kenner and Petras, 1972). Similarly to vaccinations against disease, 'vaccination' against illiteracy was carried out at a single stroke, requiring the collective effort of large sectors of a population that was either teaching or learning during eight months in 1961, when schools were closed to allow teachers and students to participate in the campaign. It is estimated that around 250,000 'teachers' reached over 900,000 people during the literacy campaign.

The literacy challenge faced by the Revolution was great. At the time, almost one in four Cuban adults was illiterate. This figure of 23 per cent almost surely hid a reality of more than 40 per cent illiteracy in the rural areas, more than 1 million adults, with fewer than 40,000 trained schoolteachers in the island. The campaign began in April 1961 by recruiting close to 100,000 secondary-school students between the ages of ten and eighteen who, after a two-week crash course in teaching, were mobilised to the rural areas of the country for six months, to live with and teach poor and illiterate peasants. Another 150,000 adults, including many workers, women and teachers, were recruited through factories, the Federation of Cuban Women, the Association of Small Farmers and the Committees for the Defence of the Revolution, to deliver 'Acceleration camps', a form of catch-up class for groups of people who had been left behind in their progress, or were being sent to rural areas as part of troubleshooting teams (Fagen, 1969; Kozol, 1978). If we take into account the mobilisation of the thousands of specialists necessary to conduct eye tests and to deliver reading glasses to the more than 150,000 people who needed them and had never had them before, the extent of the mobilisation effort required becomes clear.

The literacy campaign has acquired mythical status among those who participated in it. Equipped with a lamp, a pair of boots, a hammock and two books with which to teach adults their first reading and writing lessons, the experience is warmly reflected upon by them (Elvy, 2005). The campaign only aimed at ensuring that every Cuban achieved a level of education equal to the first year of primary school. The results were spectacular and more far-reaching than many literacy campaigns before or since. Official figures suggest that in eight months the illiteracy rate in Cuba fell to less than 4 per cent (Lorenzetto and Neys, 1965), the level required for UNESCO to declare a country free of illiteracy. The Cuban literacy campaign experience, a leading educational story of the twentieth century, became only the first stage of many aiming to raise the educational level of Cubans. Increasingly in Cuba, the authorities became aware of the need to deliver quality as well as quantity of educational opportunities. In later years, the literacy campaign was followed by attempts to make further educational achievements available to those who had started their formal education during the campaign. For example, by 1980, 1.5 million formerly illiterate adults had achieved sixth grade and plans had been made to ensure that they continued their education towards their ninth year of formal studies for all adults, with the aim of achieving permanent education for all (Leiner, 1987).

Not all observers have been uncritical of Cuba's educational successes. A number have disagreed over the island's educational achievements during the literacy campaign. Eberstadt, for example, has disputed Cuban claims that illiteracy was reduced to 4 per cent in the space of one year, arguing that discrepancies in the figures about the extent of illiteracy in Cuba before the Revolution show evidence of deliberate falsification (1988).

Although the 'Year of Education', as 1961 was called, may not necessarily have resulted in high levels of literacy in those who benefited directly from the campaign, the symbolic victory that the campaign represented for Cuba cannot be disregarded. On the one hand, enthusiasm and optimism and a sense of what was possible in a revolutionary situation thrilled participants in the campaign. Abroad, the vision of an island converted into a great school could not but increase the interest in, and support for, the Revolution, among a politicised generation of young people who shared the enthusiasm for alternative forms of socialism and who would lead the events of 1968 and 1969 in Paris, London, Berlin and Rome (Ali and Watkins, 1998).

On the other hand, there is consensus in the literature to suggest that the greatest victory of the literacy campaign lay in the message it carried as an expression of the wider social justice that the new revolutionary government wanted the new society to enjoy (Kapcia, 2005; Kozol, 1978; Lutjens, 1998). In addition, many of the same sources have pointed out that the literacy campaign's success went well beyond the issue of bringing education to the illiterate masses and that, by bringing together Cubans of different social classes, ages and upbringings, the campaign became a profound moment in the political, social and moral transformation of the country, affecting the society and the culture of the country, in addition to spreading literacy (Bhola, 1984). For others, the provision of mass adult education in Cuba became the key to Cuba's future 'alteration of the class structure' (Bowles, 1971: 492), in clear reference to the overtly political reading that the revolutionary leadership made of the campaign. After all, it is not possible to create a new social order without the full participation of every sector in society; in 1960s Cuba, an eminently agrarian society, illiteracy and poverty in rural areas made this transformation impossible. What the Cuban literacy campaign represented was the realisation of a revolutionary form of political change, by confronting society with the reality of the extreme socio-economic inequalities that existed in the country at the time. This experience brought about the gaining of *conciencia* in the masses, regardless whether their participation in the campaign included teaching or learning to read.

The process of gaining *conciencia* that the campaign brought has been described by Freire in his *Pedagogy of the Oppressed* (1970). A key author in the context of Latin America, Freire was of course primarily informed in his views by his personal experience of teaching in north-east Brazil, but his views became popular in Cuba, and the Cuban experience, in turn, informed his theoretical positions. In his writings, Freire (1970) characterises learning as freedom, a term he uses in both its pedagogical and political senses. The term carries a double meaning that directly links the process of learning with the process of human change, and development of a critical stance that can question, examine, interrogate and analyse the world around. In other words, true learning (and teaching) cannot take place without it changing us in some way. In the case of Cuba, the important lessons of the literacy campaign were equally shared by those who volunteered to teach as much as those who learned to read and write.

Freire's *conciencia* was not alone in describing the ideological processes that supported and explained Cuba's educational development in the early years of the Revolution. Guevara's writings, in particular his views on the 'New Man', serve to explain both the mass mobilisations that characterised many spheres of economic and social life in the 1960s – including the literacy campaign or the organisation of teaching at universities after staff numbers dwindled – and the high regard for altruistic displays of *conciencia* on which these mobilisations rested. Initially attributed to Guevara's writings, the New Man of the Revolution symbolised the highest stage of *conciencia* possible in the children of the Revolution – those who would be more 'complete' beings, as they would be able to fulfil their true creative nature. The New Man (and woman), Guevara argued in his *Man and Socialism,* would 'no longer think in individual terms but would direct his efforts towards the good of the collective' (Gerassi, 1968: 387–400). As health and education were the pillars of the new society, it was no coincidence that both the figures of the medical doctor and the teacher became the ideal embodiments of the New Man, that these two professions showed record numbers of registered students and that, still to this day, they can be seen as key to the task of maintenance of social cohesion and legitimacy in Cuban society. It is also no coincidence that these two professions and areas of social policy provision dominate Cuba's internationalist missions abroad.

The exploration of ideological sources of influence that can explain the role of adult education in Cuba in general and the literacy campaign in particular would not be complete without reference to José Martí, popular hero of the wars of independence and claimed by Fidel Castro as the 'intellectual author' of the 26 July Revolutionary Movement's (MR26) political manifesto (Coltman, 2003: 88). His dual role as intellectual and man of action would re-emerge as an ideal type during the 1960s, putting the emphasis, as some of the literacy campaign educational materials showed, on the need to 'be educated in order to be free', in clear reference to one of his most famous quotes that still adorns the entrance to public libraries in Cuba. Not surprisingly, the example set by Martí was partly the inspiration needed by the young and educated sections of the population who took charge of Cuba's nationalist politics from 1934 onwards, culminating in the revolutionary triumph of 1959. This mixture of cultural and revolutionary activism would have significant effects on the shape of education and culture in Cuba during this decade because, like the revolutionary leadership, new educational developments would be led by the young in their own educational territory: the university.

Thus, the literacy campaign had kick-started Cuba's educational revolution, a revolution that touched many other areas of culture and would never be far from the political developments of the island. For example, the 1960s provided many examples of projects that demonstrated the emphasis that the revolutionary leadership placed on culture and education. The number of schools in Cuba increased enormously, to cater for the needs of the high numbers of students at every level in an educational system that, just like the health system, became state-provided, universal and free. There was also a cinematic revolution in the film industry and plastic arts, as the creation of the Cuban Institute of Art and Cinematic Industry (ICAIC) in 1959 demonstrates

(King, 1990). One of the first tasks it set itself was to reach every corner of the island, popularising cinema as much as possible. Consequently, cinema audiences increased exponentially, as did the readership at libraries. The National Library reported more than a six-fold increase in the number of users from 25,000 in 1959 to over 165,000 in 1960 (Goldenberg, 1965). A related issue was the enormous increase in the number of publications on the island that took almost immediate effect after the Revolution; all this, in a country where there was really no reading tradition, where, according to the first director of the Instituto del Libro (the national publishing house) in 1967, Rolando Rodríguez, 'culture, such an important factor in the birth of a Cuban national identity had been completely pushed to one side by the mediocrity of colonial society' (Rodríguez, 1997: 2).

Cuba's educational revolution, which began with the literacy campaign, also affected university education. During the 1960s, higher education expanded enormously and ceased to be the preserve of the few. It was, in addition, the setting in which the Revolution's political and intellectual elites developed (Suchlicki, 1969). If the revolutionary leadership had begun their political careers at the University of Havana, the 1960s saw attempts to create a new class of 'organic' intellectuals, with the creation of the new Philosophy Department and journals such as *Pensamiento Crítico* for the dissemination of new ideas. The university also introduced highly experimental teaching practices – with final-year students contributing to the teaching – in order to compensate for the lack of lecturers. The importance of the university as a locus of revolutionary discourse and practice was connected to the wider importance of the university in Latin American radicalism, which went back to the university reforms of 1918 in Córdoba, Argentina. In a society obsessed with youth and the belief in youth's role as the natural leaders of political change, any changes in educational policies would affect this group more than any other (Hennessy, 1993).

The 1970s and 1980s were a period of fractures and continuity in Cuban education; the fractures came in the role and the nature of the university and higher education. Following the collapse of the 10 million-ton sugar harvest of 1970 and Cuba's closer alliance with the Soviet Union, a process of 'institutionalisation' began to take place. This had consequences for education in that higher education became more technocratic, more dependent on the Soviet Union for the content of its curriculum, and competitive instead of open to all. Continuity, on the other hand, was provided with the delivery of basic education to the masses – started by the literacy campaign – and in the export of this experience to other societies, something that began with Nicaragua in the 1980s (Leiner, 1985, 1987) but which would come to its own as part of the opportunities for extending Cuba's ideological principles through ALBA.

ALBA: Towards a New Paradigm of International Collaboration

A wave of national-popular governments has spread around Latin America since the beginning of the twenty-first century, representing popular opposition to the human consequences of the neoliberal economic thinking that dominated the region in the 1980s and 1990s. The return to democracy in many Latin American countries was soon followed by a turn to the left, a phenomenon that has come to be known as 'the pink tide' (Spronk, 2008). Regardless of the country-specific reasons for this ideological turn, it partly reflects a common critique of the neoliberal models of development, one that has brought about the political conviction that social protection has to be a key element of future developmental paths (Hall and Midgely, 2004).

This is, in fact, how ALBA, created in 2004 by Cuba and Venezuela, proposes its alternative to a model of capitalist globalisation, understood as the result of the popular rejection of neoliberal policies and competition-based forms of trade, especially the US-sponsored Free Trade Area of the Americas (FTAA) and other models of economic integration, such as MERCOSUR (Southern Common Market) (Dello Buono, 2007). ALBA currently has eight member states, including Venezuela, Cuba, Bolivia, Nicaragua, Dominica, Ecuador, St Vincent and the Grenadines, and Antigua and Barbuda. In addition, Paraguay is an observer and might join in the future. ALBA's aim is to develop an alternative model of regional integration and, as a result, is already developing a number of policy instruments, such as a regional energy infrastructure, a 'development bank of the South', independent of traditional, northern-dominated development institutions such as the World Bank or the International Monetary Fund (IMF), a digital television network and a single currency (de la Barra, 2006).

ALBA's alternative model of development is based on two key principles: international cooperation and more participative forms of democracy (Brennan and Olivet, 2007). The former is guaranteed, because ALBA constitutes a trade and solidarity bloc that is socially oriented rather than strictly in search of profit maximization. ALBA appeals to principles of social justice, well-being and human development as well as solidarity between the poorest peoples of the Americas. In this sense, it is fond of arguing that this is a form of association based on the principle of 'collaborative advantage', as opposed to the hegemonic principle of competitive advantage that informs mainstream economics. This principle of collaboration and solidarity exchanges between countries operates largely in the area of social-policy delivery, especially in health and education, making Cuba a key player within ALBA, in supporting countries' attempts to eradicate illiteracy and deliver free universal health care provision (Bossi, 2009).

The claim to participation within ALBA can be made in so far as organised civil society takes a particularly important role in its workings, as has been seen in recent ALBA summits, which include a gathering of continental-level transnational networks of civil society meeting in parallel with the formal presidential encounters. The close relationship that exists between civil society in Latin America and some ALBA members, such as Bolivia and Venezuela, suggests that ALBA goes much further than a simple set of state-level relations. Instead of following what has been termed the 'club' model of international cooperation (Benner et al., 2004), ALBA includes a network of civil-society agents closely linked to the state (Briceño Ruiz, 2007).

Thus, the argument can be made that ALBA represents a solidarity network because of its value-driven ideology that emphasises collaboration, solidarity and human development (Smith, 2009). In addition, even though it is driven by nation-states, elements of ALBA constitute a multi-level network of collaborative arrangements that includes civil society through trade unions, non-governmental organisations (NGOs), social movements, as well as governments – what has been described as a set of inter- and transnational processes where policies are driven by the interplay of state and non-state actors (Muhr, 2010). In a world in which policy transfer and aid are common features of globalised policy-making and practice, these processes of solidarity are often only explored in terms of North–South transfers. ALBA, and the Cuban contribution to solidarity transfers from within, constitute perhaps a new paradigm of development that permits us to see whether the ideological principles and institutional mechanisms that delivered the original literacy campaign in Cuba can be spread throughout Latin America. What does a literacy campaign look like in the twenty-first century and what can its outcomes be?

Cuba's Contribution to Bolivia's Educational Revolution[1]

The Cuban contribution to what Bolivians call the 'refoundation' of their country through a 'democratic and cultural revolution' has taken place mainly in the fields of education and health. In terms of education, the literacy campaign began in January 2006 with the arrival in the country of the first team of Cuban advisers, one day after new president Morales was sworn in, and ended officially on 20 December 2008. In spite of the great advances made in this three-year period, a small contingent of Cuban advisers continues to operate in the country and is currently contributing

---

1 This section builds on research materials that have appeared in a previous publication (Artaraz, 2011).

to the planning and implementation of a post-literacy campaign, initiated in March 2009, that takes its cue from Venezuela's post-literacy programme 'Misión Robinson'.

According to the last census in 2001, Bolivia had a 13.3 per cent illiteracy rate. For presidential candidate Morales in 2005, this was a major source of oppression and domination. Presenting education in very Cuban terms, as a source of personal and national liberation, we can see the ideological link made by Movimiento al Socialismo (MAS) between a campaign for the eradication of illiteracy and the 'refoundation' of Bolivia as the first step towards decolonisation. Not surprisingly, within days of his historic electoral victory on 18 December 2005, Morales signed an agreement with Cuba to offer advice on Bolivia's literacy campaign in what was the first policy of the MAS government. By 1 March 2006, the literacy campaign had already begun to be piloted around the country (interview with Benito Ayma, 2009).

Called 'Yo sí puedo' (Yes, I can), the literacy programme was based on 65 hours of face-to-face teaching in small groups, designed to be satisfactorily completed by illiterate adults in the space of three months, at a rate of five to six hours of group-work per week. As interviewed Cuban advisers recalled, the programme benefited from incorporating the lessons learned during Cuba's literacy experiment in 1961. However, one of the main features of the Bolivian campaign was that it was audio-visual, with a set of standard video-taped lessons accompanied by a reading book for each participant. As a result, group leaders and rural teachers, as well as final-year students in teacher training programmes – all paid Bolivians and not volunteers, unlike during the Cuban campaign – required minimal training to deliver a standardised literacy programme designed to bring students to the reading and writing age of a nine-year-old (interview with Alexander Avila, 2009).

The Cuban contribution to the programme was limited to advising on the pedagogical methodologies and logistics of delivery. In 2009, only around 126 Cuban advisers were present in the country, accompanied by 47 Venezuelans. Cuba also provided 30,000 television sets and videos recorded with the programme lessons, all teaching materials (methods, books and manuals for teaching staff), the 8,000 solar panels that had to be installed in rural areas without electricity that the programme was to reach, as well as the eyesight tests and reading glasses for over 50,000 adults who needed them before being able to follow the course. All of this came at no cost to Bolivia and was covered by Cuba's contribution and Venezuelan funding through ALBA.

The results speak for themselves; in the space of three years, as many as 820,000 Bolivian adults – 70 per cent of them women – have achieved the basic objectives of the programme, having learned to read and write, mostly in Spanish but also in Quechua and in Aymara for 14,000 and 25,000 people respectively. Although fewer people chose to learn to read and write in their indigenous language than was expected, the results constitute an important achievement towards the Millennium Development Goals and mean that UNESCO was able to declare the country free of illiteracy (Ministerio de Educación y Culturas, 2008).

The assessment of the literacy campaign has been extremely positive both inside and outside the country, with an enormous impact at all levels. As in the original literacy campaign in Cuba, the most important outcome was long-term political support for what Bolivians call the 'process of change', particularly in isolated rural locations where the poorest citizens made up the bulk of participants in a literacy campaign squarely identified with MAS. In addition to the narrow political gains for MAS, the literacy campaign, like its Cuban counterpart, was able to increase national cohesion in a country riddled by divisions – partly the result of high levels of cultural and ethnic diversity – by using this opportunity to teach about citizenship and inclusion, with key messages such as 'Education is a human right', 'All Bolivian cultures are equal in value' and 'Bolivian women have a right to live without fear of violence' (Ministerio de Educación y Culturas, 2006). In addition, entire communities previously isolated for lack of electricity have now, thanks to literacy and to the technical means put at their disposal in the form of televisions and solar panels, become a new politically aware section of the population.

That the literacy campaign could not possibly have been successful without Cuban expertise and Venezuelan backing is obvious. However, the literacy campaign would not have been possible without the degree of Bolivian social and political organisation that took MAS to power. In particular, the social movements such as the Confederation of Rural Workers or the Confederation of Indigenous Women have, as part of the local educational authorities, followed up progress in the campaign, providing social control of the campaign and its political legitimacy, a proviso that was included in the recent constitution (Asamblea Constituyente, 2008). Indeed, the power of Bolivian social movements is such that they are the driving force behind new educational developments that aim to go beyond the original literacy campaign.

The final and most important impact of the Bolivian literacy campaign must be the way in which it has shaped educational policy in the country. A post-literacy campaign called 'Yo sí puedo seguir' (Yes, I can continue) began in March 2009 with a first wave of 3,000 groups in 185 municipalities, followed by a second and a third wave in August and October of that year respectively. The numbers this time are much greater, with up to 1 million people taking part, a figure that includes all those who were part of the original programme, plus all those adults who have not completed primary school. The plan this time is to introduce four curriculum subjects – geography, history, maths and natural science – and to develop them until students reach the educational level of an eleven-year-old. The cost of this new plan is $50 million, a significant resource commitment for a country such as Bolivia (this post-literacy campaign is being designed and fully funded by Bolivia), but very cheap in terms of the potential gains in comparison with the costs of the formal educational system. A third phase is currently being designed for the introduction of an accelerated secondary education curriculum that is parallel to the current one and allows adults to work and study.

Bolivia has taken an enormous leap into providing basic education for the entire population, a historic first in a country known for the systematic forms of exclusion to which it subjected large sections of society. The literacy campaign would not have been possible without the support of the ALBA network. However, what is interesting is the evolution that policy thinking has taken in Bolivia during the three years that the literacy campaign lasted. Whereas the original plan was to stop at the point of having eradicated illiteracy in the country, now the policy aims are much broader and more ambitious, planning an increase in the educational level of the majority of the population and creating the basis for a working and universal educational system. This degree of ambition is linked to the political realisation that, in order to deal with illiteracy once and for all and prevent its resurgence in the near future, the country's structural conditions of inequality and oppression need to be tackled. One element of this challenge includes creating the infrastructure to ensure that secondary educational facilities reach 100 per cent of the population and that entire rural communities are not left behind, as is currently the case. The second, more difficult, challenge is ensuring that students do not feel forced to abandon their education in order to find work to survive. Until this challenge is met, functional illiteracy will continue to flourish in the country on a regular basis (interview with Alexander Avila, 2009).

Cuba's Internationalism and the Future of South–South Relations

Five decades on, both Cuba and the world have changed in ways not easily foreseen in the 1960s. With the fall of the Berlin Wall and the collapse of the Soviet Bloc, Cuba ceased to have a role as the socialist military 'emissary' to the poor South. The Revolution itself has changed, no longer willing to 'export' the type of armed insurrection that cost Guevara his life in 1967, and no longer able to punch above its weight in aid of 'liberation struggles' around the world. However, Cuba's internationalist example continues to have currency, whether on the humanitarian, medical or educational fronts (Harris, 2009). It is therefore fitting that, as the case study discussed in this chapter shows, it should have been in Bolivia, Cuba's last direct revolutionary stage more than four decades ago, that the Revolution has been able to contribute to the eradication of illiteracy, one of the latest examples of successful educational internationalism in Latin America, and something that Bolivia has only been able to dream about for most of its republican history.

Along with the Soviet Bloc, the early 1990s brought about the disappearance of the type of society that the Left considered to be its 'destination', as it struggled to imagine alternative versions of socialism (Santos, 2009). In the Latin American region, countries trying to make their societies more democratic and more just lost their political and ideological compass towards a fairer, more sustainable future as that decade saw a deepening of neoliberal economic policies that failed to deliver on both counts: higher levels of democracy and socio-economic justice. That decade was the hardest yet for the Cuban Revolution as the island had to contend with both the real crisis for survival and the apparent lack of a roadmap to socialism.

However, it seems that the internal debates in many of the countries in the region have delivered a new, invigorated set of revolutionary processes that began in Venezuela and quickly spread through the continent. These are revolutions of a different nature that do not attempt to build their understandings of democracy, justice and, increasingly, environmentally sustainable models of development by following imported recipes, as Latin America did during the twentieth century, even when, as Cuba did in the early days of the Revolution in its relations with Western European members of the New Left, it dared to look further afield. In Venezuela, Bolivia or Ecuador, the starting points are different, the conditions are unique and the social groups that have led these 'revolutions in democracy' are also special, in so far as they have often emerged from within the politics of recognition – as have indigenous peoples in the continent – to bring about political change built on indigenous forms of knowledge. These are 'refoundations', new beginnings that follow a new 'epistemology of the south' (Santos, 2010).

The result of this new continental mood is that Cuba finds herself again in fashion, not as the only beacon of a fairer society in the region but as one of a family of states attempting to put into practice the ideological principles that first informed the Cuban Revolution and its transformation of society through a literacy campaign. It is in this context that ALBA was formed and is creating the institutional mechanisms for Cuba to be able to maintain and continue to put into practice a type of internationalism that will further the principles of collaboration, solidarity and reciprocity that inform current relations between ALBA countries, just like in the case of networks of solidarity. There is a real dearth of these principles in the practice that informs North-driven international relations, even when they engage in aid transfers to the global South. This is why, in referring to Cuba's South–South social policy transfers, explanations of Cuba's reasons for engaging in internationalist cooperation that emphasise the principles under which international relations operate, such as explanations focused on the term 'diplomacy' to refer to Cuba's internationalist contributions, miss the point.

This chapter has taken a historical overview of Cuba's original literacy campaign to find explanations for its replication abroad – as was the case in Bolivia (2006–2008) – inside Cuba's revolutionary ideology. It argues that ALBA presents the Revolution with new opportunities for subverting the received wisdom informed by the logic of a capitalist mind and working instead towards making a reality the call from the World Social Forum that 'another world is possible'.

4

Floating in the Void: Ethical Weightlessness in Post-Soviet Cuba Narrative

ODETTE CASAMAYOR-CISNEROS

University of Connecticut, USA

'Still, sedentary, like moss on a stone' (Portela, 2010: 17): the words with which Zeta, the protagonist of Ena Lucía Portela's 2000 novel *Cien botellas en una pared*, describes herself 'Inmóvil, sedentaria, fija como el musguito a la piedra' (Portela, 2003: 31). Within the range of post-Soviet Cuban narrative, Zeta is one of the characters in which ethical weightlessness has been developed most coherently. She represents many young Cubans for whom, after 1989, there is little prospect of better worlds to aspire to take part in. No political system, no community, no cosmology, neither on nor off the island. Indifferent and weightless in the face of politics, history, society and the economy, these young people practise the entire suspension of moral judgment, in the tradition of the followers of Pyrrhus.

Born and currently residing on the island, the narrators Wendy Guerra (born 1970), Orlando L. Pardo Lazo (born 1971) and Ena L. Portela (born 1972) were educated within the cosmology of the Cuban Revolution, a concept through which I define the complex of ideas conditioned by the revolutionary experience that bring logic to the world that Cubans have lived in since 1959, and which sustain both the emotional and rational dimensions of their existence. Based on an epic conception of existence, moulded by the ideals of heroic sacrifice, resistance and permanent confrontation with external and internal enemies, the cosmology of the Cuban Revolution has justified the permanence of the political situation in operation, since it appeals to the notion of the liberation of the pueblo. Thus the Cuban Revolution is founded on a model of public-Kantian and libertarian-Arendtian reason.

However, these narrators, born in the 1970s, did not live through the heroic enthusiasm of the decade of the 1960s. Marked by historical facts such as the Bay of Pigs invasion in 1961, the Missile Crisis one year later, and recurrent counter-revolutionary attacks, the specifically epic quality of the 1960s was analysed by Tzvi Medin (1990), who described an ideological framework not only dominated by a total identification with the guerrilla figure and Fidel Castro, but also by 'the omnipresence of a constant situation of extremity that imposes self-definition, compromise, militancy, social cohesion cemented by the indispensable national consensus, and mobilization' (Medin, 1990: 29).

The essayist Iván de la Nuez, working on Cuban post-Soviet writers, stated that these '[h]ijos de la Revolución [...] habitan en un futuro en el que [...] la Revolución [es percibida] en una zona límite' (sons of the Revolution [...] they inhabit a future in which [...] the Revolution is [perceived] as a borderzone) (De la Nuez, 2001: 9). In his introduction to an anthology significantly entitled *Cuba y el día después,* De la Nuez explored the contradictory existential situation of young Cubans who form part of the 'engendro [...] que un día se llamó Hombre Nuevo' (malformed embryo) [...] that was once called the New Man (2001: 10), and that according to Ernesto 'Che' Guevara's pamphlet 'El socialismo y el hombre en Cuba' (Socialism and man in Cuba), would represent the perfect subject within the perfect future Communist society. De la Nuez recognised that those born after the 1960s in Cuba were educated to live the utopian society that their parents would construct on a daily basis, only to find, after the collapse of the socialist system, that they were 'conminados a imaginar y vivir un mundo diferente al prometido, como si se balanceran en una cuerda floja entre el futuro perdido y el futuro posible' (called upon to imagine and live as in a world that was very different to the promised one, as if they were balancing on a tightrope between a lost and a possible future) [(2001: 9–10). For De la Nuez, if one were to follow Guevara's parameters to the letter, one would end up with 'uncontaminated' subjects who have never known the 'pecado original del capitalismo' (original sin of capitalism), but who simultaneously have 'vivido la Revolución con el desparpajo de entender que ésta fue hecha *para* ellos [y] con la cíclica denuncia y paternalismo de sus progenitores en el poder, que no han cesado de repetirles que la Revolución no fue hecha *por* ellos' (lived the Revolution with the self-confidence of knowing that it was made *for* them [and] with the cyclical accusation and paternalism of their parents in the power structures, who have constantly and repeatedly reminded them that the Revolution was made *by* them [the parents]) (De la Nuez, 2001: 10). As a result, these young Cubans have been unable to find an epic meaning to their existence. Hence, some of Ena Lucía Portela's characters find it difficult to understand those who, at some time or other in their lives, devoted themselves to pursuing profound ideologies. With a constant recourse to sarcasm, the narrator of *Cien botellas* projects a gaze of astonishment onto the early years of the Cuban Revolution: 'Qué tumulto. Qué bullicio [...] Eran unos jactanciosos [...] Creían vivir intensamente. Creían. Los imagino rebeldes, entusiastas, dinámicos, plenos de vitalidad, optimismo e ideas novedosas. Debió ser un momento de ilusiones' (Portela, 2003: 36). (How tumultuous. How noisy [...] They believed they lived intensely [...] I imagine them rebellious, enthusiastic, dynamic, and full of vitality, optimism and new ideas. It must have been a moment of great hope.) (Portela, 2010: 20–21)

This is how Zeta describes her parents' generation, who at that time were young people living the 1960s in an atmosphere of complete epicity, convinced that the task of constructing a new society lay in their hands. In Portela's voice, those heroic years seem to have occurred in another world, a world completely alien to that which exists at the beginning of the twenty-first century. Zeta cannot understand the exaggerated emotions that characterised that period. From her perspective, her parents' existence was a serious one, where every word and every feeling carried some weight. But for her and her contemporaries, on the other hand, all affect, morality and ideology lacks value, carries no weight in their lives. Her parents' era was characterised by the weight of existence; her own is characterised by weightlessness. The dream, Portela suggests in *Cien botellas*, has been relegated to the past.[1]

Likewise, Nieve Guerra, the protagonist of Wendy Guerra's novel, *Todos se van* (Everyone is leaving) (2006), regards previous generations with the same astonishment. Nieve fears for her mother when the Berlin Wall comes down. Describing her mother, she confesses her incomprehension before a women who is devoured by politics, who is tired of carrying the weight of ideologies but who at the same time knows that she is lost without them: 'Se derrumban los muros [...] Mi madre dice que un día ella se va a derrumbar como un muro, porque no tiene fuerzas para levantar otro, ella sin muros no sabe vivir, el muro es su barricada [...] Si llegara el capitalismo, si llegara viva a tumbarse este muro de agua habría que aprender otra manera de sobrevivir. Mi madre no lo aguantará' (The walls are falling down [...] My mother says that one day she is going to fall down like a wall, because she doesn't have the strength to build another one, and she doesn't know how to live without walls, the wall is her barricade [...] If capitalism came along, if this wall of water came tumbling down, we would have to learn other ways to survive. My mother won't be able to take it) (Guerra, 2006: 249). With some amazement, she discovers that although her mother may criticise the Revolution, she cannot live without it, and what her mother suffers appears to hold little importance for Nieves: a lack of reference points, of walls against which to support herself and behind which to take refuge from the chaos.

---

1   For an interesting and intense debate on the island about *desencanto* (disenchant-ment) in contemporary Cuban literature, see Fornet, A. (2002), Fornet, J. (2006) and Pérez Cino (2002).

The Postmodern Utopia: A Global Phenomenon

Unprecedented uncertainty, worsened by the current political, ideological and economic crisis of the Cuban government, characterises the post-Soviet era. In the void created by an absence of scatological models and identity models that, from the 1990s, has dominated the island's existence, there floats the weightless subject. The positioning of this subject, nevertheless, is neither exclusively Cuban nor post-Soviet, allowing us to discover connections between this weightless posture and certain conceptualisations of global postmodernity, as developed by Frederic Jameson and Zygmunt Bauman.

What I here identify as ethical weightlessness can be related closely to the state that Jameson has attributed to postmodernity, where 'the subject has lost its capacity actively to extend its pro-tensions and re-tensions across the temporal manifold and to organize its past and future into coherent experience' (Jameson, 1991: 25). What results is a state of suspension in the present, which seems to be charged with its own substance and which requires neither to be legitimated by the past nor to incubate the seeds of the future, thus differentiating itself from modern historicity. It is worth emphasising that, in itself, the crisis of the historical *telos*, an essential element of the void that determines current existence on the island, does not necessarily lead to ethical weightlessness. This weightlessness only emerges when the subject feels indifference to history. When the subject – unable to organise its existence scatologically – can do no more than produce 'heaps of fragments', its cultural creation is transformed into the haphazard practice of heterogeneity, fragmentation, randomness (Jameson, 1991: 25). Unconnected fragments, as weightless as the 'floating organs' highlighted by Jameson in his reading of the architectural projects of Rem Koolhas (Jameson, 1994: 136), such are the characters that will be explored in the following pages. The ethical weightlessness that characterises them bears the features identified by Jameson as constitutive of postmodernity: the absence of a historical *telos*, a new 'depthlessness', the waning of affect, and the colossal impact of new technologies, a consequence of the new world economic system (Jameson, 1991: 6).

Jameson has presented the new depthlessness as being the principal formal feature of postmodernity. Postmodern depthlessness rejects those models that, within modern thought, bring a sense of depth to objects, subjects and phenomena. As for the waning of affect, Jameson refers to the 'decentering of the formerly centered subject or psyche' (typical of classical capitalism and of the nuclear family) in the world of administrative bureaucracy or, one might add, of the current existential void. Under this perspective, the conventional hero disappears when postmodernity puts an end to the bourgeois ego, to the concept of the subject as a monadic recipient whose exterior reflects its interior, as well as the resulting psychopathologies of that ego.

On the other hand, I relate here the uncertainty of post-Soviet Cuba with the ethical crisis that Zygmunt Bauman has attributed to the postmodern subject, who lives dizzyingly exposed to an infinite number of inexplicable phenomena and also to other subjects towards whom it lacks ethical norms that might regulate social interaction. The subject wanders dispossessed when (according to Bauman, they are in their greatest need), of the moral instruments that would allow harmony to be maintained when facing the highly chaotic situations of contemporary life (Bauman, 1993: 17). Bauman has thus defined postmodernity as 'a *modernity without illusions*' (Bauman, 1993: 32), in which the subject is convinced that 'the 'messiness' of the world is not transitory but will rather 'stay whatever we do or know, that the little orders and "systems" we carve out in the world are brittle, until-further-notice, and as arbitrary and in the end contingent as their alternatives'(Bauman, 1993: 32–33). According to Bauman, the 'postmodern perspective' will enable the utopian impulse that underlies the process of 'deconstructing the "without us the deluge" claims of nation-states, nations-in search-of-the-state, traditional communities and communities-in-search-of-a-tradition, tribes and neo-tribes, as well as their appointed and self-appointed spokesmen and prophets' (Bauman, 1993: 14).

As suggested by these theoretical approaches, which link post-Soviet Cuban experience with postmodern global life, the analysis of current problems should not be enclosed within an island-based perspective. It is more valuable, thus, to locate them within the spectrum of Jameson's 'late socialism', as proposed by Ariana Hernández-Reguant in the introduction to her edited volume on cultural dynamics during the Special Period (Hernández-Reguant, 2009: 2). My own research proposes that contemporary Cuba struggles at a difficult crossroads configured by what are known as Second and Third Worlds. It finds itself caught between the experience of socialism and that of underdevelopment; between the extinct geopolitical constellation of Eastern Europe and that of Latin America.

Cuban Genealogies towards Post-Soviet Weightlessness

On presenting Zeta, her author Portela, along with describing a present suspended in the void, also demonstrates the itinerary that Zeta has undertaken in order to arrive at that void. Her existence is almost a carbon copy of that exposed by De la Nuez (2001: 9–12). The contingent and de-teleologised nature that the protagonist attributes to her life is sketched in her sarcastic description of her family origins: an orphan on her mother's side – a Parisian who 'se dedicaba a ser nativa de París [. . .] leía *La náusea* y se la tomaba en serio, quizás porque la leía en francés' (Portela, 2003: 37) (dedicated herself to being a native of Paris [. . .] She read *La Nausée* and took it seriously, maybe because she read it in French) (Portela, 2010: 22), Zeta says of her birth: 'nací de pie y por poco no nazco, por muchos motivos soy la viva estampa de la casualidad' (Portela, 2003: 37) (I was born feet first and almost wasn't born at all, and so, for many reasons, I'm living proof of fate) (Portela, 2010: 22). Her father was gay and either did not know how to or was unable to concern himself with his child's education, for which Zeta would be eternally grateful. She considered herself to be 'una gordita inocente bajo la custodia de un padre soltero, más soltero que padre' (Portela, 2003: 37) (a fat little daughter in the care of her bachelor father, more bachelor than father) (Portela, 2010: 22), who emigrated to the United States as soon as possible, leaving the child behind on the island. With these letters of presentation, it is not by chance that she takes on the name of the last letter of the alphabet, an allegory of her deferred position on any value scale designed to measure human progress. A being suspended in nothingness. Abandoned in Havana in the chaos of the 1990s, Zeta can only depend on a handful of friends and on Moisés, whose mistreatment of her becomes a vehicle for his inexplicable yet profound hatred of the human race.

From birth, she lives in the ruins of a former Havana mansion, La Esquina del Martillo Alegre, as baptised by its current residents, an indescribable and innumerable collection of more or less criminal and marginal creatures. She stays there, generally drunk or high on drugs, always waiting for nothing in particular, always at the mercy of the 'business deals' and distractions provided by her friends and neighbours. Dragged along by her friend Linda, she attended university but never had the slightest inclination towards studying. In any case, as she herself explains, a university degree has no use. With the advent of the Special Period, she lost the only job she had ever held, in a 'oscura revista de temas agropecuarios' (Portela, 2003: 76) (an obscure farming magazine) (Portela, 2010: 51) since, the narrator explains, 'ya no había temas agropecuarios ni papel para imprimir la revista' (Portela, 2003: 76) (there were no more farms or paper on which to print the magazine) (Portela, 2010: 51).

Hunger seems to be the only circumstance that really affects her present life,[2] the only thing that prevents her from settling comfortably into her ideal state: a 'paraíso musulmán' (Portela, 2003: 16) (Muslim heaven) (Portela, 2010: 6), which she describes as 'la dulce complacencia del no hacer, de vegetar' (Portela, 2003: 16) (the sweet satisfaction of doing nothing at all,

---

2   See Whitfield (2008) for an examination of the influence of hunger and poverty on so-called 'Special Period literature'.

of vegging out) (Portela, 2010: 16). Within her indifference, she is able to recognise that '[p]or esas fechas la cosa económica no marchaba del todo bien. A decir verdad, no marchaba: se había paralizado. No sé si vivíamos al borde del colapso o ya dentro de él'(Portela, 2003: 76) (The economy wasn't doing so well in those days. To be frank, it wasn't doing anything at all: it was paralyzed. I don't know if we were living on the brink of collapse or in the midst of it) (Portela, 2010: 51). But nor does the protagonist find an escape route from poverty. Any conscious activity aimed at some type of progress, however insignificant it may be, lacks logic from her perspective. Following the example of her neighbours and many others in Special Period Havana, she tries to raise a pig in her apartment but considers the enterprise a disastrous initiative, because she takes care of the animal as if it was human. Gruñi Alvarez La Fronde, as she baptises the pig, dies, causing great sorrow to his owner. Also, Zeta does not want to survive from begging, as many of her compatriots do, although she is quick to recognise: 'no es que me pareciera mal vivir de limosnas, pues lo que importa es vivir [no interesa para qué, no hay que preguntarse para qué, sólo vivir]' (Portela, 2003: 79). (It's not that I thought it was wrong to live off charity, because what's important is to live [it doesn't matter what for, it makes no difference, the important thing is to live]) (Portela, 2010: 53). Nor does she succeed financially as a prostitute, because she is unable to charge for her favourite pleasure: sex. Zeta is unconcerned with everything: politics, society, her family history, her obesity and physical unattractiveness, her own future or Moisés' daily acts of aggression. She brandishes her own method, weightlessness, as protection against reality:

> Si Penélope tejía y destejía un tapiz, yo me aposentaba en el paraíso musulmán y tarareaba la canción de las cien botellas, esa que dice 'cien botellas en una pared [...] / cien botellas en una pared [...] / si una botella se ha de caer [...] / noventa y nueve botellas en una pared'[...], luego se caía otra y quedaban noventa y ocho, luego otra y otra y así hasta el final, hasta llegar a cero. De lo más entretenido, el sonsonete era también un sortilegio para conjurar la catástrofe. Me gustaba creer que, si llegaba a cero, no ocurriría ninguna desgracia. (Portela, 2003: 16)

> If Penelope weaved and undid a tapestry, I, in turn, would retire to Muslim heaven and tra-la-la that song about one hundred bottles, the one that goes: 'One hundred bottles on the wall [...] / If one should fall [...] / ninety-nine bottles on the wall [...]' Later, another would fall and there would be ninety-eight, then another and another until

the end, when there would be zero. It was quite entertaining and the little sing-song also served as a spell to avoid catastrophe. I liked to think that if I reached zero, nothing awful would happen. (Portela, 2010: 6)

However, the young protagonist never details exactly what would constitute a disaster for her. In her existence there is neither drama nor disaster. There is no solution to find because there are no problems to resolve. The Muslim heaven identifies Zeta as a floating but absolutely fixed subject. She is suspended, but she does not move towards a specific place, nor does she make any attempt to leave her situation. I thus propose that, in reality, Portela's characters have not remained balanced on a tightrope, as De la Nuez suggests. In fact, they have jumped from the tightrope and are completely indifferent to their social context. They maintain their weightlessness in the post-Soviet – and postmodern – void. They incarnate the 'depthlessness' explained by Jameson.

In her first novel of 1998, *El pájaro: pincel y tinta china*, Portela had already presented a quartet of characters alien to any of the realities that had been recreated in Cuban literature until then. Bibiana, Fabián, Camila and Emilio H are young Cubans who are indifferent and unperturbed by the turbulence of the times in which they live. Portela situates their story in August 1994, when Havana witnessed significant popular protests that would lead to the infamous Balseros Crisis during which 32,385 Cubans left the island for the United States, but these characters seem not to notice. They never question the relevance of ideas of unity or harmony, of nation and culture, of mission and destiny, nor other moral values of responsibility, humiliation or sin. They are simply unaware of all that, completing the act of *desacralización del horror* (desacralisation of horror) highlighted by Nara Araújo (Araújo, 2003: 103) in Portela's narrative. For this reason, in one section of the novel, the narrator mocks those who at the current time still preserve ideals, whatever they might be:

> [E]ran fanáticos: neoizquierdistas, neoconservadores [...] opuestos al aborto y a la pena de muerte y a la eutanasia, neonazis, neohippies [...] discotequeros, vegetarianos, espiritistas, cibernéticos, *punks*, alcohólicos, ascetas, feministas, pragmáticos, homofóbicos [...] católicos, *gays* del arcoiris, neoexistencialistas, drogadictos, anticuarios, santeros, ecologistas, psicólogos, peloteros, ateos, payasos [...] Todos tenían conexiones [...] Tenían respuestas, etiquetas, correligionarios, ídolos. Hablaban mirando hacia el frente hacia el futuro con voz altisonante y entrecejo fruncido. Se sentían en su derecho, tal vez con razón. Opinaban. Creían que pensaban, creían que sentían, creían que creían. Eran escandalosamente crédulos. Fabián, quien [...] los escuchaba

demasiado, comenzó a sospechar que por ese camino llegaría directo y sin problemas a ninguna parte.

> [T]hey were fanatics: neo-leftists, neo-conservatives [...] opposed to abortion, the death penalty and euthanasia, neo-Nazis, neo-hippies [...] disco divas, vegetarians, spiritualists, cybernauts, *punks*, alcoholics, ascetics, feminists, pragmatists, homophobes [...] Catholics, rainbow *gays*, neo-existentialists, drug addicts, antiquarians, santeros, ecologists, psychologists, baseball players, atheists, clowns [...] They all had connections. They had responses, labels, fellow believers, idols. They looked straight forward, facing the future, as they talked, with high-sounding voices and furrowed brows. They felt they were right, and perhaps they were. They expressed their opinion. They believed that they were thinking, believed that they were feeling, believed that they were believing. They were scandalously gullible. Fabián, who [...] spent too much time listening to them, began to suspect that theirs was the path that would lead directly, and with no problems, to nowhere. (Portela, 1998: 26–27)

As this fragment illustrates, Fabián is lacking in a sense of community identity. He can be explained by nothing and no-one. In such conditions of existential weightlessness, the act of forming judgments and opinions is presented by the narrator as a series of futile and socially innocuous gestures. He also lacks 'regressive nostalgia', because Portela's works do not celebrate 'the magnificence of pre-Castro Cuba' (Loss, 2007: 258).

In order to remain happily afloat in this chaotic and futureless world (in which many young Cubans currently find themselves immersed), Portela's characters arm themselves with irony and acidic sarcasm. This humour, in which I have previously found the characteristics of Gilles Lipovetsky's (1993) 'empty laughter' (see Casamayor, 2009), replaces the social agency that the protagonists neither possess nor desire to possess. Nor do they seek to avoid the suffering caused by their lack of individual impact on society. The narrator insists repeatedly that her laughter is not mockery. In *Cien botellas*, for example, Zeta considers her own laughter to be innocent, in contrast to the disapproval of those characters who surround her and who read her easy laughter as either evidence of stupidity or of her astute mockery (Portela, 2003: 52). In this way, a lover who is 'Dutch or South African Boer' – our indifferent protagonist does not know – slaps her thinking she is mocking him, because, whilst he talks to her in his incomprehensible language, she contents herself with smiling 'beatífica, para que el infeliz no se [sintiera] incomprendido' (Portela, 2003: 125) (beatific, so the poor man doesn't feel misunderstood) (Portela, 2010: 86). In addition, her sadistic husband Moisés threatens to throw her out of the window if she continues to laugh about the difficulties of the Special Period. Whilst the city outside slowly dies from its economic hardships and vanishing hopes, Zeta is either unperturbed or, alternatively, smiling innocently. It is at this point that Moisés, driven to desperation by her smile, explodes, slamming his fists on the table – a habit that the narrator highlights because the dramatic gesture contrasts with her own indifference – and reproaches her: 'que estábamos empantanados en el desastre, en la catástrofe, en la hecatombe, en el infierno, en la puta mierda [. . .] Que no había de qué reírse. Que riéndome parecía lo que en efecto era: una soberana imbécil' (Portela, 2003: 54) (that we were sinking into disaster, catastrophe, a massacre, Hell, into pure shit. [. . .] There was nothing to laugh about. In fact, while I laughed, I looked exactly like what I was: a great imbecile) (Portela, 2010: 34). Zeta, for her part, does not understand the irate reactions that her attitude provokes, because, for her, her laugh has no intrinsic motivations and is only given meaning by others.

The protagonist Nieve Guerra situates herself similarly in Wendy Guerra's *Todos se van*. She knows that she carries no weight in society, and thus, that there is no reason to worry, hope or protest. She confesses: 'Sólo quiero escapar de la política, no soporto verme metida en todo esto. Algo me dice que no sé pelear en esas ligas' (I only want to escape politics, I can't bear to see myself stuck in all of this. Something tells me that I don't know the rules of this league) (Guerra, 2006: 188). Nieve reaches this state after years of censorship and authoritarianism, of silence and whispers, of crushing patriarchy. In this novel, Guerra presents how the Revolution has gone adrift through the perspectives of Nieve and her mother. This perspective is one of abandoned women, stranded on an island that is left to its fate as long as the two women remain there: the mother, out of tiredness; the daughter, out of indifference. However, the two have experienced during every period of the Revolution the incomprehension and arbitrariness of the men who steer the destiny of the nation, of society and of the family. Authority on the island is masculine and patriarchal, and it constantly crushes or excludes them. The *machismo* of revolutionary Cuban society is exercised principally by the father, then by Osvaldo, the protagonist's lover. Both these characters, and each in their own way, betray and mistreat the protagonist, forbidding her from keeping a diary in which to empty her thoughts. Thus, Guerra draws an exact correspondence between machismo and censorship: 'No sé por qué mi padre y Osvaldo odian el diario. La historia se repite en ciclos que regresan para recordarme que nunca he sido mi propia dueña [. . .] la censura aparece siempre con cada hombre que me cruzo en el camino' (I don't know why my father and Osvaldo hate my diary. History repeats itself in cycles which return to remind me that I have never been my own mistress [. . .] censorship always appears with every man who crosses my path) (Guerra, 2006: 224).

In *Todos se van* we witness the slow process by which the ethical weight-lessness of the protagonist is constituted via the daily sedimentation of the absurd within her existence. Like Zeta, she personifies the sordid infancy of – playing with Guevara's concept – the New Woman. Her life has also been 'constructed' on the basis of family fragmentation and chaos that in this case is directly linked to post-1959 national history. Nieve's mother was a 'hija de la patria' ('daughter of the *patria'*), as, when her parents took exile in Miami and she decided to remain on the island, Nieve's mother was 'adoptada' ('adopted') by the Revolution (Guerra, 2006: 145). However, on reaching adulthood, she was marginalised and censored as an artist because, although she considered herself a revolutionary, she differed from many government postures that, in her opinion, denied the authentic nature of the Revolution.

Whilst revolutionary speeches reiterate the importance of youth for the future of the nation and present in spectacular fashion the Revolution achieve-ments in giving new generations of Cubans a comprehensive education, Nieve sees her mother leave for Angola, sent to an absurd war, and sees her return sick with malaria, whilst Nieve's school education has been damaged by her mother's absence in Angola. A few days after her return to Cuba, and still extremely ill, the mother loses custody of her daughter, who passes into the guardianship of her father, the personification of arbitrary power and mistreatment. Thus, the contradictions between revolutionary speeches and reality dominate Nieve's description of her childhood. When the time comes to go and live with her father, she recalls: 'Fui a la oficina de la mano de una señora que me dijo dos veces: "La revolución no te abandonará." No sé qué tiene que ver la revolución en esto. Mi padre me esperaba sentado en la silla del juez. La señora le dio a firmar unos papeles y me entregó como si fuera un paquete de correo [...] . Mi padre [...] ganó y nosotros perdimos' (I went to the office holding hands with a lady who twice told me: 'The Revolution will not abandon you.' I have no idea what the revolution has to do with all of this. My father was sitting in the judge's chair and waiting for me. The lady gave him some papers to sign and handed me over as if I were a postal delivery [...] My father won and we lost) (Guerra, 2006: 39).

Like Zeta, Nieve also brings herself up and, as an adolescent, she becomes one of the *becados*, boarding students living most of their time far from their families in a situation of perpetual gregariousness, as Nieve describes it. Traditional family ties and moral concepts splinter under this system. Guerra devotes an entire chapter to describing the uniformity predominant in the spirit of this generation, on which Nieve states: 'Nosotros, los hijos, a veces queremos olvidar los apellidos y hacemos verdaderas hazañas por volvernos uno más de aquellos que componen la larga fila de la bandeja de aluminio' (We children sometimes want to forget our surnames and we achieve great feats by becoming just another one of those people who make up the long line handing aluminium trays) (Guerra, 2006: 140). With the aluminium tray, Guerra alludes to the image of a line of adolescents, all in uniform, waiting for their daily portion of food (the same diet for all), in a student refectory.

From time to time there are direct confrontations between Nieve and her mother. For example, when the child has to attend, along with her classmates, the infamous *actos de repudio* (acts of repudiation) against her fellow citizens who in 1980 had decided to emigrate to the United States via Mariel; her mother forbids Nieve to attend such acts (in which those who left the country were subjected to violent and unjust attacks). However, Nieve attends them at times 'sólo por cumplir' (only to do my duty) (Guerra, 2006: 125). On one occasion, the individual under scrutiny is an acquaintance and the mother attempts to rescue Nieve from the scene, shouting: 'Vámonos de aquí, que esto no es la revolución' (Let's get out of here, this is nothing to do with the Revolution) (Guerra, 2006: 126). Nieve is thus brought up in an absurd world located between the disappointment of her mother and the demands of her own social life. Spending her time hiding so as not to have to attend the revolutionary marches in which little or nothing remains of the original revolutionary spirit, her dilemma lies in whether to disobey her mother or to disobey the political power, which is inevitably patriarchal.

Her diary allows her to understand the existential chaos that is developing within her, that is, her inability to understand that society in which she has been brought up. Her relationship to heroism, a basic element of the cosmology of the Cuban Revolution, is complicated not only because her vision of war is determined by the damaging impact that the conflict in Angola had on her own life, but also because, since childhood, her generation has been inculcated in maintaining a strange relationship with the pantheon of revolutionary heroes:

> Cada uno de nosotros le debe 'una peseta a cada mártir', dice mi madre: al asma del Che, al cuerpo de Camilo en el mar, al que escribió con sangre antes de morir el nombre de Fidel en una pared, a los que mataron en Angola, a los que se perdieron en Bolivia, a los mambises, a todo el mundo le debemos algo. Ellos son los que hicieron todo por nosotros; nosotros no podemos hacer mucho por ellos. Creo que les debíamos todo eso mucho antes de que naciéramos.

> Each one of us owes 'a penny for every martyr', my mother tells me: Che's asthma, Camilo's body lost at sea, the one who wrote Fidel's name on a wall in his own blood before he died, the ones who were killed in Angola, the ones that were lost in Bolivia, the *mambises*, we owe something to everyone. They're the ones who did everything for us; there's not that much we can do for them. I think we owed them all of that long before we were born. (Guerra, 2006: 139)

For young Cubans such as Nieve, Zeta and those described in De la Nuez's (2001) essay who do not feel part of the revolutionary epic, the logic of heroism is founded on a position of forced gratitude; gratitude for something they have known only through ideological rhetoric and history books. Thus, the absurd replaces the sense of epic in the protagonist's world. At various points in the novel, Nieve confesses her aversion towards the military training practices that, as a young student of art, she was obliged to undertake:

> Como no podemos estropearnos las manos trabajando en el campo porque somos el futuro artístico de la patria, decidieron cambiar los cuarenta y cinco días de 'escuela al campo' por otros tantos en la Escuela de Preparación Militar. [. . .] No soporto nada militar [. . .] pero si no voy me sacan de la escuela; como dice la consigna: 'Cada cubano debe saber tirar y tirar bien'.

> As we aren't allowed to ruin our hands working the fields because we are the future artists of the patria, they decided to swap the forty-five days of the 'school in the countryside' for as many days in the School for Military Training [. . .] I can't stand anything military [. . .] but if I don't go they'll throw me out of school. As the slogan says: 'Each and every Cuban must know how to shoot and to shoot well'. (Guerra, 2006: 148)

The era of urgency and epic feats, so characteristic of the first years of revolution, is clearly in the past. In the present, the young protagonist complains at being locked up in a military camp, 'aprendiendo a matar a alguien que aún no sabemos quién es' (learning to kill someone that nobody knows who it is yet) (Guerra, 2006: 154). Quite simply, this phrase contains the essential feeling of her generation in regard to the extreme situations of revolutionary life in the 1960s. Playa Girón, counter-revolutionary attacks, the Missile Crisis, are historical events described in textbooks and commemorated in political ceremonies. These are texts, not lived experiences (and even less personal projects), and are now obsolete and incoherent. Confrontation and the need to defend the Revolution have, for these young Cubans, become abstract situations, repeated in school projects and speeches, and simulated in absurd military exercises.

Sown in a void, the modern concept of heroism has its roots suspended, provoking the state of weightlessness in which Nieve finds herself. Likewise, when in her desire to stand out as an individual from the uniform masses that her generation has become, she shaves her head 'para que entiendan que yo soy yo' (so that they understand that I am my own self), her mother drops a Chinese jar that was the remaining memory of her paternal grandparents in the house. The past, 'jarrón chino, porcelana china, vida escrita en chino que no entiendo' (Chinese jar, porcelain china, a life written in Chinese that I can't understand) ends up shattered as a result of Nieve's act of individualisation (Guerra, 2006: 140).

Just as the past falls apart, so too disappear her friends, lovers and family members, as they gradually leave the country. But not even escaping from Cuba represents a real departure for the weightless subject: 'He dicho adiós tantas veces y para nada, aquí sigo anclada al fondo' (I have said goodbye so many times and what for? Here I am, still anchored to the bottom of the sea), states the protagonist (Guerra, 2006: 248). Whilst the rest leave, Nieve – like Zeta – is unable to abandon the absurd world in which she lives; nor do these two protagonists need to leave that world, because they have never been anchored to it. They have merely floated. In Nieve's case, she is floating and indifferent, but keeping her memories, noting everything in the diary that, when all the others leave, becomes her only companion. More specifically, she fills her diary with the sudden and unexpected events that accompanied the collapse of the Soviet bloc in 1989. These archived facts appear unconnected, lacking a narrative: they are the fragments that, according to Jameson, are the only remaining way to express history that is possible for the postmodern subject, a text stripped of meaning, substituting the heavy burden that history has been in the modern world. Nevertheless, despite the incoherence of her diary, it records the advice that Antonio, her last lover, dictated to Nieve: 'Respeta el pasado. No me olvides. No colabores con la desmemoria. Déjate llevar por el recuerdo aunque sea vacuo, así fue pues así nos lo dejaron entender' (Respect the past. Don't forget me. Don't cooperate with forgetfulness. Let yourself be carried along by memories, even trivial ones, that's how it was as that's how they told it to us) (Guerra, 2006: 271).

In the final pages, the author reproduces in fragmented form the history without meaning to which Nieve has known no other way to respond but like a block of ice, drifting halfway between reality and the sea depths: 'Invernando en [sus] ideas, sin poder desplazar[se], para siempre condenada a la inmovilidad' (Hibernating in [her] ideas, unable to move, condemned to eternal immobility) (Guerra, 2006: 285). For, whilst the entire world changes along with the fall of the Berlin Wall, the protagonist affirms that in Cuba, these events are silenced and daily life continues undisturbed, even with increasing numbers leaving the island – like her father who left in 1980 or her boyfriend Osvaldo who leaves in the 1990s – or disappearing as victims of political persecution, as in the case of Antonio. Nieve wonders: 'Ahora parece que son ladrillos y ladrillos al suelo, familias reencontrándose, todo vuelve. [...] No me imagino cómo podemos romper aquí un muro de agua, amorfo y profundo' (Now it seems that there are bricks and more bricks on the ground, families being reunited, everything is returning. [...] I have no idea how we can break down this wall of water, amorphous and deep) (Guerra, 2006: 250). The rest of the world is solid, with bricks that crumble and new lives that begin. On the island, the only solution available to Nieve is to float in formless, dense and unbreakable chaos.

At the end of the novel, when she has lost everything, including friends and shelter – because her mother's humble apartment collapses and Osvaldo's house is re-appropriated by the government after his exile – she runs towards the sea, throwing off her clothes to enter the cold December waters; the immediate impression here is that Nieve will abandon her life on the island, whether through suicide or, with luck, by reaching the coast of Florida. Instead, the unimaginable happens:

> Orden, tranquilidad y silencio' sentí mientras se producía la inmersión. Luego subir, subir, para nada. Cada vez me acercaba más a la super-ficie, pues de allí soy. Emergí poco a poco, mirando alrededor, pero preferí sucumbir hasta que la línea de agua tapara mi cara, separando, desprendiendo mi suerte de la realidad. De repente una lluvia blanca empezó a caer sobre el mar [...] Sigo estando viva, sigo siendo nieve sobre nieve. Ahora soy una piedra de hielo con algunas algas, unos cuantos moluscos, papeles arrugados y arena dispersa. A la deriva viajo poco a poco hasta la inmovilidad total.

> Order, tranquillity and silence', I felt as I was immersed. Then, rise, rise, but in vain. Each time I got closer to the surface, for that's where I am from. I emerged gradually, looking around, but I preferred to surrender until the line of water covered my face, separating and detaching my fate from reality. All of a sudden, a white rain began to fall on the sea [...] I am still alive, I am still snow on snow. Now I am a block of ice with a few pieces of seaweed, a few molluscs, a few pieces of wrinkled paper and some grains of sand. I drift gradually towards total immobility. (Guerra, 2006: 284–285)

Wavering between order and chaos, between the possible world of the depths and the real world of the surface, the protagonist ends up paralysed by an impossible Havana snow, neither in one place nor another. Alive but weightless.

An X-ray of Weightlessness

Also inert, surrounded by the incomprehensible fragments of history, are the characters of the short stories included in *Boring Home* (Pardo Lazo,

2009). This book has not been supported by any of the traditional publishing houses, but by the Bibliotecas Independientes movement.[3] *Boring Home* won the Novelas de Gaveta Franz Kafka literary competition, created by Radio Praga (Czech Republic) in order to offer publication opportunities to Cuban authors living on the island who write only to keep their work 'hidden in drawers', because they are unlikely to be published officially. The Czech publishing house Garamond printed 1,000 copies which were not sold but sent to Cuba to be freely distributed (and the book is also available on the Internet). In addition, Pardo Lazo is a regular blogger on aspects of Cuban reality that are not disseminated through the official media. Virtuality thus dominates his writing and penetrates the short stories contained in *Boring Home*.

Pardo's collection of short stories is built on the pun, where words continuously come undone in the confused and tedious world of contemporary Havana, through which his characters move as if suspended. Young people wander about a city that spreads out into desolate and dark neighbourhoods totally immersed in chaos. In the short story that gives the book its title, Nora and Sondra rent their garage to a Cuban-American who has returned to the island in the hope of dying in the house in which he was born, now a rental house and the property of the two young women. Weightless in true Havana style, not only do they welcome the returning exile and help him to die, but they also involve him in their Cuban 'nada', their nothingness. The moribund Orlando Woolf passes away aware that he has returned to a home that no longer exists, a maternal household that is no longer so: *boring home*, the boring house, the tedium of every day and, at the same time, a pun on the novel *Boarding Home* (1987), by the exiled writer Guillermo Rosales (1946–1993), who passed away in Miami in the midst of incomprehension from Cubans on both shores.

Orlando Woolf ends his days in Hanada, as Pardo often calls the city that appears in his short stories. In that same Hanada wander the protagonists of other stories, such as Orlando, Silvia and the recurrent Ipatria. The latter is perhaps the most virtual of all the characters in this book. In her name, the 'I' alludes to the virtual world of the Internet, and the patria refers to a nation that no longer exists, the house or 'home' that has disappeared. In the short story *Ipatria, Alamar, un cóndor, la noche y yo*, Ipatria, symbolising the drifting and indifference characteristic of the weightless subject, lives – along with the narrator – strange nocturnal adventures

---

3 Consisting of a network of over 100 libraries installed in Cuban homes since 1998, the aim of the Bibliotecas Independientes movement has been to facilitate the reading of books that are not promoted by the official institutions.

in which the past (charged with history) floats like suspended droplets in the amorphous present. Ipatria is one of the few Chileans who remained in Cuba, even after the restoration of democracy in Chile and the end of the Cold War in the 1990s. She vegetates in her neighbourhood in Alamar (East Havana), which, until some twelve years ago, was reserved for Chilean political refugees, just as another 'Zone' in Alamar also existed for Soviets residing in Cuba. The abandoned area is today a *páramo* (bleak wasteland), more deserted even than the already bleak Alamar, in the opinion of the narrator who also describes this crumbling neighbourhood as a *cementerio obrero* (working-class cementery) (Pardo Lazo, 2009: 88). In Alamar, which was built in the 1970s as the model socialist neighbourhood, lie the vestiges of socialism. There, where meaningless and nothingness prevail, 'solitarios a dúo en [...] la Siberia cubana' (a solitary duet in [...] Cuban Siberia) (Pardo Lazo, 2009: 99), is where the protagonists of this short story move, between darkness, noisy neighbours and the chaotic fragments of history. Ipatria recites history madly: Salvador Allende's coming to power, the coup d'état of 1973, the persecution and murder of many Chileans (her mother one of them), the exodus of her father and herself alongside many militants in that corner of Alamar. The narrator finds no logic in the girl's story and as such, that story – which is actually the history of Latin America and its revolutions – seems unintelligible. Life is instead lived with the body, hungry and torn apart, through the impossible love between the protagonists.

History – or its uselessness – also figures at the centre of another short story, 'Wunderkammer', where Ipatria and the narrator devote themselves to burning newspaper cuttings that the narrator's father had secretly collected. Now that the father is finally dead, they can enter his bedroom (to which access had been denied to them for the very five decades the Cuban revolution has last) and discover the strange collection that he had devoted his life to: the 'medieval cámara de las maravillas. O cualquiera que sea el nombre del acto paterno de narrar por corte y compilación' (medieval chamber of marvels. Or whatever you might call the paternal act of narrating through cuttings and compilations) (Pardo Lazo, 2009: 177). The newspapers and pieces of information preserved here would allow them to link together the history of the revolutionary Cuba in which they live, but Pardo's protagonists are indifferent to such a task:

> Aquellos ripios ya no tenían, para nuestra generación, ni siquiera un valor documental [...] Tedium vitae reconcentrado, mimesis mala: una parodia no tan simpática como patética, cuyo mejor destino sería su conversión en ceniza, peste y vapor de agua [...] [T]ranquilamente trocables en dióxido de carbono y vapor de agua: titulares transparentes,

ingrávidos, más gaseosos que graciosos, como el supuesto sentido de aquella galería curada por mi padre durante cincuenta años.

For our generation, that printed waffling no longer had even a documentary value [...] A condensed Tedium vitae, a poor mimesis: a parody that was not so much sympathetic as pathetic, whose most worthy destiny would be to become ash, stench, steam [...] [E]asily exchangeable with carbon dioxide and steam: transparent, weightless headlines, more gaseous than gracious, like the apparent meaning of that gallery that my father had curated for fifty years. (Pardo Lazo, 2009: 175, 177)

Indiscriminate burning is the only possible destination given to the newspapers – or to history. Burning that is carried out without anger or triumphalism. A simple bonfire. To convert history into smoke, weightless matter, to only make disappear the structuring myth of the society in which they live. However, the story ends with the hypothesis that the act of cremation that the characters perform also enters the paternal acts of narration (Pardo Lazo, 2009: 177). And thus to burn, to unmake history, to annihilate the myth, could constitute another narrative. A utopia. Post-Soviet. Postmodern. Because smoke exists. History does not really disappear; it remains suspended over all things and all people. Even worse, it is breathed constantly. The string of insults and incoherent phrases articulated by Ipatria fuel her madness, which is her existence. Only death can save one from history. Meaningless words, ashes suspended in the air, the stench they exude, the vapour of water that has condensed into rain, the snow falling on Nieve Guerra as she floats in the waters of Havana: they are all still history, although history takes a weightless form in the postmodern present.

The historical *telos*, the logic with which history reclothes itself in modern society, is the only thing actually destroyed by the weightless subject. But to claim to be completely disconnected from history is a gesture which is identifiable as postmodernly utopian. The persistence and survival of the utopian impulse in postmodern life was ultimately evident to Jameson, who assured that 'the most powerful arguments against Utopia are in reality Utopian ones, expressions of a Utopian impulse *qui s'ignore* [...] it can scarcely be surprising that this particular political unconscious is to be identified even there where it is the most passionately decried and denounced' (Jameson, 1994: 54–55).

The very same notion of indifference to society is the expression of a utopia. In the characters presented in this chapter, to remain unconnected and floating, suggests an idea of collective relationality, based this time on the ideal of non-relationality.

Post-Soviet Cuban Weightlessness within Latin American Postmodernity

Through analysing these topics through the prism of global postmodernity, it is not difficult to trace parallelisms between this island-based literature and contemporary Latin American literary production, even if one can no longer talk of the existence of a literature that is markedly Latin American. The aesthetic and ethical coincidences between writers on the island and in other areas of the globe demonstrate that the Cuban case is not exceptional. It is true that Cuban narrators have sought survival not only against the economic and ideological shipwreck caused by the collapse of socialism, but also against the existential void attributed to the postmodern subject, to which they were exposed once the protective armour of the Cold War disintegrated. This existential drifting is also present in the rest of Latin America, and nuanced by the specificities of each nation. Even if other countries did not experience the socialist revolution, were not directly affected by the fall of the Berlin Wall, and did not witness the avalanche of foreign capital in the 1990s in the way that Cuba did, a similar sensation of abandonment and uncertainty is noticeable in these societies. This has been recreated by artists throughout the continent, such as the narrators affiliated to the 'Manifiesto Crack' (Volpi, Urroz and Chávez, 1996) in Mexico, or those included in the anthologies *Cuentos con Walkman* (Fuguet and Gomez, 1993) and *McOndo* (Fuguet and Gómez, 1996).

More than literary circles, we are witnessing new sensibilities confronting the life and interpretation of Latin America, as Alberto Fuguet, anthologist of *McOndo*, recognises (Fuguet, 2001: 69). Fuguet describes these authors as 'Global, local, and unplugged', supporting the redefinition that they propose as Latin Americans (Fuguet, 2001: 73). Taking the space of one imaginary America, another one is advanced. McOndo vs. Macondo or McOndo after Gabriel García Márquez's (2006) Macondo? Ultimately, neither one nor the other; instead, the postmodern utopian impulse also recognisable in weightless Cuban narrative. In the new literary Latin America baptised as McOndo, magical realism was simply replaced by 'virtual realism'. Introducing a narrative that saw itself as more grounded in reality, the compilers of *McOndo* smiled ironically at the ascent of Remedios la Bella, but, once the prologue of their book was complete, they congratulated themselves for having finally produced magic, the magic which oozed from the technological simultaneity which is proper to globalisation times (Fuguet and Gómez, 1996: 18). There is, of course, a hint of self-satisfaction in the words of Alberto Fuguet and Sergio Gómez in, for example, their recognition of MTV Latina as an integrating medium for Latin American youth. Their gesture also exposes that ideological process that Jameson terms 'cynical reason': 'the empty ideology that accompanies the practices of profit and money making, and that has (and needs) no content to disguise itself [. . .] Cynical reason is simply this recognition, and it is therefore a new form of ideology or if you prefer a new ideological process rather than a new ideology as such' (Jameson, 2005: 229). It is, ultimately, a world that is positioned behind – and not after – the modern world and its revolutions, in a weightless atemporality.

In *McOndo* stubbornly also emerges the desire to offer a homogeneous vision of Latin American reality – even when the defenders of this project claimed to recognise themselves in a certain individual and conclusive heterogeneity – and even when they repeat that they have no idea or plan for the future of Latin American reality. In other words, it is nothing more than a new mythical place, another *heterotopia* in Foucauldian terms, but this time a postmodern one. Its sign is clearly opposite to that of Macondo, because now the question is no longer one of pledging allegiance to a political project, nor of defending a traditional or historical legacy, but, rather, of flatly refusing both gestures. However, the ambition to universalise, integrate and define persists in what Fuguet and Gómez called the 'moral walkman' that, according to them, characterised a hopeless generation, a generation of interference and static. They knew, nevertheless, that 'aún es demasiado temprano para saber qué va a pasar' (it is still too early to know what will happen) and they wanted to write 'desde ese punto donde se intersecta el futuro con el ahora. Un gran lugar donde mirar la puesta del sol. Un lugar lleno de posibilidades' (from that viewpoint where the future interests with the now. A great place from which to watch the sunset. A place that is full of possibilities) (Fuguet and Gómez, 1996: 11–15). In that euphoria, there is a utopian breath that does not abandon McOndian postmodernity, a postmodernity that is largely racially white and possesses sufficient resources to be able to stutter between PC and Mac, to walk with ears blocked back then by a walkman . . . and now by an iPod.

How does Cuba, which in 1989 experienced a definitive rupture at all levels of existence, fit within this panorama? There does, of course, exist a Cuban specificity – but not a Cuban exceptionalism – within the contemporary Latin American context. This singularity does not reside in the much-debated concept of *cubanía*, which, as a creation of the Cuban subject, responds to that subject's own vision of the world. What is truly singular about the post-Soviet experience of Cubans derives from the fact that contemporary life on the island can be considered a postcolonial, postmodern, post-industrial, post-Soviet and post-Cold War laboratory within Latin America. Post-Soviet Cuba thus constitutes a specific site, in which the drifting experienced by other young people in Latin America and the rest of the world is particularly visible, ever since, in the 1990s, their parents renounced the Revolution and their dreams.

5

Celebrating 50 Years – But of What Exactly and Why is Latin America Celebrating It?

ANTONI KAPCIA

University of Nottingham, UK

In September 2010, Raúl Castro shocked Cubans and non-Cubans by announcing that, over five years, around a million jobs would be cut from Cuba's overstaffed state sector (accounting for some 80 per cent of its economy), half of those in the coming six months. While, for Cubans, the shock was palpable (few having believed either his previous warnings about inefficient overstaffing or that it would affect them individually), the world's media assumed that it was the death knell for Cuban socialism. When Fidel Castro then, responding to a US journalist's question about the exportability of the 'Cuban model', joked that the model no longer worked even for Cubans, this too seemed to confirm the abandonment of the 'model'.

However, we should treat such interpretations with caution, remembering that the same death-knell had been assumed many times: in 1962–1963 (when the Revolution's first major economic crisis threatened to derail the whole project), in 1970 (with the disastrous 10-million ton sugar harvest, or *zafra*), in 1989–1994 (when Cuba seemed destined to follow the Socialist Bloc's career towards capitalism) and in 2007 (when Raúl Castro, slating the Cuban system, encouraged Cubans to add their own criticisms in a nationwide consultation). So we have certainly been here before.

This, of course, also raises another set of issues, about continuity and longevity. While the 1990s and early 2000s saw several studies seeking to explain the Revolution's survival (Fernández, 2000; Kapcia, 2000) – correcting the equally prolific literature in the early 1990s predicting or assuming its imminent demise (Baloyra, 1993; Eckstein, 1994; Horowitz, 2008), the more pertinent issue now is not *why* it survived but rather *what* has survived. In other words, as Cubans themselves were urged to consider in the 1990s, what exactly do we mean by 'the Revolution' and what might 'Cuban socialism' mean, now as in the 1960s, 1970s or 1990s (i.e. the moments when the same question was posed, in the light of then seemingly significant changes to the political direction)? Moreover, we should not forget that another aspect of longevity and continuity regarding Cuba can be detected in the fact that, just as many on the Left in the 1960s saw in the new Cuba some sort of model, both to achieve revolution and to create a desirable anti-imperialist and egalitarian system, and just as, in the 1970s, progressive Latin American and Caribbean governments turned to Cuba for advice on how to structure their social and land reform programmes, so too now, since the late 1990s, have an increasing number of politicians and governments in Latin America turned to Cuba for some sort of template. This, therefore, in turn raises the question as to whether it is the rest of Latin America that has changed in what it takes from Cuba or whether the changes in Cubans' own definition of their 'Revolution' are less important than any continuity within the whole process.

To attempt to answer this question, we should start by looking back to those key moments, posing the same question: what was 'the Revolution' about at that time? What were its politics, its underlying ideology and its implicit and explicit intentions? Clearly, given the limitations of space and the complexity of the issues, one must simplify the argument considerably, focusing specifically on selected aspects of the politics of each moment. Those are: what actions were then significant in defining the new 'Revolution' (laws passed, policies pursued and processes under way, if not always evident at the time); and what did the discourse of the time reveal about the deeper aims and possible future directions?

The Early Revolution

If we start at the beginning (1959 to mid-1960), we can in retrospect see some things very clearly, although those months were so bewildering, with rapid government changes (as the Revolution's political character became more defined), and so many apparently significant events and measures that everything seemed decisive at the time. Nonetheless, some moments can be isolated as being of special long-term significance.

Of these, the May 1959 agrarian reform was perhaps the most fundamental, although the stipulations of the law itself were not especially radical (in comparison with earlier Latin American reforms). While defending the principle of private property (and not privileging 'communal' patterns), in the guaranteed minimum of 27 hectares and the permitted maximum (which, at 402.6 hectares, was remarkably high for what many assumed was a socialist reform), it limited itself to focusing on efficiency and fair ownership.

However, nothing in Cuba in 1959 was ever that simple. As political positions radicalised, the definition of a maximum landholding meant an inevitable conflict with US corporate interests, which then accounted for about

37 per cent of Cuba's sugar production (O'Connor 1970: 27), with serious implications, given the United Fruit Company's recent involvement in the overthrow of the Arbenz government in Guatemala in 1954. Hence, a reform adversely affecting those interests was far from neutral in its implications, as recognised by some of the so-called Tarará group (the 'inner circle' of ex-rebels who planned the reform) – most notably Ernesto 'Che' Guevara (a veteran of Guatemala and one of the few rebels with a clear anti-imperialist perspective), the two Castro brothers, and Antonio Núñez Jiménez, Oscar Pino Santos and César Escalante (all three from the pro-Moscow communist party, the Partido Socialista Popular (PSP)).

Beyond those long-term implications, however, the reform's seemingly less important 'collectivist' elements were also significant, suggesting a social-democratic or socialist character that emerged more clearly as the reform's momentum developed, as cooperatives gained in prestige (guaranteeing benefits not associated with private landholdings), and then, in late 1960 and 1961, lost out to the collective *granjas del pueblo* (O'Connor, 1970), which, initially created as an efficiency measure for cattle farms (although not without an awareness of the Eastern European experience), increasingly attracted labour away from the cooperatives. The third Agrarian Reform (1963) finally confirmed this drift towards greater collectivism. Equally, the creation and scope of the all-powerful Instituto Nacional de Reforma Agraria (INRA) soon exceeded all expectations; in a Cuba where the old state had collapsed and the new one was still inchoate, INRA effectively became 'the Revolution' in the countryside, dominating decisions nationally and locally in questions of investment, infrastructure, education and political socialisation (O'Connor, 1970). In other words, in the absence of a powerful state, INRA *was* the embryonic state for many Cubans, and, while many outside observers sought evidence of the Revolution's politics in the government, the PSP or the Rebel Army, was the institution that most decisively determined the process's evolving politics.

Here, of course, lay one of the Revolution's greatest attractions for the contemporary Latin American Left, which, persuaded by the Cuban leaders' rhetoric and Guevara's writings, identified the Revolution with a peasant base, seeing the broad-brush picture of the reforms as reflecting a 'different' socialism from the old, stultifying Soviet models; indeed, it was the less radical 1959 measures that stirred their admiration (more for the priority given to the peasantry than for the detail of the distribution) than the inherently more radical 1963 measures. This, of course, confirmed that what the Left wanted from Cuba was more a reflection of its own preferences and expectations, in this being no different from the North American or European Left (Artaraz, 2009; Gosse, 1993) in reading into the new Revolution a definition that said more about them than about the Cuban reality.

The second key phenomenon of those early years was, unquestionably, the experience of participation emerging after 1960. While outsiders – witnessing rallies of protest or celebration, or Fidel's impromptu meetings with 'ordinary' Cubans – might marvel at the supposedly 'organic' relationship between 'the masses' and Fidel (Sartre, 1961), the reality on the ground was a structured process of political involvement, soon responding to the imperatives of central direction and mobilisation *of*, rather than *by*, 'the people'.

The earliest such mechanism, seminal for those involved, was the Milicias Revolucionarias, created in October 1959 specifically to counter the growing threat of counter-revolutionary sabotage and to prepare for the impending invasion (Manke, 2011). That body was seminal, shaping a long-lasting depth of loyalty among those often very young Cubans who volunteered to defend the Revolution and emulate the 'heroic' guerrillas of the Sierra. The fact that, in April 1961, those militias (based on local peasants) proved crucial in resisting the invasion at Playa Girón strengthened the *milicianos'* self-image as critical to the Revolution's survival and outcome.

The same can be said of the Committees for the Defence of the Revolution (CDR), created in September 1960, also to prepare for the invasion. Involving ordinary Cubans on a weekly basis, while a potentially overarching party was still embryonic, the CDRs proved seminal to a sense of empowerment, to political socialisation and to the many processes by which social reform was spread to the lowest level (Fagen, 1969: 69–103).

The third area of defining processes came in the cultural field. First, in March 1959, the Instituto Cubano de Artes e Industrias Cinematográficas (ICAIC; Cuban cinema institute) became the Revolution's first national institution, recognising the mobilising and radicalising potential of a revolutionary cinema and inspired by the experiences of the early Soviet revolution, the Spanish Republic and Mexico. Second, a month later came the cultural centre, Casa de las Américas, specifically to link the Revolution's culture (as yet undefined) with a wider Latin American context then finding its identity through the incipient 'boom'. By giving the new Revolution a clearly Latin American dimension, Casa clearly anticipated Cuba's later cultural definition, in its emerging *tercermundismo* (thirdworldism), exemplified by Fernández Retamar's seminal 1971 essay, *Calibán* (1980).

Finally, those early years saw the grassroots emergence of what would eventually be defined as the movement of *instructores de arte*: the attempt to 'spread the Revolution' through culture, which, teaching ordinary Cubans to perform or practice art or music in some form, and formalised and spread after 1961, was based on the ideas that all Cubans had the capacity to become artists and that culture could be the basis of national unity and radicalising integration (Kapcia, 2005: 135–136). While the outside world saw wider significance in ICAIC and Casa, striking a chord among intellectuals and writers who had long resented US cultural hegemony, the *instructores* movement passed unnoticed.

Beyond this, the Revolution's early patterns seemed unexceptional. Its first economic model was based on conventional UNECLA prescriptions, until capital flight demanded greater state intervention, eventually formalised in a more Soviet-oriented version. The political model also seemed familiar to Latin Americans, apparently echoing previous national experiences of populist mobilisation. What many missed, therefore, was the fact that all of those early reforms stressed or implied two things: the fundamental contribution to unity and integration from structured participation and the importance of the empirical in leading to a necessary radicalisation of perspectives.

If we examine, albeit cursorily, the 'official' discourse of those early years, we can see, at one level, the ideological confusion, but also, at another level, the clearly national-focused imperative, and the evolution of the latter into a more coherent version of the former. On 1 January 1960, Castro's speech celebrating the Revolution's first anniversary was unquestionably oriented towards a nationalist impulse of nation-building, with its talk of 'nuestra nación' (our nation) (Castro, 1967b: 12), of the need to 'reconstruir el Estado' (rebuild the State) (1967b: 12), and with a discourse of 'betrayal' ('los gobernantes que entregaban la Patria a los intereses extranjeros' (leaders who handed the *Patria* over to foreign interests) (1967b: 12)), which suggested that, while the United States might have been the imperialist 'problem', the Cuban elite had collaborated with that neocolonialism. In this it reflected the explicit target of Castro's most famous speech, in 1953, *La historia de absolverá* (Castro Ruz, 1961): namely Batista and those who supported him; in other words, 'tyranny' and 'oligarchy' were the problems identified then, against the backdrop of a structural neocolonialism. By September 1960, however, in the speech later known as the First Declaration of Havana, Castro's discourse – while still targeting *tiranía* (tyranny) and the oligarchies of Latin America, in his call for the peoples of the continent to follow the Cuban example and throw off the yoke of oppression – had shifted towards a greater awareness of the United States as 'the problem'. While the speech's narrative of *imperialismo* tended to be historical, focusing on pre-1930 interventions, there was a clear current of antagonism towards what was explicitly condemned as 'el imperialismo norteamericano' (North American imperialism) (Castro, 1965b: 10), responding specifically to US attempts to isolate Cuba diplomatically. Given the rapid deterioration of US–Cuban relations from February 1960, that shift was to be expected; however, even as late as September 1960, the discourse was driven not by socialism (still not mentioned) but rather by a nationalist anger, railing against the United States and being 'atentatorio a la autodeterminación nacional, la soberanía y la dignidad de los pueblos hermanos del Continente' (being alert to national self-determination, sovereignty and the dignity of the brotherhood of peoples on the Continent) (Castro, 1965b: 10–11).

1961: A Turning Point

Following the Revolution's trajectory, we find that, by the end of 1961, its direction was much clearer: in January relations were broken with Washington. On 16 April came the first public reference to a 'revolución socialista': 'Eso es lo que no pueden perdonarnos, que estemos aquí en sus narices, ¡y que hayamos hecho una revolución socialista en las propias narices de los Estados Unidos' (That is what they cannot forgive us for, that we are here right under their noses and that we have carried out a socialist revolution right under the nose of the United States) (*Revolución*, 1961: 3). In June, Castro's 'Palabras a los Intelectuales' famously defined the parameters for cultural expression ('dentro de la Revolución, todo; contra la Revolución, nada' (Within the Revolution, everything; against the revolution, nothing) (Castro, 1980: 14). By the end of the year, the path towards a new single party (Partido Unido de la Revolución Socialista de Cuba) began with the merging of the three rebel organisations of 1956–1958 into Organizaciones Revolucionarias Integradas (ORI).

However, no sooner was socialism declared than it began to be questioned. In 1962 came the public disagreement with the PSP, effectively accused of seeking to appropriate the ORI, after which the PSP was relegated to second place, behind the ex-guerrillas of the 26 July Movement. In that same year, the Second Declaration of Havana – specifically responding to the Organisation of American States' (OAS's) isolation of Cuba, but also notably more explicitly anti-imperialist than its 1960 predecessor – initiated a long campaign of actively supporting armed revolution in the continent, challenging both the United States and the Soviet policy of 'peaceful co-existence'. Also, in 1962, of course, came the Missile Crisis, which, while confirming Cuba's invulnerability to US invasion (in the secret US undertaking), created a resentment of, and distance from, Soviet definitions of socialism. Indeed, from 1962–1963, conscious Cuban efforts were made to confirm that distance ideologically, through the 'Great Debate', the 'moral economy' and the increasingly 'Guevarist' tenor of many of the patterns of thinking. Hence, if Cuba was socialist, the definition that was followed often bore little resemblance to the patterns of the Socialist Bloc, and, if the events of 1961 had seemed to confirm Cuba's client status, then the following years complicated that picture enormously.

Of what, then, did this new 'socialism' consist? Economically, in 1961, it meant centralisation, diversification and industrialisation (the latter with reluctant Soviet aid), but by 1965 it meant even greater centralisation than Moscow advised (but that Guevara had recommended), alongside a curious strategy of a short-term concentration on maximising sugar production (for the infamous 1970 10-million ton harvest) in order to finance a postponed industrialisation. In neither case did the Cuban 'model' meet Soviet prescriptions. Politically, the 1961 interim body, ORI, resembled Eastern European patterns of 1945–1948, the 1965 creation of the Partido Comunista Cubano (PCC; Cuban Communist Party) seemingly confirming this; however, that new party did not meet nationally until 1975, its Buró Político remaining dominated by the ex-guerrillas. Moreover, the growth of the CDRs after Playa Girón meant a national pattern of grassroots mobilisation that differed from anything in the Socialist Bloc.

Yet one experience of 1961 did clearly define the Revolution's emerging character: the literacy campaign. This phenomenon was clearly seminal: increasing the literate population by almost a third (converting the proportion of illiterates from around 3 per cent to 23 per cent) in less than a year transformed the possibilities for social and political integration, and created a more useful workforce for production. However, it was the experience and lessons drawn that really made it fundamental. For the experience of either being made literate or participating in the volunteer literacy workforce marked hundreds of thousands indelibly (as with the militias), radicalising them as clear beneficiaries of a genuine liberation (Jolly, 1964; Fagen, 1969: 33–68). The lessons learned, however, went even further.

First, as a campaign fusing an almost military efficiency (and discourse) and an enthusiastic mass volunteering, the campaign confirmed the value of the ethos of *voluntarismo* (voluntarism) that shaped successive campaigns and planning. Indeed, it seems likely that the emergence of the notion of a 'New Man' (although associated with Guevara's essay, originally written in 1965, 'El socialismo y el hombre en Cuba' (Man and socialism in Cuba) (Guevara, 1970), had its genesis in this experience, which – like the insurrection – suggested that, with adequate 'subjective' conditions (commitment and consciousness), adverse material conditions could be overcome. Moreover, it suggested that the more the system involved people collectively, the more radical they became.

Second, the literacy campaign confirmed that explicitly 'political' materials (e.g. the campaign's *Alfabeticemos* and *Venceremos* manuals) could, in a context of collective mobilisation, *lucha* (struggle) and 'siege', successfully persuade people; hence, it became the template for all the subsequent mass mobilisations. In fact, the campaign also demonstrated that a 'guerrilla' ethos worked in enthusing people, associating participants with a 'heroic' struggle for collective liberation and identifying the Fuerzas Armadas Revolucionarias (FAR) as the inheritors of the anti-Batista *barbudos*.

Finally, the literacy campaign confirmed the centrality of 'culture' within the whole revolutionary project of liberation; for not only did literacy radicalise those who benefited, but the campaign also generated the recognition of the need to meet new literary demands by increasing the provision of material to read. This engendered the characteristic programmes of *piratería*, whereby, to meet the needs of swelling numbers of university students and then to raise the quality of Cubans' reading of literature, textbooks and then a range of what was seen as the best of world literature were pirated inside Cuba and made publicly available (Rodríguez, 2001). This responded partly to traditional, *martiano* (Martí-based) notions of the centrality of culture, but was also reflected in the *Palabras*, whose long-term significance lay not just in its implications for writers or artists' freedom vis-à-vis the state but also in its formal encouragement to spread revolution through culture, most specifically through the *instructores* movement. For, while the cultural elite focused on its own opportunities, Castro reminded them of the other, more collectively liberating, process of 'cultural democratisation' outside the 'ivory tower' (Kumaraswami, 2009).

Much of this, however, went unnoticed in a Latin America where, while governments followed the US line in seeing in Cuba as a dangerous 'Communism' and 'Sovietisation', the Left continued to read Cuba either as it had in 1959–1961 (as an unstructured *por la libre* process of liberation) or as a radicalism that, for the first time in a continent where communists had monopolised the Left, allowed them to be 'communist' without following uncomfortable Soviet models, that is, identifying with Cuba's more idiosyncratic policies rather than with the longer-term implications of these grassroots experiences.

Once again, a perusal of the discourse of those years confirms the underlying impulses of the apparently new direction. While the January 1962 Declaration might seem 'typically' communist in its routine condemnations of US imperialism, other speeches of the time reflected a less stereotypical leftism, confirming the continuing national(ist) impulse. On 1 January 1962, for example, the emphasis was again on 'la obra de todo lo que vale en nuestra Patria' ('the work of everything worthwhile in our Patria') (Castro, 1967b: 61), with the explicit statement of the fundamental importance of the nation-building imperative: 'El proceso revolucionario de Cuba comenzó con la etapa de la liberación nacional [...] La Revolución entra en la construcción del socialismo una vez cumplidas las tareas de la liberación nacional' (The revolutionary process in Cuban began with the stage of national liberation [...] The Revolution enters the process of constructing socialism only when the task of national liberation is complete) (Casto, 1967b: 78). Indeed, this reminds us that Castro's speech the day after the first public reference to Cuba's 'socialism' in April 1961 made no mention of socialism and, instead, talked of 'la Patria sagrada y la Revolución' (the sacred Patria and the revolution) (*Granma* 1971: 1). Even the 26 July Movement's newspaper, while talking of *explotadores imperialistas* (imperialist exploiters) and 'la gloriosa Revolución de los humildes, por los humildes y para los humildes' ('the glorious Revolution of the humble, by the humble and for the humble') (*Revolución*, 1961: 2), also ended its rhetorical editorial with a determination to destroy all those who 'intenten invadir nuestro suelo. Patria o muerte. Venceremos' (try to invade our soil. Homeland or death. We will overcome) (1961: 2), that is, reaffirming the Revolution's essentially national focus and rebel tradition.

The Years of Institutionalisation

A decade later, in the 1970s, Cuba looked very different from what the admiring Latin American Left had imagined in 1960. However, at that very point Cuba began to appeal in different ways to governments then emerging in the region. Following the 1970 *zafra*, the familiar post-crisis debate resulted in membership of Comecon (in 1972), the hitherto reluctant Socialist Bloc's trading organisation. Then, in 1973, came Castro's surprising public description of the Soviet Union as the Third World's 'natural ally', having vilified them only five years earlier as betraying that world. Finally, 1975–1976 saw three further indications of orthodoxy: abandoning the old centralised 'moral economy' of 1966–1970 in favour of an economic policy following Soviet principles and enshrining Cuba's role as Comecon's sugar supplier; the long-postponed First Congress of the Communist Party, tripling its membership (Azicri, 1988: 79) and rehabilitating those ex-PSP personnel marginalised after 1962 and the 'Great Debate'; and an apparently Soviet-style pyramid electoral system, Poder Popular, whose National Assembly approved the Revolution's first Constitution. Therefore, by 1976, Cuba seemed finally to be the satellite that many had assumed in 1961–1962.

However, as usual, all was not as it seemed. Economic necessity had indeed driven Cuba closer to Soviet preferences of behaviour and policy; however, other factors had also played a part. Above all, one reality was that, by the mid-1970s, many early costs (of transformation, mass emigration of expertise, and wholesale economic reorganisation) had declined and many early investments (notably in human capital) were beginning to pay off; hence, even a successful *zafra* in 1970 might have seen some calm consolidation. Another reality was that the Cuban leadership realised that, while mass involvement through mobilisation might be necessary during the early enthusiastic collective effort and siege, the costs (to efficiency, morale and energy) were considerable, making material satisfaction and calmer institutionalisation necessary – an oscillating pattern repeated over all 50 years (Kapcia, 2009).

Beyond this, however, the notion of 'Sovietisation' is questionable. First, the delay in settling the post-*zafra* debate and holding the Congress indicated internal disagreement, demonstrated by continuing evidence of 1960s think-ing. Equally, even after Poder Popular, the CDRs continued alongside the new system of local *municipios*; indeed, with those new structures larger and more distant entities, the CDRs' survival continued the street-level localism and contact between leaders and followers.

Two moments during this presumed 'orthodoxy' revealed clues to the underlying nature of the new 'socialism'. First, in November 1975, Cuban troops began a fourteen-year campaign in Angola to defend the Movimento Popular para a Libertação da Angola (MPLA) government against South African troops and US-backed rebels. While many saw this involvement as Soviet-backed, with Cuba as a 'Soviet proxy' (Horowitz, 1977: 94), it soon emerged – and is now widely accepted – that Cuba, acting first, did not follow but, rather, challenged Soviet policy, obliging Moscow to support Cuba with material and transport (Gleijeses, 2002). Hence, seemingly 'Sovietised' activism was actually, once again, a challenge to the Soviet Union, meeting Cuban, rather than Soviet, needs.

The MPLA's call for assistance allowed a Cuban leadership, frustrated by declining political momentum in Latin America and obliged to acknowledge Soviet primacy, a new opportunity for leverage and Third World leadership, repeating the effects of the 1960s insurrectionary foreign policy. While what we might describe as the first wave of insurrectionary decolonisation had denied Cuba the opportunities that many had hoped for (to lead a worldwide movement for liberation), the new decolonisation, in Africa and the radi-calising Anglophone Caribbean, offered opportunities to reshape the world map. Indeed, as governments sought Cuban aid and followed Cuban social development models, this new 'internationalism' was perhaps less romantic than the heady expectations of the 1960s, but more practical and promising. In fact, events in Nicaragua (and, less so, in Grenada) soon suggested that Che's *foco* strategy might have worked after all, and Cuban advice and people flowed there too. Moreover, this 'internationalism' saw human aid sent to dozens of developing countries, reflecting both a new world context and the re-emergence of Cuba's anti-imperialist impetus, above all spreading an example of decolonisation through integrative nation-building.

Second, in 1976, the Centro de Estudios Martianos opened in Havana, devoted to the study and diffusion of Martí's writings and ideas. Seemingly unremarkable, this was actually quite significant because, since the mid-1960s, it had been less clear how to accommodate the non-socialist Martí into increasingly Marxist readings of Cuban history, emphasising class rather than 'nation'; hence, he had mostly been classified as a 'progressive intellectual', a paladin of an essentially 'social liberal' commitment. However, Cuban leaders and historians refused to ignore his historic contribution and their own debt to him; not only had Castro repeatedly cited Martí as the *autor intelectual* (intellectual author) of the Moncada attack of July 1953 (as part of the Generación del Centenario, i.e. of Martí), but all the ex-guerrillas felt that Martí should be recognised as more than just 'progressive' and the Revolution's moral inspiration. Therefore, at the very moment of apparent 'Sovietisation', the Cuban leadership officially encouraged Cubans to study, learn from and exalt the 'national hero', thereby confirming the Revolution's historical and national legitimacy within *martianismo*.

Clearly, therefore, something deeper than global clientelism lay within the evolving process. For it was clear that the Revolution's leaders were determined to emphasise a national focus more than ever, and that the new 'internationalism' was driven by a nation-focused campaign to challenge imperialism, as much as capitalism, spreading a Cuban example of radical decolonisation as much as socialism.

The discourse of those years shows this clearly. While *Granma* in 1971 might replicate eastern European talk of 'fraternal' relations, workers and *el pueblo*, that same year's popular weekly, *Bohemia*, made clear references to Cuban national, and not class, history: the edition celebrating the Moncada anniversary began with a portrait of Martí (preceding images of 1953) and included an article by Mariano Moreno Fraginals on nineteenth-century Cuban reformism, a more explicitly Marxist article by the old PSP historian, Julio Le Riverend, on the 1933 revolution (which, nonetheless, exalted its traditional nationalist heroes), and a piece by Mario Mencía on the Moncada that argued that the 26 July Movement was the natural successor to Martí's Partido Revolucionario Cubano (PRC), 'un partido para hacer la Revolución' (a party fit to make the revolution) (Mencía, 1971: 34). The latter reference was especially revealing, for it implied that other parties, including the PSP, were not so defined.

The 'Special Period'

By 1994, much water had passed under many bridges. Institutionalisation and greater consumerism had turned out to be as problematic as some had warned, creating dangerous material expectations, while the PCC expansion and strengthened role had, as many ex-guerrillas had feared, seen the growth of a relatively privileged *apparatchik* layer and a bureaucratic mindset, slowing down the Revolution's ideological impetus. Moreover, with Comecon already entering what soon transpired to be a terminal crisis, the threat posed by Gorbachev (both his internal reforms – which appealed to younger Cubans – and his determination to improve US–Soviet relations at the expense of Cuba) gave stark warnings of the dangers of the Socialist Bloc links.

Those problems partly inspired the post-1986 strategy of 'Rectification' (of Past Errors and Negative Tendencies), following a contentious Third Party Congress, although the new direction was detectable from the early 1980s, as discontent simmered and the costs of consumerism and Soviet links became clear. Rectification, indeed, was a complex process: while it meant preparing for the end of the comfortable Soviet relationship – especially through economic reforms and efficiency, starting within the FAR – it also resurrected Guevara's economic precepts. In fact, the new political campaign confirmed Rectification's retrospect vision, as the cleansing of the PCC sought a leaner, more responsive and more revolutionary body, marching in the opposite direction from Moscow, resurrecting the early Revolution's imperatives and stressing its roots in Cuban history.

This reappraisal was, of course, rudely interrupted by the 1989–1994 economic collapse following the successive disappearance of the Socialist Bloc, Comecon and the Soviet Union, and was aggravated by the tightening of the US embargo in 1992. With an impending Armageddon that shook the morale of the most loyal and determined supporters, by 1994 the Revolution – however defined and however 'socialist' – seemed fated to follow the Socialist Bloc's transition to capitalism. The leaders' recourse to seemingly vacuous slogans 'Socialismo o Muerte' (Socialism or Death) and an economic strategy based on the principles of a 'war economy' (*the Período Especial en Tiempos de Paz* [The Special Period in Peacetime]) seemed to confirm an unrealistic and anachronistic Revolution under an ageing leadership, incapable of resisting the 'transition'. Indeed, when the 1991 PCC Congress agreed a platform of unprecedented economic reforms (especially legalising the use of dollars, restoring self-employment possibilities banned in 1968, and turning from sugar to tourism), and when, in August 1994, disturbances broke out in Centro Habana, transition and the Revolution's end seemed imminent.

It was, however, precisely then that a small, but sustained, economic recovery began, that the political system showed signs of strength (especially in the morale-boosting march in response to those riots), and when a deep internal debate began about 'the Revolution'. For, if the 1991 Congress had agreed a strategy to 'save the Revolution', a new debate now began to agree on what that 'Revolution' actually was, seeking to identify which of its components were sacrosanct, especially as the social and ideological costs of reform were already evident in rising crime and prostitution, resurgent racism and inequality, and a more obvious individualism.

This debate was wide ranging, involving not only the mass organisations and the PCC, but also new magazines (such as *Temas*) and new forums (including churches and new academic centres). Its conclusions emerged gradually rather than in one Congress, but a consensus became increasingly clear: that 'the Revolution' was essentially – as much as it had been in 1959 – about *la nación*. Indeed, the 1991 Congress (and subsequent constitutional changes) had indicated that by stressing the Revolution's *martiano* character, as did two successive Nación y Emigración (Nation and Emigration) conferences in 1994–1995 (to include some of the diaspora in a broader *nación*) in the depths of the crisis. Henceforth, repeated indications were given: in the opening to, and dialogue with, the Catholic Church about the growing consensus on the *crisis de valores* (crisis of values) and the importance of social integration; in the encouragement to historians and the media to reassess Cuban history, stressing especially the nineteenth century, and the hitherto problematic 1930s, 1940s and early 1960s; but also in the hand held out to many formerly *non grata* émigré writers and artists whose achievements began to be recognised.

The second aspect of the emerging consensus was the realisation that, while some (Cubans and non-Cubans alike) might have looked back nostalgically to the late 1960s as the 'heroic' moment of 'true' revolution, it was actually in 1959–1961 that the Revolution's nature and purpose might be found. That became clear after 2000, when the Batalla de Ideas (Battle of Ideas) (launched to reinvigorate ideologically and to resist the corrosive effects of crisis and reform) consciously took up many of the Revolution's early mechanisms as a template for addressing problems of disintegration and disunity.

There was, however, another curious aspect to the new consensus and definition: a new emphasis on 'localism'. For, while everyone, from 1991, was focused on the economic reforms necessary to rescue the Revolution (accepting the hitherto unacceptable), many outside Cuba focused more on 'the political' – often assuming that, as in eastern Europe, the reforms adopted were simply the inevitable transition to a capitalist free market. Hence, the outside world tended to look at Cuba's political system in one of two very different ways.

On the one hand, Western media assumed that Cuba was either headed in a 'Chinese' direction (economic liberalisation with control under a monolithic party) or towards a capitalism which would loosen the PCC's (and hence Fidel's) hold, leading many to focus on the illegal opposition (whose media and academic profile rose significantly) or on human rights questions. Thus, when the EU, from spring 2003 (with the controversial sentencing of 75 dissidents), began to move closer to the US position, supporting US condemnation of Cuba in the UN Human Rights Commission and briefly isolating Cuba diplomatically, this was partly following the growing academic consensus in the United States and Western Europe.

However, simultaneously, other political issues inside Cuba were attracting attention from non-Northern countries, specifically the key question: how had Cuba managed to survive a crisis which should have been terminal, a 'siege' that intensified after 1992 and the collapse of most of its trading partners? While Western academia focused on factors inside Cuba (the FAR, the 'Fidel factor', coercion, ideology, social benefits, and so on), much of the developing world – whose friendship Cuba had courted or won over two decades – tended to watch in admiration as the Cuban 'enclave' clung on. Hence, as the 'pink tide' began to take shape in Latin America from the mid-1990s, and as the independent Caribbean moved away from the Washington Consensus, political forces there focused more on the political, rather than economic, factors that might explain it. Curiously, therefore, while North America and Europe saw survival in economic terms, assuming the inevitable collapse of the political system, the developing world tended to see it in political terms.

What they focused on was, essentially, two things: the character of, and loyalty to, Fidel (thereby reflecting the West's overwhelming traditional 'Fidel-centrism'), but also the key question of a popular loyalty seemingly ensured through participation. In this respect, however, what mattered now was less the grand national schemes of before (although the literacy campaign still attracted admiration and fostered emulation) than grassroots experiences, especially in the post-1990 years.

For what had actually happened in Cuba from 1991 was not simply the atomisation of collective solidarity into rampant individualism that most observers saw (Eckstein, 1994) but rather a partial dismantling of the state, creating spaces into which various entities stepped: individuals (many simply seeking immediate economic solutions but some grasping more criminal opportunities), families (whose networks, even more extended than in many countries because of patterns of remarriage, provided a context for collective self-help), churches (whose access to external aid made them valuable sources of material charity), but also local PCC and Mass Organisation activists who saw their immediate responsibility as defending the Revolution through local, but collective, solutions to the problems of supply, distribution and order. Here, they were helped considerably by the *barrio*-level Consejos Populares, which had begun to emerge in some localities in the late 1980s, attempting to fill the distribution and communication gaps left by the more distant Poder Popular system. As the Consejos were expanded to meet new needs in 1991–1993, they formalised what was emerging more haphazardly: a new localism, through local initiatives of collective endeavour, created to meet the new needs, develop new networks and create local manifestations of the state – most notably the *talleres de integración formal*. The latter were in fact not as organic as they seemed at the time, and were often directed by local activists, with national encouragement from a leadership aware of the short-term inadequacies of the national state.

It was in fact the emergence of this more disaggregated state, through local mobilisation, that now began to attract outside attention and foster emulation, most visibly in the Cuban-led Misión Barrio Adentro in Venezuela. Indeed, as political change in Latin America created a more receptive regional environment for Cuba, coinciding with Cuba's emergence from crisis and the start of the Batalla, this generated a new 'internationalism'.

Cuba under Raúl Castro

Finally, of course, Raúl Castro succeeded his brother (*de facto* in 2007 and formally in 2008) and launched a reform programme that, though stalled by internal resistance, was formalised by the 6th Party Congress of April 2011. Those reforms shocked many Cubans (used for half a century to guarantees of state provision, protection and employment) and persuaded many outside observers that Cuba was heading for either a future based on the Chinese model (of untrammelled marketisation and political control, i.e. a form of state capitalism) or a model replicating the capitalist transitions of post-1989 Eastern and Central Europe.

While space does not allow for a full discussion here of the likelihood of either scenario, it is worthwhile commenting that neither outcome currently seems likely. While some Cuban economists (often eagerly awaiting 'transition' in the early 1990s) argue for a Chinese, or at least Vietnamese, 'model', many in the Cuban leadership clearly find aspects of the Chinese experience (widespread corruption and increased inequality) unpalatable and dangerous; for a political system that gained early legitimacy by eliminating corruption, pursuing a moral imperative and emphasising a tangible egalitarianism, the dangers of allowing either problem to grow (more than already evident since 1990) are all too clear.

As for a capitalist transition, Raúl Castro has long advocated a role for the market, as a tool to protect and enhance rather than as a tenet of belief. This reflects his pragmatism towards whatever is available to achieve the Revolution's objectives or defend its gains, without undermining its basic ethos; indeed, his perceived role for the market does not apply to key economic sectors, health provision, education or welfare, confirming that reform does not stray from a shared belief in the state's responsibility to protect, balance, regulate and provide.

Today's Revolution

Given this juncture, what actually remains of 'the Revolution' of 1959–1962? First, the most obvious characteristic, as important as ever, is the overriding emphasis on unity; as was initially the case, this is evidently still seen as being ensured through social benefits, but also through mass participation, single-party rule and institutions such as the FAR. Indeed, the latter seems now more fundamental to that imperative; for, having survived the trauma of the 1989 Ochoa case and the post-1993 mass demobilisation, it has clearly managed to rescue most of its established legitimacy as the popular heir to the 1956–1959 Rebel Army (establishing the Revolution) and the 1960s militias (defending it against external challenge) (Klepak, 2005).

Second, today's Revolution reaffirms the same historical legitimacy of 1959–1962; indeed, following the 1990s debates, its leaders evidently seek to rehabilitate new elements of Cuba's pre-1959 past. In 1959–1961, the new Cuban historiography largely focused on the legacy and figure of José Martí and of radical nationalists such as Antonio Guiteras, as legitimate antecedents of the emerging radical process of nation-building. In the more 'orthodox' (i.e. pro-Soviet) 1970s, historians instead examined the Revolution's class roots. Now, however, attention is focused on those in the radical tradition of the 1950s, ignored after 1959 – radicals and social democrats such as Manuel Bisbé and the Catholic Rafael García Bárcena. Hence, this past is being exhumed to honour the extended family of the national canon.

Third, it is clear that today's Revolution stresses the national in almost everything, as was true in the early years. Not only does this repeat the early willingness to challenge the United States if Cuba's material improvement is made conditional on US terms, but also includes a renewed sense of pride abroad. That was briefly lost in the 1980s (Havana being occasionally seen as too close to Moscow) and then again in the 1990s (with the new isolation and a widespread perception of Cuba as an irrelevant anachronism); now, however, it is clear that some of that pride has been regained.

Finally, Raúl's post-2011 'Revolution' again tolerates and even extols the virtues of small-scale private and cooperative initiative, exactly as the 1959–1960 process assumed would be the case. The 2011 reforms do not look forward to the capitalist future (as most outside commentators assume) so much as look backwards to 1959, resurrecting a pattern that many Cubans regretted losing.

Conclusions

Where, then, does this trajectory lead us in understanding the Revolution's essential nature and Cuba's renewed attraction in the wider Latin American context: is there another remarkable similarity between 1959–1960 and the present day?

The most convincing element of both periods seems to be the continuing emphasis on, and motivation by, the imperative of nation-building. Indeed, the post-1993 debates and characteristics have confirmed a reality visible in 1959–1960: that what united those Cubans who welcomed and continued to support the Revolution, regardless of its changing ideological definitions, was a belief in the urgency of taking up the nation-building project promised by Martí in the 1880s and 1890s, but subsequently frustrated (not least by a 'Plattist' neocolonialism) and weakened (by the distortions of the post-1934 dependency). For what other Latin American nations experienced at different stages after the 1820s – with varying degrees of success and enthusiasm – had never been achieved, even to that limited extent, in a Cuba that was until 1898 still colonial and thereafter more intensely and more legally neocolonial than any other country, apart from Puerto Rico.

This essential reality, indeed, should remind us that, far from being unique (the habitual academic claim about Cuba), the Revolution of 1959–1960 reflected many of the features, imperatives and discourses of contemporary nation-building projects in Africa and Asia; this included the drive to unity (decolonising movements arguing that disunity – created or encouraged by imperialism – had allowed colonisation to survive), and the emphasis on a single-party, accelerated economic development, and defiant (if often distorting and badly targeted) cultural decolonisation.

However, what made Cuba 'different' from these other projects, and more essentially attractive, was its unusual geopolitical position and its rapid ideological challenge to the Superpowers' hegemonic positions. Hence, Cuba was admired as much for its image and message as for the details of its own, often disorientated (and disorienting), process of nation-building. In the 1960s, Cuba was seen by many radicals – in both the decolonising world and a supposedly long-decolonised Latin America – as a model, firstly of the victory of a movement for genuinely radical change, and then, even more significantly, of resistance to both 'imperialism' and Soviet hegemony. This was especially true for the Latin American Left: while many African post-colonial governments approached Cuba for lessons in attacking the problems of decolonisation, nation-building, rapid development and so on, it was Cuba's image (in the idea, rather than details, of land reform, political involvement, nationalisation, and equality) that resonated among the less activist politically aware rather than any deep knowledge of the reality or specific policies.

Hence, after 1997, Cuba was once again appreciated, rather than admired, as a model of survival (because Cuba's collapse was greater than any recession suffered during the region's 'lost decade'), and also, emotionally and morally, as an example and inspiration. Indeed, the latter helps explain the widespread respect for Fidel Castro, despite evident political differences between the doyen of anti-imperialism and the admiring leaders who trek in 'pilgrimage' to Havana after taking power. The latter also realise, of course, that their own domestic political legitimacy gains through public sympathy with Cuba's plight, although this in turn confirms the continuing appeal of 'Cuba' (as an idea) beyond the political class. Yet, there is another motivation for many of these leaders' attraction to the still magnetic 'pole' of Havana: namely, the reality that their formal sympathy for Cuba is a way of acquiring historical legitimacy from clearly leftist forces while they themselves are obliged to drop their former radicalism and move towards variations on neoliberal economics.

However, even allowing for such self-serving motivations, the reality is also that, if there is any lesson to be learned from Cuba by these new governments or movements, it is that Cuba's nation-building project is still based on the unusual and vital element of participation. In other words, the new admirers seem to have realised that, while Cuba's commitment to nationalisation, a state-run economy and single-party rule, with a formally Marxist ideology, are no longer as acceptable as in the 1960s to a redefined Left, Cuba does perhaps teach something to a post-military, post-recession, post-Washington-Consensus and post-democratisation regime, in a context where previous nation-building processes (including populist structures from 1930) have been dismantled by the combination of military rule, neoliberalism, recession and debt.

Latin America's historical experience has actually been that the 1820s–1890s period had not in fact seen successful nation-building projects, but, instead, post-colonial elites' universal preference for an essentially weak state. While many 'liberal' modernising elites from the 1870s sought ways to cement 'national identity' (through 'invented traditions' or Europeanising projects) – many not taking convincing shape or striking deep roots until the cultural nationalisms of the twentieth century – a strong nation state was the key element missing from the nation-building project, and the reality of post-colonialism was a necessarily weak state, leading to conflict and allowing elite politics to dominate and individuals to seize power. For that very reason, late-nineteenth-century middle-class radicalism and similar movements sought to strengthen the state (also enabling them to enter the political system, via the public sector, and the economic system by protectionism), as did 1930s and 1940s populist strategies, to modernise and make up for lost opportunities. However, the military state of the 1970s and 1980s was able to exist precisely because of that populism, adapting the post-1930 state for its own purposes, while dismantling the economic state on ideological grounds; hence, by the 1990s, the idea of the strong state needed once again to be addressed.

In fact, this made Cuba's post-2000 Batalla de Ideas curiously relevant; for its purpose was less a desperate and anachronistic attempt to save Cuba's socialist ideology and persuade Cuba's youth of the virtues of socialism (the common external interpretation) than an attempt to mend Cuba's structures, ethos, processes and morale, damaged and undermined by the trauma of the Special Period. In other words, the Batalla was essentially a revolutionary nation-*rebuilding* process, seen by many Cubans as just as necessary as the nation-building had been in 1959. This largely explains the post-2000 emphasis on nation, community, and 'ideas' (stressing and again expanding education and culture), seeking to repeat the successful impetus of 1959–1961.

6

Cuban Medical Internationalism Under Raúl Castro

JOHN M. KIRK

Dalhousie University, Canada

Raúl Castro has been leading Cuba for a relatively short time – since 31 July 2006, when he assumed many of his elder brother's state functions, and formally as president since February 2008, when he was elected at the National Assembly gathering. During that time significant changes have occurred in Cuba, largely in reaction to difficult economic circumstances. Between 1998 and 2008, for instance, sixteen hurricanes caused over $20 billion in damage. Meanwhile, the Cuban economy, extremely inefficient and laden with layers of bureaucracy, had stagnated. Raúl Castro has therefore brought in some major initiatives, ranging from massive distribution of 1.2 million hectares of unused land to 180,000 small farmers to the introduction of sweeping legislation designed to encourage an estimated 500,000 Cubans (roughly 10 per cent of the workforce) to find alternative employment. Joint ventures with foreign capital, cooperatives and self-employment are now proposed. At the same time cuts in benefits and long-held subsidies have been implemented, and income tax introduced – for the first time for most Cubans. In his speech of 26 July 2009, the anniversary of the start of the Revolution, Raúl Castro outlined the major challenge of import substitution, also encouraging Cubans to put political slogans to one side and, instead, to work the land; it was time to overcome empty rhetoric and instead develop a significant economic reform programme. Speaking on 4 April 2010, the president outlined in greater detail some of the major challenges facing Cuba, showing how the country was living beyond its means, and calling for national unity in order to face grave economic difficulties:

> En resumen, continuar gastando por encima de los ingresos sencilla-mente equivale a comernos el futuro y poner a riesgo la supervivencia misma de la Revolución. Nos enfrentamos a realidades nada agrad-ables, pero no cerramos los ojos ante ellas. Estamos convencidos de que hay que romper dogmas y asumimos con firmeza y confianza la actualización, ya en marcha, de nuestro modelo económico.

In summary, to go on spending more than the income we are receiving is the same as eating up our future, as risking the very survival of our Revolution. We indeed face some very unpleasant realities – but we refuse to close our eyes as we face up to them. We are convinced that we have to reject all forms of dogma, and we assume with firmness and confidence the continuation, which has already started, of our model to reform the economy. (Castro, 2010b)

Since then the Cuban government has accelerated these reforms, seeking to encourage Cubans to be less dependent on the state, to substitute imports (particularly in the food sector), and in general to make the economy more efficient.

It is clear that the economic challenges facing Cuba are serious indeed – as is the medicine applied. Given the enormous sweep of Cuba's medical internationalism programme (with some 41,000 health workers currently working in 68 nations), the question of the impact of current economic difficulties on its successful cooperation programme is clearly pertinent. (In addition there have been criticisms in Cuba by patients, concerned at the absence of their doctors, since about 22 percent of them are working abroad as *internacionalistas*.) Accordingly this chapter examines the evolution of medical internationalism since 2006, analysing the degree of changes undertaken by the revolutionary government, and offering some comments on probable future developments.

Setting the Scene: The Context of Medical Internationalism since 1960

Cuba's record of medical cooperation around the globe is extraordinary, and at present Cuba has more medical personnel working in the developing and underdeveloped world than all countries of the G-8 combined. This is a tradition that dates back to 1960, just a year after the Batista dictatorship was overthrown – and at a time when approximately half of Cuba's 6,000 doctors were in the process of leaving the island. In other words Cuba's first internationalist mission (to Chile in the wake of a devastating earthquake) could not have come at a worse time in terms of the economic conditions and the availability of medical personnel. Three years later a larger delegation of medical personnel went to newly independent Algeria to set up the bases of the national health system. The essential point to bear in mind is that, even 50 years ago, ideology and a spirit of humanitarianism trumped domestic economic challenges (Kirk and Erisman, 2009).

In all, almost 130,000 Cuban medical personnel have served on such inter-nationalist missions. The largest contingent sent on an emergency mission was to Haiti, although, since the founding of the Henry Reeve Contingent (inaugurated in 2005 shortly after Hurricane Katrina, to provide medical cooperation at times of natural catastrophes), Cuban emergency medical missions have been sent to Guatemala, Pakistan, Bolivia, Indonesia, Belize, Peru, Mexico, Ecuador, China, El Salvador and Chile, a phenomenon often ignored by the media.

This response to medical emergencies is noteworthy, especially if one takes into account that these missions have all taken place since 2005. Another key dimension of Cuba´s approach is the focus on training medical person-nel – particularly those sectors of the population who would not normally be able to afford to study medicine. The theory is that, once they have been trained as physicians, they would have 'buy in' to their local commu-nity, and would be prepared to work with those people who traditionally could not afford access to the appropriate treatment. As a result, Cuba has been involved in teaching medicine, establishing nine medical schools in the developing and underdeveloped world. At present teachers from Cuba's 22 medical schools are teaching in fifteen countries around the globe. Back in Havana, the impressive Latin American Medical School (known better by its Spanish acronym ELAM) currently has almost 10,000 students – from 60 countries – registered. Since 2005 9,900 have graduated (República Boli-variana de Venezuela, 2011). The impact of five decades of Cuban medical cooperation (a term consistently employed, instead of the paternalistic 'aid'), is enormous. According to Feinsilver (2010), medical personnel have 'saved more than 1.6 million lives, treated over 85 million patients (of which over 19.5 million were seen on "house calls" at patients' homes, schools, jobs, etc.), performed over 2.2 million operations, assisted 768,858 births, and vaccinated with complete dosages more than 9.2 million people'.

The record is impressive indeed. But much of this had long been established when Raúl Castro took over the reins of power. In light of the pressing economic difficulties facing Cuba, the question remains: how did these massive challenges affect decisions of the Cuban government concerning its commitment to medical internationalism? How has this important aspect of Cuban foreign policy fared under current economic difficulties? What can we expect in the future in terms of Cuban commitment to this enormously successful policy – at a time of major economic challenges? In particular, will there be the same interest in medical internationalism, or will this be cut in order to focus on domestic public health concerns?

Continuing Initiatives in Medical Internationalism

It is widely recognised that healthcare and education are the two jewels in the Cuban crown. It is also understood that, among the various modalities of medical internationalism, providing free medical education to students from developing countries is a longstanding facet of Cuba's most important solidarity activities with the developing and underdeveloped world. This trend began under the leadership of Fidel Castro, and was developed for almost 50 years. There is no evidence that, since Raúl Castro came to power in 2006, Cuba has in any way reduced its interest in training doctors for the Third World. In fact, as noted later, it has become even more interested in doing so, mainly through non-traditional medical training and particularly in Cuba and Venezuela, but also in other countries – from Bolivia to East Timor. Within the traditional sphere, however, the support provided in terms of medical education remains a strong as ever. In early July 2011, for example, 115 Haitian medical graduate students graduated from the Caribbean School of Medicine based in Santiago, bringing to 731 the total of Haitian physicians trained for free in Cuba (Agencia de Información Nacional, 2011). Many from earlier graduating classes joined their Cuban colleagues and fellow medical students from ELAM in January 2010, when they flew back to provide medical care to the victims of the earthquake there. Students from scores of countries continue to study medicine in Cuba, spending the first two years at ELAM or in Santiago (a campus mainly for Francophone students) before being distributed around the island to work in clinics or hospitals while continuing their university medical education for a further four years. It is expected that, upon graduation, they will return to their own countries and work with underserved communities there – or to other developing countries that need their assistance. (The latter opportunity is pursued by those students who at times encounter difficulties imposed by traditional – and conservative – medical federations in their home countries, and cannot have their titles recognised. As a result many return to Cuba for more specialised training, or volunteer in other developing countries. Many, for example, have joined the Cuban medical brigade in Haiti). In this way the traditional 'brain drain' of medical personnel in developing nations in fact becomes a 'brain gain'.

Cuban medical personnel are currently working in almost 70 countries literally around the globe, while students from developing countries continue to study in Cuba. The largest contingent is in Venezuela (roughly some 30,000 medical personnel), but more typical is the case of Guyana, where some 200 Cuban medical staff are working – while over 400 Guyanese are studying medicine in Cuba. Under Raúl Castro there has not been any noticeable change, either in terms of the numbers of Cuban medical personnel working abroad or studying at ELAM (where there is an annual intake of some 1,400 students from approximately 50 countries, including the United States). Both programmes have functioned well, are relatively cost-effective, and have produced a variety of benefits for both host country and recipient.

Another of the ongoing initiatives revolves around the victims of the Chernobyl nuclear meltdown in April 1986, who have been treated in Cuba (at no charge) since 1990. By March 2010 an astonishing 25,457 patients (including 21,378 children) had been treated (Pérez, 2010), and at that time there were 160 Ukrainian patients receiving medical treatment. It is worth noting that the largest number were treated in the 1990s, just as the Soviet Union was imploding, and economic aid to Cuba and trade were disappearing. This was undoubtedly Cuba's most difficult economic situation since 1959, and Cuban society suffered greatly. Yet despite the disastrous economic conditions in Cuba during the 'Special Period', following the collapse of its principal trading partner (responsible for over 80 per cent of its trade), Cuba continued to receive patients, mainly from the Ukraine. The patients are based in Tarará, some 20 km east of Havana, where they are evaluated upon arrival; those needing specialised medical care are then treated in the appropriate hospitals. Room and board and all medical services are provided at no cost by Cuba, an extremely generous act, since medications alone have cost approximately $350 million (Grogg, 2009). With reason, former president Leonid Kuchma, visiting Cuba in March 2010, noted that, while other richer countries had shown pity, Cuba had supported the victims in concrete terms (Álvarez, 2010). Yet again, despite dire economic circumstances (and it is worth remembering that gross domestic product (GDP) in Cuba contracted approximately 35 per cent between 1989 and 1994), humanitarianism, and medical support for those less fortunate, predominated. This project for the Chernobyl victims continues, although the number of patients continues to decrease as the impact of the nuclear meltdown does likewise.

Fresh Initiatives in Medical Internationalism

One of the most significant developments in recent years has to do with what is often referred to as the 'new paradigm' or the 'Polyclinic Project' in medical training, designed for students from non-traditional backgrounds who otherwise would probably not be able to afford a medical education. Cuba and Venezuela have stated that they will train – at no cost to students – 100,000 doctors for the Third World within a decade, and are well on its way to doing so. Dr Juan Carrizo, president of ELAM, noted that 24,000 students are currently being trained through this method in Cuba, with a further 25,000 being trained in Venezuela (Agencia de Información Nacional, 2010). The complete name for the medical training programme is the Nuevo Programa de Formación de Médicos Latinoamericanos (NPFML), although in fact it has also been employed in Africa and Asia, adapted to local conditions. It was introduced in 2005, largely in the wake of commitments made by Cuba and Venezuela in various agreements related to the Alianza Bolivariana para las Américas (ALBA), when Cuba offered to provide the massive training in medicine of young Latin Americans. A similar programme was instituted in Venezuela, using Cuban medical personnel, and called the Programa Nacional de Formación de Medicina Integral Comunitaria en Venezuela (PFMIC). The first 8,000 students of this programme graduated in 2011, and are working in traditionally underserved regions of their country. The initiative was born from discussions between Fidel Castro and Hugo Chávez in 2005, the central idea being to train doctors for Latin America, and in particular for those areas where medical care was either exorbitantly expensive or not available. As is the case with ELAM students, the focus was on selecting medical students from non-traditional backgrounds, because it was believed that they would be more likely to return to their home communities upon graduation.

The essence of the new programmes, wherever they are established, is to emphasise a hands-on form of medical training. The community itself becomes the 'laboratory' for the training, with extensive work carried out by students in the various popular clinics, diagnostic centres, and technology and rehabilitation clinics. Between the two programmes (in Cuba and Venezuela), almost 50,000 doctors were being trained in 2011. Students are taught alongside a professor (the vast majority of whom are Cuban) who is a specialist in Medicina General Integral or comprehensive general medicine. Significantly, most of these medical mentors already possess experience abroad, and are familiar with conditions in the developing world. The practicum assumes far more importance in this new approach, as the student learns in the consulting room alongside the doctor, and in the polyclinic. The central idea is to produce physicians who will be engaged with the community, and not just work in their offices. They will emphasise preventive medicine, be prepared to work wherever they are needed, and will always place community needs before individual ones (Alvelo Pérez, 2010). Clearly this constitutes the professional formation of a radically different form of medical practitioner. The impact of the presence of Cuban medical personnel was great indeed in Venezuela, where the national Medical Federation was displeased with the new approach of the Cuban physicians, their work ethic, their ability to work in chronically poor neighbourhoods and their low salaries. With the advent of a new wave every year of Venezuelan medical graduates, it is clear that there will be major tensions over the model of public health to be implemented.

Perhaps the most outstanding example of recent developments in Cuban medical initiatives is the attention given to East Timor and other small countries in the South-West Pacific. The initial contact dates from 2003, with East Timor, followed by ties with Kiribati, Nauru, Vanuatu, Tuvalu and the Solomon Islands between 2006 and 2008. As Tim Anderson has pointed out, 'by 2008 there were around 350 Cuban health workers in the region, with 870

East Timorese and more than 100 Melanesians and Micronesians engaged in medical training' (Anderson, 2010: 77). The first cohort of eighteen Timorese have now graduated as medical doctors following studies in Cuba (with their training being completed back home). It is worth pointing out that as late as 2002 there were only 47 physicians in that country.

The Cuban role in East Timor, and increasingly in the South-West Pacific, is multifaceted. In the first instance it represents the major component of public healthcare delivery in the country. By 2008 there were some 300 Cuban health workers, and their role had been extremely important since their arrival: more than 2.7 million consultations had taken place, and an estimated 11,400 lives had been saved because of their medical interventions (Anderson, 2010: 82). Cuba is also training 658 Timorese medical students in Cuba, with a further 186 in Timor (De Araújo, 2009: 1). The first contingent of interns graduated in August 2010. They will be followed by 64 doctors for the academic year 2010–2011, 501 in 2011–2012, 245 in 2012–2013, and 17 in 2013–2014, with an average of 50 students being admitted in each subsequent year. In other words they will produce an astonishing seventeen times the number of physicians who were working in their country as late as 2002. There is no indication to date that this programme will be curtailed or reduced by Havana.

One of the fundamental purposes of Cuban medical internationalism in 2010 is to provide the basics for recipient countries to train and replace Cuban co-operants – in other words, to help them to help themselves. In the case of East Timor, this can be seen in the Faculty of Medicine, established in 2005 in the National University with the support of Cuban medical professors. Until this point Timorese students had either been trained in Cuba or in small groups by Cuban physicians working at local hospitals and district health centres, somewhat along the lines of the NPFML programme noted above. Increasingly students from the region will be trained locally, instead of travelling to Cuba. Cuban medical personnel will also gradually withdraw, as the need for their cooperation decreases and their role as physicians and educators is filled by Timorese – who in turn will be able to use their Faculty of Medicine to train medical students from several South Pacific islands. The multiplier effect of medical personnel is thus the goal, with the intention of gradually reducing the number of Cubans as local practitioners fill the vacuum.

The first *internacionalista* medical experience came in the wake of a major earthquake in Chile in Valdivia, while the most recent response to a major natural catastrophe was also in that country in February 2010, following another earthquake off the coast of the Maule region. Common to both was a determination to provide humanitarian assistance at a time of major domestic challenges. Given the enormous importance of Cuba's response to natural disasters (especially under the auspices of the Henry Reeve Brigade, formed in 2005 following President George W. Bush's rejection of the support of 1,500 Cuban medical personnel), it is likely that this highly trained contingent, several thousand strong, will continue its tasks. Again, it is important to emphasise that this commitment to sending medical contingents to assist after major natural emergencies can trace its roots to 1960, when the first mission was sent to Chile. This rich tradition is deeply rooted in the Cuban medical psyche, and could not easily be terminated. The formal establishment of the Henry Reeve Brigade in 2005, and the record of Cuban emergency missions since, also make this unlikely.

This commitment to employ Cuba's medical prowess to serve people facing major challenges can be seen most clearly in the commitment to Haiti, both during the massive earthquake of January 2010 and in the cholera outbreak in 2010–2011. In both cases, Cuban medical personnel took the lead, despite the international media ignoring their contribution. To a large degree Cuba was well suited to respond to the earthquake, because it had maintained a large medical presence since the devastation of the hurricane ('Georges') in 1998. Indeed, by 2007, Cuban medical personnel were already treating almost 75 per cent of the Haitian population, with corresponding decreases on a large scale of infant and maternal mortality rates (Kirk and Kirk, 2010). In the case of the cholera outbreak, Cuban medical staff treated some 40 per cent of the victims throughout the country.

A year after the earthquake the Cuban role has become of paramount importance. Indeed, within 24 hours of the earthquake, the first group of trauma specialists of Cuba's Henry Reeve Contingent arrived to support the work being carried out by the hundreds of Cubans and ELAM-trained Haitian graduates already working on the island. (Cuban medical personnel had in fact been working in Haiti since the devastation of Hurricane Georges in 1998, when some 500 arrived to help there; there were still some 340 working there at the time of the earthquake.) After the worst of the earthquake emergency was over, Cuba volunteered to provide the principal support for the restructuring of the public healthcare system in Haiti, supported by Venezuela and Brazil. The outbreak of cholera in October 2010 posed a fresh challenge to the Cuban medical personnel, who were soon joined by reinforcements, both Cuban and ELAM graduates (from 23 countries). By the end of 2010 there were 1,398 members of the Cuban-led medical team, of whom 61 per cent were working actively in cholera-affected areas. They had established 66 cholera treatment centres, treated 56,967 patients, and had a mortality rate of 0.48 per cent, significantly lower than the national average (Gorry, 2011; Somarriba López, 2011). Sadly again, their enormous contribution was widely overlooked by the international media.

Medical Internationalism in the Face of the *Lineamientos*

In November 2010 the Communist Party of Cuba published the *Lineamientos de la política económica y social*, a 32-page discussion document on the suggested plans for the restructuring of Cuba's political economy. It was distributed throughout the country – in workplaces, mass organisations, neighbourhoods, schools, unions and in the public media, where it can be downloaded daily from the websites of Cuba's major newspapers (*Cubadebate*, 2010). Tens of thousands of meetings were held to discuss the suggested prescription for the country's ills. An estimated 8.9 million people attended these meetings, some three million spoke, and in the end two-thirds of the guidelines were either amended or new ones were formulated. In terms of medical internationalism there were several key areas where government suggestions could have a major impact upon this policy. From a western capitalist perspective it would be normal to expect that, in times of financial belt-tightening, 'frills' such as medical assistance abroad would be among the first cuts to be made. In the case of Cuba, this is not necessarily so, for reasons analysed below; in essence it comes down to balancing a mixture of five decades of successful humanitarian solidarity with stark financial challenges. Also to be added into the analysis are factors such as the immense diplomatic value of Cuba's medical internationalism, the financial opportunities it provides to medical personnel frustrated at the inverted social pyramid in Cuba (and the corresponding poor financial remuneration), the process of socialisation according to which Cuban medical personnel see this as a rite of passage and the commercial value for the Cuban state resulting from the impact of having 40,000 working abroad.

In terms of market potential for Cuban medical internationalism and the sale of pharmaceutical products, this is clearly articulated in the *Lineamientos*. Number 74, for instance, notes the desire to create a strategy for market development in terms of exporting medical services and pharmaceutical products. In terms of the latter commercial interest, it is not widely known just how advanced (or how profitable) the Cuban biotechnology industry is. The *polo científico* in Havana, where thousands of scientists work in some 52 research institutions, has produced many valuable pharmaceutical products for export – as well as 83 per cent of the medicines consumed in Cuba.

As of 2010, Cuba was producing some 38 pharmaceutical products, exported to 40 countries (Reuters, 2010). A few examples will help to illustrate this. Over 120 million doses of a Hepatitis B vaccine have been exported in recent years. Vaccines against Meningitis B and C, leptospirosis and typhoid fever have long been established and exported to many developing countries. Cutting-edge work on cancer and AIDS vaccines have resulted in successful trials and are soon to be commercialised. The medication known as

Nimotuzumab has been used in clinical trials in 25 countries, and has shown an ability to significantly reduce tumour sizes in patients suffering from brain and oesophagus cancer. After fifteen years of research into its ability to stop tumour growth, Vidatox (based upon properties of the blue scorpion) has been recently launched. Particularly promising is Herberprot-B, an invaluable find for diabetics suffering from foot ulcers (who otherwise could face amputation). In addition two Cuban pest control products, Griselesf and Bactivec, are widely used in Africa to control the breeding of mosquitos, and thereby reduce mortality rates from dengue, malaria and other transmissible diseases. Significantly, transfer technology of these products has resulted, with factories in China and Argentina now producing them, and several others to be opened in a further six countries. Likewise Cuba and Brazil are producing a meningitis vaccine, mainly for distribution in Africa. Finally, Cuban scientists have initiated Memoranda of Understanding with Syria, established joint operations in India, China, Vietnam, Iran and Brazil, and set up agreements for further research with the governments of Algeria and Belarus. In all these cases, a combination of commercial potential and solidarity (because the pharmaceutical products are sold at substantially lower prices than those charged by transnational drug corporations) can be seen.

The potential for the export of pharmaceutical products is enormous, particularly if the United States drops the economic embargo against the island. Cuba has already been extremely active in the developing and under-developed world, but the largest potential market is Europe and, ultimately, the United States. The sale of over $300 million of pharmaceutical products in 2009 (placing it in second place behind nickel as Cuba's most valuable exported products) illustrates this potential (Grogg, 2010).

The export of Cuban professional services – particularly those in the medical and educational fields – has been generously supported by Venezuela, where some $6.6 billion in payments for professional services were disbursed in 2008. The official figures for 2009 in terms of the exportation of goods and professional services (mainly medical services) was $11.171 billion, while a Reuters report in November of 2010 referred to $9.9 billion resulting mainly from the contribution of medical personnel broad (Reuters, 2010). There are approximately 39,000 Cubans working in Venezuela, of whom some 30,000 are in the healthcare field – roughly 75 per cent of the total of Cuban medical personnel working abroad (Romero, 2010: 110). There is little doubt that, as long as financial support is provided Cuba by Venezuela in return for these professional services, Cuban medical services will continue at this rate. Once again commercial logic, combined with medical humanitarian spirit, has proved to be a successful model.

Cuban medical cooperation is currently being provided around the globe, and in a variety of different formats. These range from subsidies provided by

Venezuela to Cuba for medical services in countries that belong to ALBA to the poorest country of the western hemisphere, Haiti, where there are a dozen 'triangulation cooperation' agreements from countries that pay the expenses of Cuban staff there. Norway, for example, pledged $885,000 to Cuba for supplies and medicines just ten days after the January 2010 earthquake. There are also many desperately sub-Saharan countries where a symbolic contribution is made to Havana – while at the opposite end of the scale are Qatar and Kuwait, which pay substantially for the supply of Cuban medical personnel in their hospitals.

The *Lineamientos* have two clauses with a direct bearing on this situation, stressing the need to seek financial self-sufficiency while also repeating Cuba's ongoing internationalist solidarity. Article 104 emphasises the need to seek, where possible, at least compensation for medical services rendered abroad. It is significant that the sections of the document dealing with healthcare in Cuba emphasise the same two basic elements: a sound financial footing, and the need for humanitarian medical collaboration. This approach will be employed in the field of medical internationalism, with solidarity and economic efficiency being key goals.

Concluding Thoughts

For over five decades Cuba has shown a remarkably consistent record of medical collaboration with nations around the world. Significantly, in good times and bad, humanitarian needs have always been seen as more important than basic financial considerations. Under the government of Raúl Castro the need for financial stability and sound economic planning have become of paramount importance, and at first glance there would appear to be an impossible gulf between the longstanding humanitarian tradition of the Cuban Revolution and the current financial exigency. Yet a study of events since he assumed power in 2006 shows clearly that, while all efforts will be made to cover costs of these ambitious programmes, international cooperation will not be affected to any great degree. Instead, as history has shown, it will remain more or less constant, ultimately diversifying in new directions.

A few examples help to illustrate this phenomenon. In the past years the size of the Cuban medical brigade in Mozambique has been increased from 130 to 160. In June 2010 a new eye clinic was established in Botswana. Eleven Cuban medical school professors arrived in Ghana to teach in Tamale University. Early in 2010 some 31 Cuban doctors arrived to work in Rwanda, on a project financed by the government of South Africa. In Pisco, Peru there are now three contingents of medical personnel. They had originally arrived after an earthquake in 2007, but their emergency mission has evolved into the staffing of community clinics. There has been an increase in the production of biotechnology products in joint ventures in India and China. Cuba has initiated a programme of mosquito and malaria control in Ghana. In Tanzania, Malawi, Congo and Ethiopia sales of medical products by the Cuban company Labiofam have increased sharply in the past year. Mobile clinics have been set up in the south of Belize. Argentina has seen the rapid development of ophthalmology clinics staffed by Cuban personnel since 2005 (with over 30,000 patients treated). Likewise the vision-restoration programme Operación Milagro (Operation Miracle) has increased its role in Jamaica (where a new ophthalmology clinic was opened in Kingston in 2010), and some 61,000 Jamaicans had been treated. In May 2011 sixteen Cuban nurses joined 35 others in Jamaica following the signing of a bilateral agreement. In February 2011 Cuban medical personnel initiated a new programme for patients with diabetes in Algeria. In the summer of 2011 Cuba initiated the coordination of an eight-nation project to carry out research and control the spread of dengue. Many of these projects do not provide any financial gain for the Cuban economy, but are nevertheless pursued at the request of the host government, and with the support of Havana. They give a general idea of the multifaceted role of Cuban medical personnel abroad – and all these initiatives have been established in the last two years.

There are several loose threads that need to be considered in seeking to appreciate the future path of this complex reality. It is abundantly clear that Cuba has no plans to expand its ambitious programme abroad in any major fashion. At the same time it is important to recognise that for the foreseeable future it will not make any major reductions in its medical cooperation. Indeed the Cuban medical presence in the ALBA nations, where Cuban medical personnel are subsidised by the Venezuelan government, will probably continue to grow. Operación Milagro, for instance, continues to flourish. By September 2011, for example, some 600,000 patients had been operated on by Cuban doctors at twenty eye clinics in Bolivia. Of these, approximately 500,000 were Bolivians, the remainder being from Argentina, Brazil, Peru and Paraguay, who had travelled to clinics on the Bolivian border (*Granma*, 2011). In addition Cuba had sent in 2009 a medical brigade of 213 people to Bolivia in the Brigada Moto Méndez, to undertake a nationwide survey of health needs there. In all the Cuban *misión* visited over 3 million homes, making an inventory of people with physical and mental challenges, and their needs (Elizalde, 2010). Similar fact-finding health missions were also undertaken in Venezuela and Ecuador, and other similar public health initiatives are probable.

The Henry Reeve Brigade will also continue its exceptional programme of relief in natural emergencies around the globe – it has done so on several occasions since 2006, most recently in Haiti and Chile in 2011. Likewise the Cuban role in Haiti will remain strong, both because of Cuba's contribution since 1998 and thanks to trilateral financial support from a number of countries to support Cuba's actions there. Supported by Brazil and Venezuela, Cuba has already made a commitment to restructure the public health system, and will undoubtedly maintain a large presence. Cuba's successful Operación Milagro vision-restoration programme, currently found in dozens of developing countries, requires comparatively little funding, delivers operations in a highly cost-effective manner, and brings tremendous symbolic capital in each of the dozens of countries where it operates. Funded by Venezuela, and employing Cuban ophthalmology personnel, it has restored sight to over two million people since its inauguration in 2005. It too will emerge largely unscathed from any considered cuts.

Furthermore, while there are no plans to develop large-scale medical faculties, it would not be surprising to see the development of the 'hands-on' medical training now being employed by Cuba in several countries, such as Gambia, East Timor and of course in Venezuela. The first 8,000 students of Medicina Integral Comunitaria graduated in Venezuela in 2011, following their training by Cuban medical school teachers. Until the graduation of 50,000 in Venezuela (with a similar number in Cuba), Cuban medical faculty will remain fully engaged in this project. In East Timor, the Faculty of Medicine at the National University established by Cuba in 2005 will continue to broaden the intake of students from other South Pacific nations. During this rapid increase of medical training the Cuban medical profile will understandably increase in the region. That said, when the mission is completed, the number of Cuban personnel will be reduced, leaving public health responsibilities to the local staff – and moving elsewhere.

In sum, despite the many economic challenges facing the government of Raúl Castro, medical internationalism remains a major priority of the Cuban government, which views it as both a long-term investment and a necessary obligation, with a tradition stretching back to 1960. Medical cooperation abroad also brings in a substantial amount of funding – some of which is used to subsidise medical cooperation in poor underdeveloped countries. It opens the door for the sale of Cuban pharmaceutical and surgical goods, and this has risen remarkably in recent years. (In August 2011 Ecuadorean president Rafael Correa announced that his country would prioritise the purchase of Cuban medical products over those produced abroad. In all, $1.3 billion would be spent on pharmaceutical goods: they would first try to source them from local producers, but after that would look to Cuba – before seeking medicines from transnational companies. It is likely that this trend will continue to rise dramatically, both through joint ventures with other developing countries, and through direct exports. The quality of Cuban medical products is well-known, and if the US embargo is ever lifted, biotechnology will become crucially important for the Cuban economy). It is also a significant part of the profoundly rooted essence of Cuban foreign policy. Moreover it enhances Cuba's international image, winning much goodwill in international fora. Indeed, so important is this 52-year old programme that it is enshrined in the Preamble of the Cuban Constitution.

Raúl Castro, presented as the quintessential pragmatist, desperate to balance the financial books in Cuba at a crucial stage in its development, has said little about medical internationalism. But he is hardly blind to the traditions and the international prestige that it has brought, the badly needed hard currency from Venezuela, or the massive needs in the developing world. In his speech to the summit of the Latin American and Caribbean Community, held in Cancún in February 2010, he spoke about Cuba's commitment to support the Haitian population. This speech in many ways can be taken as a symbolic declaration of the broad sweep of Cuba's programme of medical internationalism:

> La solidaridad del pueblo cubano no llegó a Haití con el terremoto. Ha estado presente desde hace más de una década … Les aseguro que la colaboración médica cubana y su modesto esfuerzo permanecerán en Haití los años que sean necesarios, si el Gobierno de esa nación así lo dispone… A nuestro país, férreamente bloqueado, no le sobra ningún recurso, más bien le falta de todo, pero está dispuesto a compartir su pobreza con los que tienen menos, en primer lugar con quien hoy más lo necesita en el continente.

> The solidarity of the Cuban people did not arrive in Haiti with the 2010 earthquake. It has been present for over a decade […] I can assure you that the modest efforts of Cuban medical cooperation will remain in Haiti for however many years it is needed, providing that the Government of Haiti wants this to continue […] Our country is the victim of a harsh blockade, and has little to spare. Quite the contrary – we are short of everything. However we are prepared to share our poverty with those nations that have even less, and especially today the country in our continent which needs it more than anybody. (Raúl Castro, 2010a)

One way or another, Cuban medical internationalism is here to stay…

Acknowledgement

Funding for this research project came from the Social Sciences and Humanities Research Council of Canada (SSHRC). I would also like to thank Emily Kirk, a doctoral student at the University of Nottingham, for her editorial assistance.

7

Peripheral Visions? Literary Canon Formation in Revolutionary Cuba

PAR KUMARASWAMI

University of Manchester, UK

The aim of this chapter is to begin to develop a more subtle framework within which to understand the construction of multiple canons of Cuban literature. Especially in view of Cuba's specific trajectory of postcolonial development and revolutionary nation building after 1959 (and the centrality of culture within these) but also the new landscape for literature that emerged after 1989, the chapter ultimately analyses the mechanisms and criteria that have operated on the island to question and transform not only conventional views of literature, but also conventional expectations regarding the literary canon. In so doing, it argues that canon construction is so closely bound to literary policy and practice – as part of a wider project of creating a national literature and literary culture – that the two must be considered together if one is to avoid essentialising and over-simplifying what is a complex process.

Theoretical and Empirical Approaches to Defining a Literary Canon for Revolutionary Cuba

The complexity of the task of defining a literary canon for revolutionary Cuba was recently summed up by two of Cuba's most prominent literary scholars, Ambrosio Fornet and Sergio Chaple, who each highlighted in very different ways the necessity, but impossibility, of constructing a valid literary canon. Fornet drew attention to the need to locate canons within their time and place, as well as to some of the invalid comparisons that are drawn between individual works: referring to the conventional (and always negative) measuring – and questioning – of revolutionary literature against the 'classics' of Cuban literature, such as Carpentier's *El siglo de las luces*, he noted:

> Este es el tipo de pregunta que denota mala fe o deseos de terminar abruptamente un debate, porque no estamos hablando tanto de valores literarios como de las relaciones entre una determinada época y su

expresión en el terreno de la literatura. [. . .] Tendríamos que asomarnos al repertorio de obras de la época para saber cuáles son las más representativas y qué aporta cada una por sí misma o como parte del conjunto'.

This is the kind of question that denotes a lack of faith or the desire to terminate a debate abruptly, since we are not talking so much about literary values as about the relationships between a particular historical moment and the expression of that moment in the literary domain. [. . .] We would have to look beyond, to the repertoire of literary works belonging to that moment, in order to find out which were most representative, and what each work brought, both in its own right and to the whole. (Espinosa, 2009: 28)

He continued that the process of establishing canonical works was always in flux, with different criteria and values (including representativeness, genre, generation) functioning at different times to revalidate the same text in different ways. In addition, and responding to the impetus from the 1990s onwards to incorporate the notion of a Cuban *diasporic* community within Cuba's literary canons (often including émigré writers who had fallen out of favour with the system), he highlighted a more explicitly political aspect of canon formation, in that it is also bound by commercial and ideological interests and agendas. Commenting on the decision in the 1990s to consider notions of diaspora and thus overcome the exclusivity and intolerance that had kept many of these émigré writers out of the island-based canons, he stated: 'Hubiéramos estado condenados a una especie de esquizofrenia histórica y crítica. Así que lo que salvamos, al "recuperarlos", no es más que una parte de nuestro patrimonio cultural, es la integridad de nuestra memoria histórica' (We would have been condemned to a kind of historical and critical schizophrenia. And so, what we salvaged by "recuperating them" is no more and no less than a part of our cultural patrimony, the integrity of our historical memory) (Espinosa, 2009: 29). He went on to explain how the exclusivity that had, for political and ideological reasons, featured in Cuba's rejection of the *diasporic* community until the early 1990s, was practised – for political but also economic reasons of copyright – by the 'gatekeepers' of much émigré-authored Cuban literature: 'Ahora la pelota de la intolerancia está del otro lado de la cancha, porque resulta que los herederos o los albaceas de Cabrera Infante, de Padilla y de Arenas – para citar los casos más notables – se niegan a autorizar que sus obras se publiquen en la Cuba castrista' (Now, the ball of intolerance has fallen on the other side of the pitch, because it has turned out that the inheritors or executors of Cabrera Infante, of Padilla, of Arenas – to name the most significant cases – refuse to authorise the publication of their works in Castro's Cuba) (Espinosa, 2009: 29).[1] For Fornet, then, the task of constructing a representative and inclusive canon of Cuban writers was an impossible one; perhaps the best conclusion one could draw would be that the literary canon is always partial, incomplete and subjective.

Indeed, the recently published third volume of the *Historia de la literatura cubana*, published by Letras Cubanas in 2008, brought to life some of the difficulties and risks inherent in just such an enterprise. The last volume in a trilogy that was initially discussed and approved in the 1980s, Volume III was first conceived of in 1988, under the auspices of the Instituto de Literatura y Lingüística, and brought together the contributions of over 30 individual literary specialists. However, the 20 years that this volume took from initial conception to final publication (despite constant re-editing over that period) already indicate that it was always going to be necessarily incomplete and partial, if not already out of date in terms of providing a reliable or representative account of canonical texts and authors in revolutionary Cuba.[2] The introduction to this third volume, by the writer, former Director de Literatura and literary critic Sergio Chaple (his role here was as editor-in-chief of Volume III), clearly set out just how ambitious – but also necessary – a task the series had been. With specific reference to the long-awaited Volume III, and its delayed and somewhat fragmented nature, he noted:

> Circunstancias ajenas a la voluntad de nuestro colectivo de autores determinaron que el proceso de confección de este tomo transcurriera en dos grandes momentos. En el primero de ellos, el estudio de la época inaugurada en nuestra historia literaria por el triunfo de la Revolución se extendía [...] hasta 1988 (sus primeras tres décadas). Concluido éste, y listo el volumen para su entrega editorial, las harto conocidas dificultades por las que atravesó el país en la década de los noventa – particularmente en su primera mitad – imposibilitaron la pronta publicación del tomo, por lo que se tornó imprescindible una actualización, en forma de apéndice panorámico, el cual abarca de 1988 a 1999, año escogido para el cierre definitivo de la información contenida en él.

---

1 This little-researched aspect of the complex economic relationships between island-based and international publishing houses is a problem which is regularly discussed in meetings of cultural institutions in Cuba.
2 The series is composed of three volumes covering (albeit somewhat unevenly) the span of Cuban literary production from colonialism to the present: (a) colonial period; (b) 1899–1958; and (c) 1959–1988, with an appendix on the 1990s.

> Circumstances outside the control of our group of authors resulted in
> the fact that the elaboration of this volume took place at two significant
> moments. In the first of those, the study of the era inaugurated in our
> literary history by the Revolutionary triumph went as far [...] as 1988
> (its first three decades). Once this was complete, and the volume was
> ready to be submitted to the publishers, the now infamous difficulties
> experienced in this country in the 1990s – particularly in the first half
> of that decade – made it impossible for the volume to be published
> promptly; for this reason it became indispensable to update the volume,
> by way of an appendix, that runs from 1998–1999, the final year chosen
> to conclude the information contained in the volume. (Chaple, 2008b: 3)

What, then, are these 'difficulties' that Chaple referred to so obliquely? He was
of course referring to the economic crisis – the Special Period in Peacetime,
declared in 1990 – that paralysed so much of the infrastructure of daily life for
Cubans, made scarce even the most basic commodities and, disarticulating
as it did many of the social and family networks and collective practices
that had become part of the revolutionary *habitus* for the island's population,
necessitated a survivalist mode on the part of the government, institutions
and mass organisations and ordinary Cubans, in which literary production
could hardly be considered a priority. Chaple's discrete phrasing, then, drew
attention to a combination of factors – shortages of material and human
resources, the emigration of key writers and literary scholars, and, after 2000,
the difficulties of accessing literature enabled by new technologies – which
made the task of tracing the shape of a national canon virtually impossible.

Given these admissions of the difficulties that plague the enterprise of
canon construction in Cuba, why should it be important to conceive of and
realise such a project? A brief exploration of what is meant by the literary
canon and how and why it is constructed can help to highlight its functions,
both general and Cuba-specific. The conventional definition of a literary
canon has itself been a moving target, following trends of literary theory
and criticism. At the centre of all these definitions, however, is a recognition
of the politics of representation and of the authorising function that the
construction of a literary canon encapsulates (Fowler, 1979; Altieri, 1983).
More recent explorations have investigated the methods used to construct
the literary canon (Guillory, 1993) and explored the impact of decentered
or peripheral literary cultures on the canon (Gugelberger, 1997). In sum, all
ideas of the canon are based both on commonality (of genre, 'field', purpose,
context) and authenticity (of text and of belonging to a single author). At
times, this common ground can consist of the prestige, both socio-cultural
and political, that is attached to the figure of the individual writer, the literary
group or the wider literary movement; for others, the canon can be shaped

by themes and responses that emerge in literature as a response to the development of external events, political debates or philosophical currents, or the emergence of particular identity groups. But in all cases, the formation of the canon is dependent on the Bourdieusian notion of 'consecration' of a number of literary works by various 'disinterested' mechanisms and agents, that is, through critical or scholarly reception, evaluation and recording in the public sphere. In other words, circulation, visibility and some level of permanence are prerequisites for any text to gain entry to the canon, although, in order to preserve the traditional integrity of the process of canonisation (which, Bourdieu would argue, distinguishes the intrinsic worth of cultural activity in the capitalist world through opposition to the more strategic or self-interested fields of economic or political activity), the process is rarely explored and deconstructed, or the inequalities exposed in global terms.

Pascale Casanova's groundbreaking work *The World Republic of Letters*, published in English translation in 2004, uncovered many of the mechanisms and strategies by which entrance to the apparently autonomous world of literature is achieved by peripheral nations and their literatures, and by which a global literary geography is constructed over time, obscuring inequalities in trade and competition between nations. Through developing a relational framework of competing literary spaces, Casanova described how the recognition of writing as literature is a highly contingent and conditional phenomenon, especially when this recognition takes place in the context of the political and economic imbalances of power that have characterised colonial, postcolonial and neocolonial relationships across and between nations. As such, she identified a series of oppositions and hierarchies, between but also joining (i) national/international; (ii) periphery/centre; (iii) politics/literature – which form the foundations for the judgments and evaluations implicit in canon construction.

Despite the centrality of literary production to independence struggles and the creation of nation-states, she argued, 'Literatures are therefore not a pure emanation of national identity; they are constructed through literary rivalries, which are always denied, and struggles, which are always international' (Casanova, 2004: 36). The power imbalances of such struggles for 'littérisation' – the recognition of writing as literature – often follow the political trajectories of their respective nations and are thus always based on models of periphery and centre: Casanova used the analogy of 'GMT' – the Greenwich Meridian – to describe the precise centre, or multiple centres, against which all peripheries measure their worth. If this was Paris for the Latin American independence movements of the nineteenth century, it could in the twentieth century also have been found in New York, Barcelona or, in more recent times, in transnational publishing conglomerates. However, the GMT or centre is bestowed with a level of authority that bestows it with the aura of the universal, beyond time and place. Thus, for any writer from a literarily deprived country to come to be regarded as literary by the legitimate authorities within the centre, their text must incarnate a canny combination of the familiar and the unfamiliar in order to be understood and recognised by the centre: 'In order to achieve literary recognition, dominated writers must therefore yield to the norms decreed to be universal by the very persons who have a monopoly on universality. More than this, they need to situate themselves at just the right distance from their judges: if they wish to be noticed, they have to show that they are different from other writers – but not so different that they are thereby rendered invisible' (Casanova, 2004: 156). Finally, the relationship between literature and politics in any one peripheral nation – and the terms of that nation's recognition at 'GMT' – are also complex matters: for a nation to be considered literarily mature, it must demonstrate in its literary production its evolving disregard for its political objectives, and thus embark on a gradual journey away from the national and political profile of its writers towards an international 'apolitical' or autonomous profile.

Through the interventions of cosmopolitan and polyglot intermediaries (Casanova, 2004: 21), themselves 'naively committed to a pure, de-historicized, denationalised, and depoliticised conception of literature' (Casanova, 2004: 23), literary recognition – literariness – is eventually conferred upon individual writers and, by extension, their nations. Through processes of repetition and recitation, these national literatures, or those texts that fulfil the centre's conditions of literariness – purity and autonomy – are granted access and integrated into the global literary system. The resulting canon, then, merely reflects the central articulation of literature as 'a kingdom of pure creation, the best of all possible worlds where universality reigns through liberty and equality' (Casanova, 2004: 12), but is in reality enabled by a complex network of mechanisms designed to confer literary status. For Casanova, then, the act of consecration through recognition and canon-formation is reciprocal and relational, but also clearly unequal, creating a vertical hierarchy linking national and international (often through the capital of the nation), and periphery and centre, through which the 'world republic of letters' emerges as the highest and only valid arbiter of a nation's literary worth (and, by extension, of political maturity). Whilst her work offered few detailed insights into the world of letters in Latin America (apart from a few pages dedicated to the invention of the Latin American literary 'boom'), its global scope makes it generalisable to any nation that has experienced colonialism and independence, and in which literary production and the contribution of writers, artists and intellectuals has formed an intrinsic part of an *independentista* and postcolonial project of nation-building.

In this sense, the 'delayed' independence of Cuba, its proximity and strategic importance to the United States, its cultural ties with its former Empire and, most importantly, the centrality of Cuban thinkers and writers to the various attempts at independence in the late nineteenth century and early twentieth century could provide an ideal illustration of Casanova's central theses. Furthermore, the central role of polyglot intermediaries, such as translators and journalists, who were able to negotiate centre and periphery through use of the expanding technologies enabled by the printing press in order to further the project of Cuban independence – José Martí is a prime example –, provides additional compelling evidence to support Casanova's model (see, in particular, Lomas, 2008); whilst in the first half of the twentieth century, the prominence of select literary figures such as Alejo Carpentier and Nicolás Guillén in negotiating Cuban cultural identity and Cuban literary production from both within and outside the nation indicates Cuban letters' reliance, until 1959, on exogenous models and sources of patronage and dissemination.

In addition, the state of contemporary letters across many parts of the world – and specifically the impact of theories, policies and practices focused on the global/transnational on our understanding of how nations represent themselves through culture – could provide a wealth of opportunities to explore the relational aspects of literary production in a context such as Cuba that, since the 1990s at least, has been obliged to engage with neoliberal economic practices, including entering a more globalised arena for cultural production where commercial or economic decisions have had a more prominent (although not predominant) role. Indeed, there have been several recent works that explore the impact of transnational publishing spaces and groupings on Hispanic culture (Robbins, 2003), on Cuban culture specifically (Fernandes, 2003; Stock, 2008; Whitfield, 2009), which refashion the 'centre' or GMT as a de-territorialised, multi-centred or cosmopolitan space.

Whilst these recent studies are correct in recognising Cuba's sustained dependence on – and increased participation in – the 'world republic of letters' through publishing abroad or electronically, they occasionally run the risk of reproducing two principal assumptions: first, that Cuba's political and cultural 'isolation' from 1959–1989 excluded it from the necessary processes of 'littérisation' that, it is assumed, are awarded only by transnational or international bodies; and, second, that where international relationships existed, specifically with the Soviet sphere, these were predominantly political rather than cultural, subjugating the 'pure' literary field to the strategic and contingent dictates of ideology and politics. As a result, under these perspectives, true participation in the 'world republic' was impossible, shackled as Cuba was by (i) insistence on its national sovereignty;

(ii) dependence on Soviet models; and (iii) duty to subordinate literary production to politics.[3]

As a result, a picture emerges of Cuban letters during this period that is predominantly focused on emphasising its aesthetic mediocrity, its peripheral or parochial concerns and its essential conformity. Set against this backdrop, the implications of the economic crisis for the world of letters on the island are inevitably positive: emigration and the possibility of publishing abroad are considered as releasing writers and texts from the restrictions of political conformity, and allowing them a first taste (since 1959) of 'pure' literature. A brief critical review of the external treatment of literature produced on the island since 1959 indicates the pervasiveness of these assumptions, as well as their power in shaping external canons of Cuban literature.

After a brief 'honeymoon period' in the early 1960s when the new Cuban revolutionary literature was embraced and celebrated, the sustained, albeit fraught, project to create a notion of Cuban literature on the island after 1959 was increasingly viewed from the outside as an essentially peripheral and futile enterprise, lurching from crisis to crisis and essentially doomed to reproduce underdevelopment, isolation, provincialism, conformity and mediocrity by rejecting art in favour of ideology and politics. An alternative vision thus emerged that focused almost exclusively on moments of extreme crisis and conflict where art (and the individual, autonomous artist) was subjugated to the demands of collective politics and ideology. As a result, the dominant narrative reproduced the opposition of the individual writer vs. the state, constructed the state as all-powerful, monolithic and largely unchanging, and art emerged as the only possible form of resistance. By focusing on moments of crisis (the *caso Padilla*, the *quinquenio gris*, Mariel) that were predominantly narrativised through the lens of exiled or émigré writers, a very particular model of Cuban literature on the island was constructed. Even the most subtle commentators on the new literature tended to assume an inevitable dichotomy between the state and the writer (Casal, 1971; González Echevarría, 1985), a focus that was further reinforced by theories of cultural resistance emerging from Latin American cultural studies, which often explored contexts of dictatorship and violence bearing little relevance to the Cuban case.

---

3   One recent study, for example, looks in imaginative ways at how Cuba–Soviet relations, both economic and political, and the movement of people between the two, were represented in literature and daily life. Further studies of this kind – exploring the impact of cross-fertilisation with other parts of Latin America and, more recently, literary transculturation under the auspices of the Alianza Bolivariana para los Pueblos de Nuestra América (ALBA), could provide evidence of Cuba's literary porosity since 1959. See Loss (2009).

Throughout the decades, and often simply owing to the difficulty of accessing literary texts published (in relatively small numbers) on the island, the vast majority of scholars working outside Cuba preferred to study selected individual writers – mostly the 'greats' such as Carpentier or Guillén (with their literary production often decoupled from the Revolution) or, alternatively, the 'problematic' writers, such as Lezama Lima, Cabrera Infante, Arenas, Piñera, this time creating a clear link between the writers and their milieu, often repressive or intolerant. Through these processes of selection, coupled with the considerable exposure given to émigré writers and intellectuals, the authority and appeal of émigré memoirs led to the clear assumption that, given that Cuba had lost or silenced its best literary talent after 1959, those who remained on the island had no choice but to 'trade in' artistic quality for political conformity, and thus become mediocre artists. The only valid Cuban canon, therefore, consisted of writers against the system (having left or having remained but been silenced or forced into conformity). Even the most respected and prominent scholars of Cuban letters have been seduced by this assumption: as recently as 2002, in an edited collection of articles on Cuban literature, the highly respected Latin Americanist Roberto González Echevarría noted that the canon of Cuban literature experienced a sudden 'decadencia' after 1959 (González Echevarría, 2004: 28), producing no writers comparable in artistic quality to Lezama Lima, Guillén, Carpentier, Cabrera Infante, Ortiz or Gastón Baquero, and describing 'los que se quedan' ('those who stay behind', i.e. on the island) with a very particular kind of humour: 'Burócratas y comisarios con abultadas obras sobran: la historia los absorberá' (There is no shortage of bureaucrats and commissars: history will absorb them) (González Echevarría, 2004: 29).

The changing focus of external canons since 1990 followed closely the socio-economic and cultural phenomena particular to the Special Period, which led to the privileging (through translation and international marketing opportunities) of a handful of Cuban writers and, additionally, to an emphasis on internationalising the literature produced by particular identity groups, such as women writers, through the publication of anthologies. Although the picture is far more complex than a simple desire outside Cuba for now-familiar narratives of disenchantment and dystopia or for texts that fulfil formulaic expectations of dirty realism, the distorting effects of commercial activity after 1990 on the changing canon of Cuban literature, and on our understanding of the changing position of the writer, are hard to ignore.

Finally, and most importantly for the purposes of understanding canon formation in the Cuban case, the concept of nation and identity in literature was broadened to include the *diaspora*, both as a result of the emigrations of the 1990s and as part of a wider scholarly interest in *diasporas*, migration and transnational movements. Ariana Hernández-Reguant's recent edited volume, for example, examined how the force of *diasporic* perspectives, both political and cultural, transformed notions of *cubanidad* into 'multicubanidad' in the decade of the 1990s. However, although noting that the embracing of a de-territorialised discourse on the island was merely a pragmatic response to economic crisis, her essay, and many others in the volume, negated the validity of discourses of national sovereignty in favour of transnationalism. She stated: 'In the island, being Cuban no longer meant, necessarily, being revolutionary – in the sense of being committed to a nationalist political project. It meant, more than ever, being cosmopolitan' (Hernández-Reguant, 2009: 10).

Blind Spots and Distorted Lenses

How, then, to explain these critical tendencies that have been so influential in moulding external canons of Cuban literature? Perhaps the most obvious explanation for these analytical and canonical decisions can be found quite simply in the disproportionate prominence, recognition and textual space awarded to writers living outside Cuba compared to those living, writing and publishing predominantly on the island. Whilst the attempt since the 1990s to unite across national borders and thus heal cultural rifts between the island and the Cuban *diaspora* is entirely praiseworthy, it once again obscures imbalances in access and exposure that are less desirable, and that have significant impact on the transformation of canons. Through removing Cuban literary production from its territorial anchoring and temporal limits (before and after 1959) in order to articulate a broader notion of nation and history, such practices not only reproduce and support the structural imbalances implicit in literary production systems and mechanisms between centre and periphery, but also assume that Cuban cultural policy and practice has been unbending in its reproduction of national sovereignty through culture. To follow critical methods that question and reject a so-called revolutionary narrative of *dentro* (within) and *afuera* (outside) (*sic*) (Birkenmaier and González Echevarría, 2004: 16) in favour of a transnational 'community', is to tell only one side of the story, and a rather conventional story at that.

The result of these dynamic trends in literary and cultural analysis has been that over the period of the Revolution, most commentators outside Cuba have focused their scholarly attention – and thus created a canon of Cuban literature – in ways that fulfil a series of expectations about literature and the writer, a hermeneutic circle that, if impossible to avoid, should at least be interrogated and problematised. For those cultural commentators who follow these paradigms, state repression has indeed become a useful shortcut for evaluating and ultimately identifying literary quality, and thus establishing literary canons in revolutionary Cuba: As González Echevarría expresses it, with considerable irony: 'el hostigamiento es el premio literario más sincero en Cuba, el verdadero juicio de valor de los mediocres que ven sus prebendas y privilegios amenazados' (harassment is the most genuine literary prize in Cuba, the real value judgment by those mediocre figures who see their benefits and privileges being threatened) (González Echevarría, 2004: 23). In other words, in what is considered an underdeveloped and peripheral system (still doggedly persisting with national identity in an era of internationalisation, still subordinating literature to politics), only those who are excluded – or who exclude themselves – from the system can be considered worthy of the 'world republic'.

Perhaps the most startling distortion in these approaches is the way in which the dominant external perspective has 'fixed' in time and place what is in reality a dynamic and complex trajectory and landscape. As Fornet described it in his speech during the much-publicised Encuentros of 2007:

> A veces, hablando ante públicos extranjeros sobre nuestro movimiento literario, encuentro personas – hombres por lo general – que insisten en preguntarme únicamente sobre hechos ocurridos hace treinta o cuarenta años, como si después del "caso Padilla" o la salida de Arenas por Mariel no hubiera ocurrido nada en nuestro medio. A ese tipo de curiosos los llamo Filósofos del tiempo detenido o Egiptólogos de la Revolución cubana.

> At times, speaking before foreign audiences about our literary movement, I come across people – generally men – who insist on asking me only about events that occurred thirty or forty years ago, as if, after the Padilla affair and Mariel, nothing had occurred on our island. I call these inquisitive souls Philosophers of a land where time stood still or Egyptologists of the Cuban Revolution. (La política cultural, 2008: 46)

In other words, rather than recognising that the 'internal' canon of Cuban literature is as multiple, partial and dynamic as any external canons, in ways reflected by the comments of scholars such as Chaple and Fornet, Cuban literature – or a small selection of it – is fixed contextually, with that context itself assumed to be determined by a number of paradigms of the writer and literature, such as notions of the 'captive mind' and culture as resistance against (internal, socialist) political repression.

Whilst external commentators are keen to expose the ideological foundations of literature in the socialist system, however, the natural opposition in this model – the literary texts as a commodity under capitalism – emerges magically free of ideology. Likewise, although usefully employing the work of Stuart Hall, Bourdieu and others in their exploration of cultural production as a social activity capable of generating individual and group agency (especially when applied to the complex terrain that emerged in the Special

Period), many external commentators are unable to recognise individual and group agency and autonomy unless it is associated with enterprise and commerce. Hernández-Reguant, for example, states that her edited volume on Cuba in the Special Period will 'track the agency of various social actors faced both with the constraints of the socialist bureaucracy and the possibilities opened by both new commercial stakeholders and foreign constituencies' (Hernández-Reguant, 2009), thus associating repression with socialism and, by definition, opportunity with capitalism.

What all of these approaches have excluded, therefore, are a number of critical factors or dimensions that allow us to gain a more comprehensive view and thus present a more diverse and nuanced interpretation of the evolution and contemporary state of Cuban literary canons. Excluded, for example, is a broadening of the notion of 'the canon' to include those writers who are less known because they do not fit the patterns indicated above; that is, excluded because (i) they are simply not published or studied outside Cuba, in Spanish or translated versions; (ii) they are assumed to be invisible or mediocre because their literary authority or cultural capital – in the form of texts, public appearances and international recognition – exists predominantly in Cuba rather than in the centres of international and transnational canon formation; and (iii) their cultural capital, always subordinated to political demands, is insignificant or compromised.

A More Complex Understanding of Literary Canons

Use of this complex but apparently natural and universal model and the perspectives and values that comprise it thus leads to an exclusive and distorted canon that altogether omits the particularities of Cuban policy and practice that have created a very different set of criteria for inclusion in the canon and, therefore, a rethinking of the canon itself. These specificities relate to the very conscious and sustained drive since 1959 (but with roots during the earlier stages of the insurrection) to approach the relationship between nation and cultural identity in very different ways, which emphasised the centrality of culture to individual and national development, and which was conscious throughout of the potential for culture to transform minds and behaviours. Thus, the rules of the game would be changed: literature and nation would be validated not through increased exposure on the international stage and Cuba would not trespass in the world republic in order to be recognised by it and ultimately be awarded membership of it. Instead, and more radically, literature could serve as an instrument of internal cohesion and national development, with external influences providing 'peripheral' inspiration or new directions, but with the nation – and the nation as a territorial entity – at the centre of any process.

However, and in contrast to the fixed positions often assumed by Fornet's 'Egyptologists' of the Revolution's literature, the processes of nation-building and canon-formation are inevitably bound by criteria of inclusion and exclusion that shift according to the contextual factors of time and place. This dynamic picture is further complicated when the context is a fast-changing one. Is it even possible to establish a canon of national literature in a context (such as that of revolutionary Cuba) characterised by rapid and constant socio-economic change, emigration, changing international alliances and economic restrictions? If so, what risks are associated with such a task? Even if one were to restrict the canon to the revolutionary period (i.e. after 1959), as Volume III of the *Historia de la literatura cubana* did, the task would be made more difficult by the complexity of the evolution of literary culture on the island, and its shifting importance within the wider project of Revolution and reconstruction of the idea of the Cuban nation. This complexity can be traced through cultural policy and the debates that crystallised the range of opinions expressed by practitioners and policy-makers at any given time over the past 50 years, and specifically, in the tensions and conflicts that lay at the centre of policy and practice. The following section offers a brief summary of these. (The entire trajectory of literary culture on the island – with a focus on the contemporary situation – is explored in Kapcia and Kumaraswami (forthcoming).)

Several seminal initiatives from 1959–1989 contributed to a radical reshaping of the literary environment and thus the foundations upon which the canon might be constructed: the 1961 literacy campaign created not only a potential mass readership of Cuban literature on the island, but also a model for individual and collective self-transformation through mobilisation and participation, which had a considerable impact on the value systems underpinning Cuban society. The campaign also established through principle and practice the idea that the barriers that had existed between the hitherto exclusive categories of class, gender, urban/rural population, formal/non-formal education could be transformed, if not wholly dissolved, through active participation in a collective project that united the nation. Perhaps most importantly, the emphasis on creating readership made clear, at least in principle, that the right to evaluate literature and recognise its merit – to contribute to canon-formation – also fell to new arbiters and gatekeepers – the *pueblo*.

This participation could also, as warned in Castro's 1961 'Palabras a los intelectuales' (Words to the intellectuals), quite possibly take the form of new authors and texts that – clearly not possessing the formal or aesthetic qualities that would facilitate their inclusion in traditional literary canons, in Cuba or elsewhere – had the potential to transform the canon. A significant example – amongst many – of the potential for transformation came in the 'new' testimonial literature that was produced from the early 1960s, with the resulting debates indicating the extent of the threat that they posed to a conventional perspective on what constituted literature (especially the importance of genre). Allowing the newly literate *pueblo* to compose and also evaluate its own narratives meant that the symbolic capital and prestige linked to the author – the aesthetic, formal or intellectual complexity and coherence of the text, the status of the author within authorising communities such as literary circles, publishing houses or cultural magazines, the relationship of the text or author to international literary currents and genres – could be hijacked and replaced (or at least threatened) by capital and authority of a very different kind – the authority of lived experience (and mostly hitherto un-narrated, therefore original experience) as a basis for literary production and reception. Indeed, the strident declaration of the 1971 Congress of Education and Culture made explicit precisely – and controversially – how the gatekeeping role should be reconfigured: 'La conciencia crítica de la sociedad es el pueblo mismo y, en primer término, la clase obrera' (The critical conscience of society is the pueblo itself, and, first and foremost, the working class) (Montaner, 1976: 152). Thus, the traditional reliance on the intellectual as arbiter of literary merit was ancillary, to 'coadyuvar a esa crítica con el pueblo y dentro del pueblo' (contribute to that critique with the pueblo and as part of the pueblo) (Montaner, 1976: 154). Equally importantly for the question of canon formation, the publishing system was to prioritise the internal readership.

Thus, the potential to change the rules of the game would require an infrastructure in order to provide the training and conditions for this massi-fied vision of literary production to become reality. Initially, the creation of a national publishing house, the Imprenta Nacional, along with the rejection of copyright through the practice of *piratería* (piracy), or the mass copying of published foreign material, allowed the possibility for new readers to have access to Cuban and international literary texts. The founding of cultural institutions in Havana for all kinds of cultural production and reception (Instituto Cubano de Arte e Industria Cinematográficos (ICAIC), Casa de las Américas), of institutions to organise, regulate but also protect cultural practitioners (Unión de Escritores y Artistas de Cuba (UNEAC)) and of innumerable textual spaces (daily newspapers, weekly magazines, cultural magazines) provided a national network for literary culture to be publicised, disseminated and debated. As controversially as the *testimonio* debate, the system of *talleres literarios* (literary workshops), formalised in the 1970s, cre-ated the potential for readers to become writers – and for aspiring writers to be published – whilst the processes of formalisation continued through-out the late 1970s and 1980s to establish a nationwide system of libraries, cultural centres (Casas de Cultura) and publishing houses, where specialist practitioners and non-specialist audiences could share physical and symbolic spaces and exchange their respective cultural and political capitals.

Despite the fact that the principle of egalitarianism provided a level of coherence to all of these initiatives, it would be disingenuous to suggest that there were not also many moments of rupture and crisis during the first 30 years of the Revolution, with the emigration of key figures – and the marginalisation of others – illustrating vividly the problems associated with perceived or real disagreement with this version of the national project and its implications for political and literary development. The central question underpinning the ongoing debates regarding literary culture under Revolution, then, was how to develop literature as a mass socio-cultural practice – as production or reception – and as an important contribution to the project of delayed postcolonial nation-building without 'diluting' its quality or prestige; and, specifically, how to achieve this under conditions of economic and political 'siege' and insecurity.

At stake in the debates – and in ways that created an intermittent but ever-present tension between the types of value (Frow, 1995) assigned to literary activity – was the understanding that any perception of the strengthening of the political value of literature inevitably meant a perceived weakening of its aesthetic value; in other words, it proposed that the two types of value were incompatible. Equally problematic was the question of the massification of literary production and the implications for the prestige and authority of the writer as public figure: the testimonial mode and the *talleres literarios* movement, in particular, were perceived by many writers not only as overly instrumental and prescriptive, but also unhelpfully mass-based, implying as they did that a mass movement of writers could be constructed through experience, education and practice, and thus threatened the status of the author as individual – or at least minority – figure and skilled specialist creator.

Moreover, since the existence of a canon and tradition required the use of the mechanisms and technologies associated with the centre (circulation, visibility and permanence), the role of the minority specialist gatekeeper was also essential: thus literary criticism – in the form of anthologies, reviews, literary histories and dictionaries such as the *Diccionario de la literatura cubana* (Instituto de Literatura y Lingüística de la Academia de Ciencias de Cuba, 1980) and the three-volume *Historia de la literatura cubana* (Chaple, 2008a), both published by the Instituto de Literatura y Lingüística – would serve the crucial function of tracing, ordering and recording the trajectory of Cuban literature of the Revolution. The binding force or common ground between the literary and the political, the individual and the masses as creators and arbiters, thus lay in the social value of cultural activity in the Revolution.

For 30 years at least, the omissions and incompleteness of these initiatives were minimised by a relatively coherent social project and vision. The economic crisis that followed the collapse of the Soviet Union, however, inevitably meant a paralysis of this project, with cultural life taking a back seat to basic and very pressing concerns. The main 'difficulties' were, of course, of an economic nature: the sudden disappearance of some 90 per cent of Cuba's imports and 60 per cent of her trade, of the secure and vital sugar markets, and of essential imports of oil, fertiliser and some staple foods, and a 35 per cent collapse of the economy in the early 1990s all meant an immediate crisis of production, energy generation and transport, and desperate shortages, with demoralising and prolonged power cuts, short-time working and increasing pressure on Cubans to find individual and often informal or illegal solutions in search of employment and hard currency. All of this threatened the basis of loyalty and commitment built since 1959, with emigration and social fragmentation weakening any sense of unity.

There were several other complicating factors – some ultimately productive, others much less so – which also had significant consequences for the process of canon-formation implied in the creation of a literary history, such as that attempted by Chaple et al., and which highlighted in dramatic fashion the impossibility of creating a representative and reliable canon of Cuban literature on the island. The first of these was the emergence of limited, but very significant, new opportunities for publishing in the international literary marketplace, coupled with the virtual paralysis of the considerable publishing infrastructure that had existed until 1989. With writers seeking publishing contracts and literary competitions abroad (which would guarantee publication plus some financial recompense in hard currency) for a whole variety of reasons – sometimes based on a complex and often contradictory blend of personal, moral, ideological, political and economic decisions – and with Cuba still extremely limited in its incorporation of virtual textual spaces, many works written in Cuba, but published elsewhere, simply disappeared from the normal tracking mechanisms for the continuation of the internal canon. Although, as mentioned, the *diasporic* question was addressed and debated (not without problems) in theoretical and conceptual terms in the early 1990s, the practical matter of adapting the canon to include such writers and texts was an even harder task. Indeed, it was only until the late 1990s that many of these lapses of information were addressed, with a recovering publishing industry slowly attempting to recuperate and evaluate work published abroad within the remit of the island-based canons, and again, in the context of often prohibitive political decisions and economic transactions.

Other contextual factors further complicated the process. If one of the cornerstones of a literary canon is its authenticity or representativeness (of form, content, themes), the profound and sudden change and the new social and cultural concerns that emerged in the 1990s (and were almost immediately reflected in cultural practice) also proved a challenge to existing notions of the internal canon. Radical social change, the rupture (through emigration and social inequalities) of communities at all levels and in all sectors, the sudden recognition of new realities and value systems, the emergence of new identity groups and social actors and the mere fact that new writers were occupying spaces left by émigrés all meant that there was little commonality to be found between the before and after of 1989. In terms of literary genre, the shortage of fuel and paper had a profound influence on the hierarchy of genres that made up literary production: short stories and poetry assumed a new dominance, with anthologies taking the place of author-based collections and with the novel genre impossible to contemplate until a publishing recovery was more firmly in place. Although many of these conditions had featured in the literary landscape from 1959 onwards, the crisis of the 1990s brought them into sharp relief. In a sense, then, the publishing crisis brought not an entirely new problem but rather a new moment of recognition of a problem: quite simply, that a general model of accumulation of writers and texts had occurred over 30 years as the effects of cultural policy – the massification of literary culture in terms of readers, texts, publishing mechanisms and writers – had led logically to both a quantitative increase and a diversification of the literary canon published on the island. If, as was indeed the case of the third volume of the *Historia de la Literatura Cubana*, an attempt was to be made to compare before and after, and (in the interests of safeguarding unity) to find some element of commonality, on what terms could that comparison be drawn, and how could a canon be fashioned that could do justice to the accumulations and transformations of the preceding 40 years?

However, there was one phenomenon – the result of both top-down policy and bottom-up practice – that changed the terms of the literary landscape, and thus the understanding of canon, in two even more profound and irrevocable ways. First, whilst the policy of massifying and diversifying the canon over 30 years had largely rejected the importance of international or transnational trends in favour of the national model, this model had mostly equated the nation with its capital Havana. The RISO publishing phenomenon changed all of this. This Fidel-led initiative, by which photocopiers (under the RISO brand name), imported from Japan by the Cuban government in order to palliate the national publishing crisis, had led to the creation of small provincial publishing houses and changed the existing publishing model (and therefore writing and reading practices) by decentralising and deregulating literary production, with texts – even those of prominent Havana writers – published more efficiently, although also much more modestly, by small-scale provincial publishing outfits across the island. Thus, whilst during the pre-1989 period there had been some attempt in policy and practice to change the rules of the game of 'littérisation' in order to incorporate new types of literary texts, new writers, with new types of symbolic capital, new gatekeepers of the canon, the model had still largely been centralised and hierarchical, with Havana always a kind of hothouse and arbiter for the quality of literary production and, thus, its suitability for the canon. Now, however, there was significant literary activity taking place outside the capital and 'under the radar' of the central mechanisms of canon-construction. After all, a book published in a provincial RISO publishing house possessed cultural capital that a manuscript waiting for evaluation in Havana did not.

Outside visions of the Cuban literary canon both on and off the island have stressed the processes of de-skilling, de-professionalisation and crisis of faith that created an impoverished context for Cuban writers – with emigration, the embracing of transnational agreements or publishing abroad as the only remaining options that carried value; in other words, that crisis led to a belated recognition by writers that the 'world republic of letters' was indeed the natural and inevitable model to be followed, and that any canon that was limited to the national was doomed to a peripheral existence. When seen from within the island, however, a very different picture emerges: that the 1990s also witnessed significant processes of localisation and decentralisation that meant that both the nation and the multiple national canons were rebuilt from the local outwards. According to this narrative, any sense of opening up or *apertura* – through joint ventures or (individual and institutional) contracts established with foreign partners – were a means to an end, a survival strategy to retain national sovereignty, rather than an admission of defeat. Moreover, most surprisingly, the decentralisation of literary production and the canon could serve the important function of re-launching a drive to reconfigure the nation and its letters. Indeed, developments regarding provincial literary culture outside Havana were eventually formalised from 2000 into the Sistema de Ediciones Territoriales (SET), whereby there was some attempt at least to recognise and chart centrally the entirety of literary production across the island (Resumen Estadístico, 2009). Whether this attempt will translate into a coherent and systematic network of agents and mechanisms to evaluate and award merit to this range of production – to shape new canons – remains to be seen, as does the question of whether the subsequent volume of the *Historia de la literatura cubana* will be able to the incorporate local and provincial into the concept of the national canon.

Conclusion

To return to Casanova's conceptual model, which emphasises the impossibility but necessity of constructing literary canons, Cuba has painted a different picture since 1959, and never more so than in the new millennium. As can be seen, the conventional path towards recognition as a literary nation follows a certain model: that the peripheral nation embarks on a gradual movement towards recognition on the international stage, as assigned by elite gatekeepers, and based on specific notions of cultural capital that inhabit a seemingly pure, absolute and apolitical realm, the 'world republic of letters'; a model, as Casanova argues, that merely serves to re-inscribe the nation's place in the periphery. In Cuba, this model clearly still has some currency, as the evidence of émigré and disenchanted writers makes clear. However, it exists alongside – and sometimes uneasily with – parallel and alternative sources of prestige and capital as assigned by an increasingly diverse network of internal gatekeepers. Furthermore, since the Special Period, its path has increasingly looked inwards, and not always via Havana, towards the provincial and the local, to mark the parameters of the canon at any given time. At the same time, however, through the new regional alliances emerging via ALBA, the possibility of a new transnationalism, clearly neither apolitical nor universal but, rather, characterised precisely by its political affinities and resistance to dominant models, also promises to inflect and transform the Cuban literary canon in novel ways.

8

Regime Change and Human Rights: A Perspective on the Cuba Polemic

STEVE LUDLAM

University of Sheffield, UK

Since the Cuban Revolution overcame the US-backed Batista dictatorship, the struggle for civil rights has been intense: against colonial oppression, against apartheid, against segregation, against military juntas, and against the loss of liberties across the divisions of the Cold War. In these conflicts, the work of human rights Non-Governmental Organisations (NGOs), such as Amnesty International and Human Rights Watch (HRW), has secured civil liberties, and saved the lives of many social critics and activists. Therefore it is challenging, for those who try to analyse the Cuban Revolution free of Cold War prejudices, when such NGOs attack the Cuban government's human rights record, a government whose achievements in securing its people's social rights and those of others around the world are widely acknowledged. The fact that human rights diplomacy aimed at Cuba also forms part of an active US strategy of regime change, itself an attack on Cuba's sovereignty and right to self-determination, does not, of course, justify every act of every state actor in Cuba, or place beyond criticism every clause of every law designed to protect Cuba's sovereignty. However, the history of US–Cuba relations demands contextualisation of such diplomacy. As the United Nations (UN) Human Rights Commission Special Rapporteur on Cuba noted:

> While not overlooking the urgent need for specific measures, as proposed above, the Special Rapporteur nevertheless wishes to point out that any analysis concerning the situation and implementation of human rights in Cuba must, as a point of departure, accept the fact that the Government is, and has for a long time been, surrounded by an international climate extremely hostile to many of its policies and, in some cases, even to its very existence. This hostile international climate does not seem to have been affected by the vast political, military and economic changes that have taken place in the world in the last few years. (United Nations, 1992: paragraph 89)

This chapter returns to this point of departure and considers: the origin of the US campaign on human rights in Cuba; the contradictions surrounding that campaign; the privileging of some kinds of human rights over others; the stance of human rights NGOs and the issues they raise.

Origin of the US Campaign on Human Rights in Cuba

US governments have long made easing their hostile policy on Cuba dependent, from the Cuban perspective, on Cuba surrendering its Revolution, and the Constitution approved in 1976 by 97 per cent of voters on a 98 per cent turnout, and becoming a liberal democracy with a free-market economy. Human rights diplomacy has grown in prominence since the end of the Cold War and the United States' reduced dependence on alliances with dictatorships. It contrasts starkly with the cordial relations that the United States maintains with states such as China and Vietnam, and with many other governments that fall short of liberal democratic norms.

Since the Soviet collapse offered the opportunity of normalising relations, US policy has paradoxically intensified against the rebel island in its Caribbean 'backyard'. When US presidents have faltered, they have felt the full force of the largely right-wing Cuban-American lobby. This lobby, long integrated into US covert anti-communist strategies in Latin America, wields the threat of the loss of electoral support in the crucial state of Florida (Ludlam, 2011). Until Barack Obama's election in 2008, no US President since 1959 had won Florida without the support of the so-called 'Miami Mafia' of Cuban exile organisations. Crucial examples are the two embargo-tightening laws of the 1990s, promoted by the Cuban American National Foundation: the 1992 Cuba Democracy (Torricelli) Act and 1996 Cuba Liberty and Solidarity (Helms–Burton) Act, both initially opposed by incumbent Presidents George Bush Sr and Bill Clinton, who both reversed their position in presidential election years when the Miami groups attacked them.

Both laws intensified US human rights diplomacy against Cuba in two significant ways that continue to frame policies and polemics. First, they entrenched a legal obligation on the presidency to overthrow the Cuban state, and provided for tens of millions of dollars in federal funding of 'Track 2' activities, to complement the embargo's 'Track 1'. 'Track 2' channelled funds into Cuban-American and other groups' activists engaged in regime-change activities in Cuba, and directly into groups inside Cuba with the aim of creating an oppositional 'civil society' force to bring down the Revolution. The strategy of organising oppositional groups and challenging governments with actions designed to justify *coup d'etats* and external intervention, is of course a long-standing and well-known US approach, against which Cuba has been permanently on the alert.

The G. W. Bush government, going to war 'on terror', listed Cuba as a terrorist state in 2002, claiming, and then withdrawing claims that Cuba was manufacturing and selling chemical weapons. In the run-up to the Iraq invasion of 2003, US diplomats in Cuba distributed funds and materials to US- sponsored civil society groups. The subsequent publication of the reports of the presidential Commission for Assistance to a Free Cuba presented detailed plans for regime change, emphasising again the US strategy of using human rights and civil society promotion as the central planks of the planned transition. The first (2004) report referred to 'encouraging multilateral diplomatic efforts to challenge the regime in international organizations and to strengthen policies of proactive support for prodemocracy groups in Cuba should form a cornerstone of our policy to hasten an end to the Castro regime' (Commission for Assistance to a Free Cuba, 2004: xvi). The 2006 report established an $80 million Cuba Fund for a Democratic Future, of which $31 million was earmarked for 'support to independent civil society on the island' (Commission for Assistance to a Free Cuba, 2006a: 20). This second report contained a 'Secret Annex', which, Cubans assumed, meant new plans for assassinations and military intervention. In a parallel *Compact with the Cuban People* in 2006, Bush promised, without irony, that, after regime change, the United States would 'discourage third parties from intervening to obstruct the will of the Cuban people' (Commission for Assistance to a Free Cuba, 2006b). President Obama's first administration continued the strategy: in 2011, the Cuban courts jailed Alan Gross, an employee of a US contractor paid by the United States Agency for International Development to smuggle communications equipment to dissident groups (Carter 2011).

Second, the 1990s legislation introduced an extraterritorial threat to non-US citizens doing business with Cuba. Title III of the Helms–Burton law made possible the arrest of representatives of companies whose trade involved the use of properties legally nationalised in Cuba, whose owners had refused (on US advice) to accept compensation. The threat was condemned as illegal by other states, and especially by the European Union (EU). Helms–Burton, however, enabled the United States to drive a new bargain with the EU, with the US president suspending Title III, and the EU adopting a 'Common Position' that stated: 'The objective of the European Union in its relations with Cuba is to encourage a process of transition to pluralist democracy and respect for human rights and fundamental freedoms' (European Union, 1996). The EU's deal put it in a diplomatic vice that the United States could tighten whenever it intensified its human rights diplomacy, as it did in 2003, when a large number of US-funded activists were arrested on the island, and the EU adopted new diplomatic sanctions.

Against this background, US human rights diplomacy against Cuba can easily appear as just another instrument, alongside the economic embargo (called a 'blockade' by the Cubans) and US-based terrorist attacks on the island, for pursuing regime change. This appearance is reinforced by other contradictions in US policy.

'Double Standards and Politicization'

There are obvious contradictions in US polemics on Cuba's record. First, the US government is itself arguably a human rights abuser: the worldwide 'rendition', torture and detention without trial machinery, epitomised by Abu Ghraib, Bagram, and, of all places, the US-occupied Cuban territory at Guantánamo, is the most recent example. The US record of support for dictators of the foulest kind, and of training their 'counter-insurgency' torturers, is well-known, above all in Latin America. In this sorry history, the US role in sustaining the apartheid regime in South Africa also stands out, alongside violent racial segregation within the United States itself in the past. When Cubans fought in Angola to expel the South African army, they were accused of exporting tyranny; when Cuba gave asylum to persecuted US black activists, it was accused of harbouring terrorists.

Second, the United States has a selective history of signing and ratifying human rights accords. It has twice withdrawn from the jurisdiction of the International Court of Justice (ICJ). The first time was in 1986 when the ICJ found against the United States after it had mined Nicaraguan harbours, as part of its 'dirty war' against the Sandinistas who had overthrown a US-backed dictator. The second withdrawal, in 2005, followed an ICJ finding against the United States for refusing 51 Mexicans on death row in US prisons access to Mexican consular officials. Similarly contradictory has been the attitude to the International Criminal Court (ICC), which is restricted to war crimes, genocide and crimes against humanity. The United States first tried to prevent its establishment, has since refused to ratify it, and still refuses to allow US troops to work under the UN flag unless they are exempt from ICC jurisdiction. The United States and Somalia are, in fact, the only states not to have ratified the Convention on the Rights of the Child, the United States is one of only seven states that have not ratified the Convention on all Forms of Discrimination Against Women, and has so far signed only three of the nine international UN human rights treaties.

Such seemingly self-serving human rights diplomacy has been particularly flagrant over Cuba. The annual battle around the United States' anti-Cuba resolution in the UN Commission on Human Rights (UNCHR) so poisoned that institution that the Commission collapsed as a viable international institution. The disproportionality in Cuba's case is striking considering the state of the Americas. A French study of Amnesty International reports on the Americas and the Caribbean listed 93 categories of recorded human rights abuses, ranging from extrajudicial assassination to forced sterilisation of women, and where they occurred. Not one case, in any of the 93 categories, had been recorded by Amnesty International in Cuba. The author concluded that, from the perspective of Amnesty's reports, Cuba had the best human rights record in the hemisphere (Lamrani, 2008: 95–101). The Inter-American Commission on Human Rights recorded that in 2009 it had received 1,431 complaints of human rights violations involving 24 states. Three concerned Cuba, 77 concerned the United States, and the three countries with highest number of complaints were staunch US allies in the region: Peru (201), Mexico (232) and Colombia (237) (Inter-American Commission on Human Rights, 2009: Chapter III).

When the UN General Assembly adopted Resolution 60/251, to replace the UNCHR with a new Human Rights Council, the text referred to 'the importance of ensuring universality, objectivity and non-selectivity in the consideration of human rights issues, and the elimination of double standards and politicization' (United Nations, 2006: 2). Cuba was elected to the new Council from its outset; under G. W. Bush, the United States refused to join. When the Special Representative to Cuba of the High Commission on Human Rights, a product of US diplomacy, was abolished in 2007, Cuba responded by noting that now it could act as a sovereign nation and, in 2008, it signed the International Covenant on Civil and Political Rights and the International Covenant on Economic, Social and Cultural Rights. Helping to destroy the UN Commission on Human Rights, though, has been a minor example of double standards when set alongside the half-century of aggressive US policy and actions against what many see as the civil rights of the Cuban people.

Cuba – Target of State-sponsored Terrorism

In the Universal Declaration of Human Rights, Article 3 states that 'Everyone has the right to life, liberty and security of person' (United Nations, 1948). This right has been repeatedly denied to Cubans by terrorists, mostly trained in the United States, often by US agencies, and operated from US territory (Bolender, 2010). In 2006, the Cuban Foreign Ministry summarised the consequences as follows:

> The many different forms of terrorism used against Cuba include: the destruction of economically important and civilian facilities; attacks on coastal facilities, merchant ships and fishing vessels; attempts on Cuban facilities, equipment and personnel abroad, including diplomatic bodies, airline offices and planes; attempts at assassinating main government leaders; the introduction of agricultural and animal germs

and plagues and strains of human diseases, among others. More than 3,478 men, women and children have lost their lives and another 2,099 Cubans have been physically handicapped for life as a result of at least 681 proven and well-documented acts of terrorism and aggression against Cuba. It is worth mentioning that these actions have not stopped over time: 68 took place in the 1990s and another 39 in the last five years. (Republic of Cuba, 2006: Part 1, Chapter 3)

The origin and tolerance of these attacks has been summarised in a paper co-authored by a former US Head of Interests (*de facto* ambassador) in Cuba:

Many Cuban exile terrorists got their start by working with the CIA on acts of violence against targets in Cuba. But as the CIA closed its base in Miami and de-emphasized such tactics, its former 'operatives,' among them Orlando Bosch and Luis Posada Carriles, turned freelance. Declassified CIA and FBI documents leave no doubt that Bosch and Posada were then involved in acts of terrorism, such as the bombing of a Cubana airliner in 1976 with the loss of 73 innocent lives. Bosch was also reported to have been behind the 1976 assassination in Washington of former Chilean diplomat Orlando Letelier and his American assistant, Ronnie Moffitt. And Posada acknowledged to *The New York Times* that he was responsible for the 1997 bombings of tourist hotels in Havana, resulting in the death of an Italian tourist and the wounding of several other people. These were but the tip of the iceberg. There were many other exile terrorists, many other assassinations and other acts of violence against Cuban-Americans who disagreed with the exile hardliners, in addition to intense efforts to intimidate those advocating dialogue with Cuba and/or those who insisted on traveling to the island. Most disturbingly, almost none of these terrorist acts, even those in the U.S., have been punished by U.S. authorities. On the contrary, there has been a clear pattern of tolerance. (Smith, Harrison and Adams, 2006: 1)

This tolerance takes various forms, beyond giving sanctuary in Miami to notorious activists such as Bosch and Posada Carriles, who are wanted in Cuba and elsewhere for terrorist offences. In 1999, the FBI published *Terrorism in the United States 1999: 30 Years of Terrorism, a Special Retrospective Edition* (Federal Bureau of Investigation, 1999). In an appendix on 'terrorist activity in the United States 1980–89', Cuban-American groups were blamed for 27 acts, mostly bombings. The main group, Omega 7, had been described by the FBI as, 'the most dangerous terrorist organization in the United States' (Levine, 2001: 188) Yet, in 62 pages of analysis, there was no mention of the Cuban–American link. One FBI agent, discussing attacks on Cuba, complained that, 'Every day we have a Neutrality Act violation because people leave to do runs on Cuba. But no one will allow us to do our job' (Bardach, 2002: 117). HRW reported that:

> The official response to the violence and intimidation in Miami has been marked by a notable failure to prosecute criminal acts directed against dissidents. While in the last few years there have been over a dozen bombings aimed at those who favor a moderate approach to the Cuban government, there has not been a single arrest or prosecution in that time. Moreover, the authorities responsible for enforcing the laws more often appear to be concerned with discrediting activists than with apprehending those responsible. (Human Rights Watch, 1993)

As expectation grew that post-Soviet Cuba would collapse, new terrorism campaigns targeted Cuban tourism and foreign tourists. In 1998, an Italian tourist was murdered in a Havana hotel bombing. At the FBI's request, the Cuban authorities presented the FBI with extensive evidence against US-based terrorist groups. The response was not action against the terrorists, but the arrest of Cuban anti-terror agents infiltrating the Miami groups, resulting in the imprisonment of Cuba's 'Miami Five'. As the veteran US civil liberties lawyer Leonard Weinglass, one of their attorneys, wrote, 'The Five were not prosecuted because they violated American law, but because their work exposed those who were. By infiltrating the terror network that is allowed to exist in Florida they demonstrated the hypocrisy of America's claimed opposition to terrorism' (Weinglass, 2005: 124). It also demonstrated the limited legitimacy of US attacks on Cuba's human rights record.

The US Embargo and Human Rights in Cuba

The US embargo has had an extensive impact on the human rights of ordinary Cubans; indeed its explicit purpose has been to create enough hunger and misery to drive Cubans to overthrow their government. The embargo on Cuba is 'the most comprehensive set of U.S. economic sanctions on any country' (United States Government Accounting Office, 2007: 1). As the UN reported in 2008: 'The negative impact of the embargo is pervasive in the social, economic and environmental dimensions of human development in Cuba, severely affecting the most vulnerable socio-economic groups of the Cuban population' (United Nations, 2008: 83). In the same year, the UN Human Rights Council reported that:

> According to the Personal Representative, Cuba's efforts are all the more significant given the disastrous and lasting economic and social

effects – compounded in 2004 – of the embargo imposed on the Cuban population over 40 years ago, as well as its impacts on civil and political rights. CEDAW, CERD, CRC, CAT and the Special Rapporteurs on the right to food and on violence against women also recognized the serious social and economic difficulties that Cuba has experienced as a result of the embargo and the repercussions this has on the enjoyment of human rights in the country. [. . .] United Nations agencies also stressed the negative impact of the embargo on opportunities for development (UNDP and UNFPA); food security of the vulnerable segments of the population (FAO); food-based social safety nets (WFP); fundamental rights of children, adolescents, women and families (UNICEF); in the area of health (UNFPA, WPF and WHO/PAHO); human settlements, planning and management and environmental health (UNHABITAT); education (UNICEF and UNESCO); science, culture, communications and information (UNESCO); and the quality of life of the most vulnerable groups (UNFPA) and the people in general (WPF and WHO/PAHO). The 2008–2012 UNDAF report noted that the blockade represents an obstacle to the process of development of the country. (United Nations Human Rights Council, 2008: 10–11)

After its study of the embargo's impact, the American Association for World Health concluded that it was responsible for killing Cubans:

After a year-long investigation, the American Association for World Health has determined that the U.S. embargo of Cuba has dramatically harmed the health and nutrition of large numbers of ordinary Cuban citizens. As documented by the attached report, it is our expert medical opinion that the U.S. embargo has caused a significant rise in suffering – and even deaths – in Cuba. [. . .] A humanitarian catastrophe has been averted only because the Cuban government has maintained a high level of budgetary support for a health care system designed to deliver primary and preventive health care to all of its citizens. [. . .] Even so, the U.S. embargo of food and the de facto embargo on medical supplies has wreaked havoc with the island's model primary health care system. (American Association for World Health, 1997)

In its more recent study of the embargo, Amnesty International argued that, although the United States has not ratified the International Covenant on Economic, Social and Cultural Rights, it has signed it and therefore is obliged under international law not to defeat its purpose:

The economic, trade and financial sanctions against Cuba, compounded by the lack of measures from the US government to monitor and alleviate the negative impact of the embargo on the Cuban population, are defeating the purpose of the provisions of the ICESCR, in particular with regards to advancing the rights of the Covenant through international co-operation. The US government is also acting contrary to the Charter of the United Nations by restricting the direct import of medicine and medical equipment and supplies, and by imposing those restrictions on companies operating in third countries. (Amnesty International, 2009: 20)

The embargo has also undermined the human rights of US citizens, imposing restrictions and penalties in terms of travel to Cuba and to support family members there (United States Government Accounting Office, 2007: 56).

US Action and its Impact on Civil Rights in Cuba

Another contradiction of US policy is that its history of unremitting aggression has contributed directly to the restrictions on its citizens that the Cuban authorities have adopted in the defence of its sovereignty. As noted above, the UN Special Rapporteur made precisely this point in 1992; Amnesty International reiterated it, two decades and four presidents later:

The embargo legislation contains provisions for 'democracy building' in Cuba which include the allocation of significant amounts of aid and support for Cuban NGOs and individuals opposing the government. The strengthening of the embargo with the Helms–Burton Act in 1996 prompted the Cuban authorities to respond with harsh legislation which has ultimately been used to condemn prisoners of conscience to long prison terms. The Cuban authorities portray non-violent political dissidents and human rights activists as foreign sympathizers supporting US policy against Cuba. The embargo has helped to undermine the enjoyment of key civil and political rights in Cuba by fuelling a climate in which fundamental rights such as freedom of association, expression and assembly are routinely denied. (Amnesty International, 2009: 6)

This passage highlights the frequent argument that Cuba's leaders use external hostility as a pretext for internal repression. Leaving aside the question of whether Cuba treats all dissidents the same, irrespective of their links with US agencies, this argument is weak. Cuba's leaders do not need to exaggerate the external threat; Cuba's 2008 submission to the UN report on the embargo detailed the evidence of intensified US civil society strategy (United Nations, 2008: 20). US aggression remains a permanent threat to Cuba's independence, not just the embargo, but other policies and actions: the overt and covert military attacks; infiltration of terrorist groups; toleration of US-based terrorist groups that have dropped and planted explosive, and chemical and biological weapons in Cuba; the treatment of the Miami Five as spies rather than counter-terrorism allies; the constant diplomatic attacks; and the full-scale regime change programmes. The combination of this bellicosity with funding to provoke domestic opposition inevitably impacts on dissidents. According to President Carter, who investigated inside Cuba in 2002, leading dissidents believe that US activity undermines them:

> We then had extensive meetings with a wide range of the most notable dissidents, each the leader of an organization and many having completed prison sentences for their demands for change in the socialist regime. They were unanimous in [...] opposition to any elevation of harsh rhetoric from the United States toward Cuba and to any funding of their efforts from the U.S. government. Any knowledge or report of such financial support would just give credibility to the long-standing claims of President Castro that they were 'paid lackeys' of Washington. (Carter, 2002)

Former US Head of Section (*de facto* ambassador) Wayne Smith told the G. W. Bush government, when the second Commission for a Free Cuba report appeared, what the funding of civil society opposition would mean to those groups:

> The report two years ago called for support to dissidents and representatives of 'civil society' as a means of confronting the government. The new report calls for more of the same, and even for the establishment of an $80 million fund to increase that support. But as in an earlier report we quoted one dissident on the island summing up the effect of that support: 'The good news is that most of that money remains in Miami; the bad news is it makes our position more difficult even so'. What he meant is that much of the money is given to organizations in Miami, some of it, supposedly, to pass on to groups in Cuba, but that little in fact gets through; it stays with those in Miami. Further, when the U.S. says its objective is to bring down the Cuban government, and then says that one of its means of accomplishing that is by providing funds to Cuban dissidents, it in effect places them in the position of being the paid agents of a foreign power seeking to overthrow their

own. Inevitably, that puts them in an even more difficult position and severely limits their effectiveness. (Smith, 2006: 3)

Every state faced with such threats has tried to ensure that its internal security is not undermined. This is not to excuse every such act of self-preservation by states, in Cuba or anywhere else. Cuba's own response to the charge that it uses the external threat to suppress internal opposition has often been repeated by its spokespersons: if you are serious in this belief, end your aggression and remove our 'excuse', and see what we do.

Privileging Some Kinds of Human Rights over Others

Another contradictory aspect of the polemic is the privileging of some kinds of human rights over others. The first part of the UN Declaration of Human Rights contains articles covering civil and political rights; the second part covers economic and social rights. There is nothing in the Declaration that gives the former prominence over the latter, either morally or in international law. The UN has stated unequivocally that, 'the Declaration gives equal importance to economic, social and cultural rights and to civil rights and political liberties, and affords them the same degree of protection' (United Nations, n.d.). Nevertheless, US human rights diplomacy against Cuba has focused overwhelmingly on civil and political rights. Social democrats and socialists, and many social liberals for that matter, have repeatedly insisted that, without basic economic and social rights, individuals will not have the opportunity or the means to the equal exercise of civil and political rights. To give just one obvious example, freedom of expression is limited if you are illiterate. But in international human rights politicking, the downplaying of economic and social rights has been the norm. As the UN Committee on Economic, Social, and Cultural Rights informed the historic Vienna World Conference on Human Rights in 1993:

> The shocking reality [. . .] is that states and the international community as a whole continue to tolerate all too often breaches of economic, social and cultural rights which, if they occurred in relation to civil and political rights, would provoke expressions of horror and outrage and would lead to concerted calls for immediate remedial action. In effect, despite the rhetoric, violations of civil and political rights continue to be treated as though they were far more serious, and more patently intolerable, than massive and direct denials of economic, social and cultural rights. (United Nations Committee on Economic, Social, and Cultural Rights, 1993)

It is hardly surprising that this selectiveness has been applied to the Cuban Revolution, given its achievements in terms of economic and social rights, which are particularly impressive in the Latin American context. In the UN's *Economic Commission for Latin America and the Caribbean Annual Statistics 2010*, which covers 41 countries, Cuba ranks as follows (all statistics are for 2008, unless otherwise stated): fifth lowest illiteracy (2010), highest primary education enrolment, fifth highest secondary education enrolment, highest tertiary education enrolment, highest primary and secondary teacher-pupil ratios, sixth lowest maternal mortality, lowest infant mortality under five years (2009), highest infant measles vaccination (2009), highest physicians and hospitals beds per inhabitant, highest dietary calories per person per day (2005–2007), highest proportions of GDP spent on education and on health (Economic Commission for Latin America and the Caribbean, 2010: 49–62). The UN's *Social Panorama of Latin America 2010* contains a striking bar chart comparing social spending as a percentage of gross domestic product (GDP) in 21 countries from 1990 to 2008. Cuba stands out like a skyscraper from a mainly low-rise social skyline. Even in the depths of its post-Soviet crises, Cuba spent the highest proportion. By 2008, its social spending took 38 percent of GDP, with the next highest, Brazil, spending 24 percent, and the average state spending around 14 percent; even in cash terms, Cuba was the third highest social spender (Economic Commission for Latin America and the Caribbean, 2011: 34). The privileging of civil over economic and social human rights reflects the long historic struggle between liberal and socialist ideas about equality, democracy and the role of the state, so it is no surprise to find the Cuban example treated as a threat to the liberal order in general.

The Stance on Cuba of Human Rights NGOs

The direction of NGO reporting tends to run alongside two main aspects of the US position: the privileging of civil over social and economic rights; and a disproportionate volume of complaints against Cuba. Overwhelmingly, the Cuba country reports of human rights NGOs focus on political and civil rights, making only passing references to economic, social and cultural rights, and (though only recently) to the impact of the US embargo. This is partly a result of the NGOs' histories; Amnesty, for example, began life fighting only on the issue of prisoners of conscience, although it has since expanded its horizons, as illustrated by its recent report on the US embargo (Amnesty International, 2009). The central focus on civil rights has indisputably been an enormous strength, and secured the lives and liberties of many activists, and of course part of Amnesty's legitimacy derives from its 'plague on all your houses' approach to states.

Human rights NGOs will properly point out that the right to self-determination does not mean the right to abuse human rights. NGOs tend to make two kinds of complaints about Cuba. One kind concerns, as noted already, the absence of multi-party democracy and private enterprise. Such criticisms, self-evidently, reject the legitimacy of socialist models. However, demands that Cuba conform to liberal democratic norms in its political system are also demands that Cubans abandon their right to choose their own sovereign political system, a right enshrined in the International Bill of Rights, as the core UN Charter, Declarations and Covenants are collectively known. Article 1 of the International Covenant on Economic, Social and Cultural Rights states that 'All peoples have the right of self-determination. By virtue of that right they freely determine their political status and freely pursue their economic, social and cultural development' (United Nations, 1966). The Cuban people made this choice in a free and secret vote in the constitutional referendum of 1976. When, in 2002, the opposition Varela Project exercised the constitutional right to petition the National Assembly to hold a referendum on introducing multi-party elections and restoring capitalist enterprise, by collecting 11,020 signatures, over 8 million Cubans signed a Communist Party-organised counter-petition declaring the socialist system irrevocable. Even allowing for social pressure, this is an overwhelming determination. The opportunity to vote on their national constitution is one that few people have ever enjoyed.

The second kind of concerns focus on the treatment of individual opposition activists, and related criticisms of Cuba's legal system. Cuba's constitution enshrines all the standard civil and political rights, and of course a whole set of economic, social and cultural rights that are normally absent in national constitutions and that underpin its socialist project. Of course there are ongoing debates, above all within Cuba itself, about improving the reality, for example, of legal non-discrimination against women, black Cubans and homosexual Cubans; but these take place against a background of historical achievement that is indisputable. The formal scope of Cuban rights and their historical context have recently been comprehensively set out in Cuba's 2008 report to the UN Human Rights Council, together with explanations of existing procedures for protecting citizens' rights, and of the prison system (Republic of Cuba, 2008). NGOs do not generally challenge the existence of these rights, but draw attention to their limitation by national security and other legislation. For example, the Constitution guarantees freedom of expression, but rules out private ownership of the media, although the Catholic church has its own media, something that the US State Department seems to find difficult to square with its views: on successive pages of its 2010 report it declared that, 'the government directly owned and the CP [Communist Party] controlled all print and broadcast media outlets and did not allow editorial independence', but that, 'priests and senior clergy openly and publicly criticized President Castro and the country's leadership in church publications and media interviews without reprisals, openly questioning how the country's leadership dealt with criticism and managed the economy' (United States Department of State, 2011; 14–15). Most significantly, in terms of NGOs' concerns, the Constitution contains a general Article that makes most dissident activity potentially illegal. Article 62 states:

> None of the freedoms which are recognized for citizens can be exercised contrary to what is established in the Constitution and by law, or contrary to the existence and objectives of the socialist state, or contrary to the decision of the Cuban people to build socialism and communism. Violations of this principle can be punished by law. (Republic of Cuba, 1992)

Two further pieces of legislation have developed this Article. Article 91 of the Penal Code prohibits 'acts against the independence or territorial integrity of the state'. Law 88 was adopted in 1999 in response to the dissident-funding provisions of the 1996 US Helms–Burton legislation. Law 88 punishes a range of activities deemed to constitute collaboration with the US embargo, including receipt of US funds to further US objectives. These were the laws used against the 75 Cubans arrested in 2003, whose cases provoked a storm of protest by human rights NGOs, and as noted above, diplomatic retaliation by the EU. The 2003 cases exemplify the politicisation of the rights agenda. In the run-up to the invasion of Iraq, the United States was, as far as the Cuban government was concerned, intensifying its subversive activities inside Cuba, its diplomats touring the country organising dissident groups and distributing money and materials. Evidence was presented that the arrested opposition figures had been collaborating with this, and receiving money and materials, a context acknowledged in the major NGO report on the cases (Amnesty International, 2003; Elizalde and Báez 2003). In having such laws to protect its sovereignty against subversion and collaboration with enemy states, Cuba is arguably acting no differently from other states. Needless to say, whatever criticism might be levelled at the judicial process, in Cuba such opposition activists are charged and tried, not assassinated, 'renditioned' or 'disappeared'. In 2010 and 2011, all of the 2003 group still in prison were released, following negotiations with the Spanish government, brokered by the Catholic church in Cuba.

Of course, NGOs do not therefore generally argue that the dissidents whom they defend are not guilty of the charges brought against them. They reject, though, the laws under which they are tried, and register other complaints about the administration of such laws, such as trial procedures, the system of elected professional and lay judges, and about the prison system itself. Examples can be found in the 2009 HRW report on Cuba, and similar issues dominate the US State Department's 2010 *Human Rights Report on Cuba* (Human Rights Watch, 2009; United States Department of State, 2011: 1–14). Issues of judicial procedure are the subject of concern and dispute in every state in the world. One crucial issue is adequate means of redress and appeal against administrative and judicial errors or abuse. Cuba's reports to the UN identify such procedures (Republic of Cuba, 2008: Chapter VII). It is not the purpose of this chapter to make any claim about the robustness of Cuban citizens' access to such means of redress; nevertheless, it is worth recalling that in the Cuban legal system a confession alone (forced or voluntary) cannot secure a conviction, and unlike similar legal systems based on Spanish procedures, in Cuba innocence is presumed until a conviction can be secured (Evenson, 1994: 161 *et passim*).

The 2009 HRW report also draws attention to other laws that can be used to harass dissidents: laws punishing forms of 'insubordination' and 'dangerousness' are highlighted. These appear to be the equivalents of UK offences and laws such as insulting behaviour, outraging public decency, public nuisance, the Mental Health Act, the Criminal Justice and Public Order Act, and the Crime and Public Disorder Act with its Anti-Social Behaviour Orders; most states have such laws in some form. This does not mean that they are not used disproportionately against dissidents, but the portrayal by HRW of the 'dangerousness' law as specifically 'Orwellian' and 'pre-criminal' is difficult to understand. The law, translated in an appendix to the HRW report, states:

> Article 72.
> A state of dangerousness is considered to be the special propensity of a person to commit crimes, as demonstrated by conduct observed in manifest contradiction to the norms of socialist morality.
> Article 73.
>
> 1. The state of dangerousness is seen when any of the following hazardous indicators occur concurrently in the individual:
>
>   a) habitual drunkenness and dipsomania;
>   b) drug addiction;
>   c) antisocial behaviour
>
> 2. A person is considered to be in a state of dangerousness due to antisocial behaviour if the person routinely breaks the rules of social coexistence by committing acts of violence, or by other provocative acts, violates the rights of others or by his or her

general behaviour weakens the rules of coexistence or disturbs the order of the community or lives, like a social parasite, off the work of others or exploits or practices socially reprehensible vices.

Article 74.
Mentally ill persons and persons of delayed mental development are also considered to be in a state of dangerousness, if, because of [their mental condition], they do not have the ability to comprehend the scope of their actions nor to control their conduct, provided that these represent a threat to the security of others or to the social order. (Human Rights Watch, 2009: 120)

Article 73 Part 2, it seems obvious, defines the 'state of dangerousness due to anti-social behaviour' as applying to someone who 'routinely breaks the rules of social coexistence by committing acts of violence, or by other provocative acts, violates the rights of others' in a manner that might already have resulted in arrest for a variety of reasons. This does not seem to be 'pre-criminal' in the Orwellian sense implied by HRW, even if, as with any such legislation, it is open to abuse by those in authority. This last point may be rejected, but it does highlight a further problem that muddies the waters in which human rights NGOs operate: the fact that some, at any rate, of the NGOs appear to campaign against Cuba in a manner very disproportionate to the degree of abuse claimed to exist. Reporters Without Borders, for example, ranks Cuba among the very worst abusers of journalists, in spite of the fact that in other, less 'abusive' states on its Index, dozens of journalists are murdered every year (none in Cuba). Reporters Without Borders, it has been noted, accepts funding from the US National Endowment for Democracy, one of the funding mechanisms for US oppositional civil society strategies across the world (Lamrani, 2007).

Conclusion

It would be ludicrous to assert that there are no abuses of civil rights by Cuban authorities. But it is valid to point out that the human rights NGOs, whose reports influence media and diplomatic behaviour, share a diplomatic agenda that privileges some kinds of rights over others, in a manner unjustified in international law; and that, in their stance on the political rights of opposition dissidents they appear to be demanding that the Cuban people abandon the post-dictatorship society they have spent 50 years creating. Even if every accusation of human rights NGOs against Cuba were justified, the scale and seriousness of the abuse pales against the situation in a multitude of other states. Two wrongs do not make a right, and the NGOs have an obligation to deal with rights issues, however narrowly defined and irrespective of the numbers involved. The use of NGO materials in anti-Cuban lobbying and media treatment, however, supports a US 'regime change' policy that is not simply determined by humanitarian concern, but by a refusal to accept the right of the people of Cuba to choose a different economic and social system and defend it through half a century of military and economic aggression.

The United States' dependence on Latin American allies to bolster its anti-Cuba strategies has largely failed, as a 'new continentalism' in the region now confronts the White House with an assertive 'backyard', demanding equal treatment for Cuba and the end of the embargo, and welcoming Cuba's internationalist contribution to the introduction of social rights across the continent (Kirk and Erisman 2009; Lievesley and Ludlam, 2009). The final conclusion is thus a rather obvious one: the best way to improve human rights of all kinds in Cuba, civil and political as well as economic, social and cultural, is to end the US embargo and its failed regime-change policy, which are the greatest sources of direct and indirect restrictions on human rights in Cuba. As the UN Special Rapporteur on human rights in Cuba commented in the early 1990s:

> International sanctions, especially if accompanied by conditions imply-
> ing the adoption of specific measures, be they political or economic, are
> totally counterproductive if it is the international community's inten-
> tion to improve the human rights situation and, at the same time, to
> create conditions for a peaceful and gradual transition to a genuinely
> pluralist and civil society. Any suggestion along the lines that the future
> sovereignty of the Cuban people could be contingent on external powers
> or forces would, in the collective memory of the Cuban people, evoke
> traumatic experiences of their not-very-distant history and their fight
> for independence, and would be a very effective obstacle to the achieve-
> ment of changes which could be very welcome in other circumstances.
> (United Nations, 1992: paragraph 89)

Twenty years later, the point remains equally valid. Although the effect would not be immediate, it is difficult to see how the removal of the US threat of regime change would not dispel the siege mentality, and give the Cuban people the opportunity of extending their existing culture of political participation.

9

Creating the Quiet Majority? Youth and Young People in the Political Culture of the Cuban Revolution

ANNE LUKE

Birmingham City University, UK

La juventud es ante todo un potencial en términos de capital humano para el desarrollo, recreación de la base cultural de la sociedad y nuevos proyectos colectivos. Concebirla sólo como un problema – para sí misma y para el resto – es una perspectiva equivocada pues tiende a estigmatizarla en función de sus riesgos y sus falencias.

Youth, above all, is a potential in terms of human capital, renewal of the cultural base of society and new collective projects. Seeing it only as a problem – for itself and for others – is a false perspective that tends to stigmatize it in terms of its risks and failings (Taken from a report jointly written by the Economic Commission for Latin America [CEPAL] and the Organisation of Ibero-American Youth [OIJ]). (CEPAL-OIJ, 2007: 14)

Since 2000, no fewer than twelve Latin American countries have established new youth directorates, responsible for plans and programmes related to youth (CEPAL–SEGIB–OIJ, 2008: 318). The year 2008 was declared 'Año Iberoamericano de la Juventud' at the meeting of the XVII Cumbre de Jefes de Estado y Gobierno and the following year's summit was convened under the theme Juventud y Desarollo (Youth and Development) (OIE, 2008). Youth, it is fair to say, is a hot regional theme. Yet there is often a disjuncture, as picked up in the opening quotation, between the actual lives of young people and impressions of the lives of young people deriving from both media coverage and academic studies of youth, which often focus on the obviously spectacular or the evidently problematic. This leads to the blaming of young people for all manner of social problems. In Mexico, for example, there is a fear that a lost generation will be created, termed the *generación ni-ni*, referring to young people who neither work nor study (*ni trabajan ni estudian*) (Murayama, 2010); concerns regarding youth generally repeatedly refer to this group. Cuba is not immune to this tendency, and this chapter explores how, after more than 50 years of a culture that elevates young people to an exalted position (and over 50 years of existence of *its* own youth organisation), there is still a perception of a youth problem.

Notions of youth as problematic derive from the sense of there being a critical period when the woman or man is forged from the girl or boy and that this happens when a person is over sixteen perhaps, but under 30. In Cuba this belief is embodied through the reference, made by Fidel Castro in a speech to students in 1963 at the University of Havana, to the proverb, of 'El árbol que crece torcido jamás su tronco endereza' (the tree that grows crooked can never be straightened). In parallel to this worry that problems, if they develop during youth, are somehow irredeemable if they are untreated at source, is the belief that young people also hold the answer or solution to social problems because they can act in a unique manner, unblemished by the faults that are built up over adult life. It is because of this concern that the *generación ni-ni* (or, to use the Cuban term, the *desvinculados*) dominate popular debate on youth. In 2009 daily newspaper *Juventud Rebelde* asked the question 'Cómo vincularse a los desvinculados' (How do we re-engage the disenfranchised) (Morales Agüero, 2009). Yet this issue is not a new one; it has emerged at intervals over the course of the Revolution as the sting in the tail of Cuban youth policy to trouble policy-makers who feel that this group of young people should not exist in a socialist country. In the wake of the most recent manifestations of this issue in Cuba – in 2000/2001 and 2007 – this chapter examines the historical and ideological context in which the issue can be located, looking back to the origins of the revolutionary understanding of the notion of youth. It explores what youth has come to mean in the political culture of the Revolution and examines the politics of youth that have emerged within this culture. In so doing it argues that the constrictions of the meaning of youth, built into the 1960s discourse of the Revolution, have had two results: first, moral panics over youth occur, often (but not only) centred upon those young people who neither work nor study; and, second, the discourse on youth that is generated is not deemed relevant by the majority of young people, thus creating a quiet majority, about whom we know little, except at moments, such as the Elián González affair, when they become critical to the revolutionary process. The bipolar understanding of youth leads to a youth policy that excludes at the same moment as it attempts to be inclusive, because the voice of those in the middle, in the grey area between youth-as-problem and youth-as-solution, is drowned out.

Rationale: Revolutionary Morality and the Contemporary Debate

Young people's return to prominence for positive reasons in the past decade has been twinned with worries about their work ethic; indeed, it is impossible to understand what could be meant by a 'youth problem' without first exploring where the ethics of work fit it. Kapcia (2005) points to an ethics of education, which was espoused in the new post-Elian educational initiatives. To his foci of morality (socialism, communitarianism, family and *martiano* morality) I would add work ethic. Of course, in practical terms – for productivity – and in political terms – to enable and enhance participation – the workplace is of central importance to the Revolution (Ludlam, 2009); but in revolutionary Cuba work has a further importance. The slogan of the Union of Young Communists (UJC) (*Estudio, trabajo, fusil*) is a moral as well as a practical slogan, and so it is unsurprising that the second of these, work, is an issue taken up by the Youth Research Centre (CESJ) in Havana. Luis Luis, from the CESJ, uses the triple ideological forces of Fidel, Ché and Martí to explain the revolutionary ethos of work – from Guevara's belief in the socialising effects of work – 'Para ello, el trabajo no sólo sería medio y garantía de vida individual, sino elemento integrador al proceso de construcción de la sociedad socialista' (for him, work would be not only a means to individual well-being, but also an integral element of the process of building a socialist society) – to Fidel's vehement hostility towards 'toda forma de explotación y parasitismo, a los especuladores, a los que quieren hacerse ricos sin trabajar, a los antisociales y lumpen' (any form of exploitation and parasitism, toward speculators, towards those who want to get rich without working, towards anti-social and lumpen elements) (Luis Luis, 2010: 59). The two perspectives make up two sides of the same coin – Guevara's idealistic promise of the socialising benefits of work operates in tandem with Fidel Castro's patent loathing of those people who do not work. From either side of the coin, those who neither work nor study are problematic. Luis Luis argues that 'La política laboral cubana se desarrolla con un enfoque ético' (the politics of work in Cuba take place within an ethical framework) (Luis Luis, 2008a: 72). Other articles in the CESJ journal reinforce the focus on work, including encouraging young people into agricultural work (Avalos Boitel and Pérez Rojas, 2008), and, perhaps crucially, the theme of *desvinculación juveníl* (Luis Luis, 2008b). Luis Luis argues that *desvinculación* 'adquiere una connotación sociopolítica e ideological, por contraponerse a los principios humanistas de la Revolución y expresar la desintegración de esos jóvenes del proceso de construcción de la sociedad socialista' (aquires a sociopolitical and ideological connotation, through being in opposition to the humanistic principles of the Revolution and conveying the alienation of those young people from the process of construction of a socialist society) (Luis Luis, 2008b: 32). It is for this reason that in Cuba moral panic and the question of work go hand in hand. Moral panic is, according to Stanley Cohen's original text, conveyed through the mass media and the 'moral barricades are manned by editors, bishops, politicians, and other right-thinking people' (Cohen, 1987: 9). In the Cuban case, the moral panic comes partly via a generational angst, but much more significantly through the leadership texts and through centre-stage position of such texts in the Cuban media,[1] and through the statements and positions of youth organisations.

It was in the context of these moral forces that the first decade of the twenty-first century saw a new emphasis on youth unparalleled since the 1960s. This was as a result, in part, of a renewed appreciation of the importance of youth within Cuba's national identity, partly triggered in 2000 by the Elián González affair (see Kapcia, 2008: 170–171 for a summary of this affair). The latter brought about a return to mass intensive youth activism, reminiscent of the 1960s, in the form of mass public assemblies (Tribunas Abiertas) and marches across the country, and blanket media coverage of these. In only seven months (between 5 December 1999 and 1 July 2000), there were 106 Tribunas Abiertas, 84 Round Tables and eleven marches (Gómez, 2003). These events were coordinated by the UJC, the Federation of Secondary School Students (FEEM) and the Federation of University Students (FEU), and, according to Kapcia, 'highlighted the reality that Cuban youth, rather than being "the problem" [. . .] might actually constitute "the solution"' (2008: 174). Perhaps there was a sense of Elián fatigue by the time the campaign came to its successful conclusion, but it had had the effect of reinvigorating participationism, and reasserting the fundamental importance of youth.

Ironically, it was the reminder that young people were activists who could help build a movement from the grassroots that also triggered a new worry over those young people who neither worked nor studied. A renewed belief in the importance of young people led to the adoption of new youth-focused and youth-led policy initiatives, including a major educational initiative to deal with this group. The Cursos de Superación Integral were launched to reintegrate the *desvinculados* into society, and, according to Fidel Castro, counted 100,591 students in September 2002 (Castro, 2002).[2] The success of these courses, however, did not succeed completely in quelling the emergence of a moral panic over the *generación ni-ni* that occured more recently.

---

1   Since the outset of the Revolution, leadership speeches have been printed in full or reported upon in the daily newspapers, as well as magazines.
2   This initiative was part of several educational initiatives that emerged at the start of this century, with a view to expanding levels of participation in education (Kapcia, 2005: 401–2).

This most recent media moral panic can be identified in the words of a letter published in January 2009 in *Granma*, complaining about young people, stating that 'sólo en el Ministerio de educación hayamos 9000 educadores en edad de jubilación que seguimos laborando mientras jóvenes vigorosos viven de actividades generalmente ilícitas' (in the Ministry of Education alone we have 9,000 educationalists of retirement age who are still working, while energetic young people are living off illicit means) (Rondón Velaquez, 2009). More serious than this generational-based panic, the like of which can be seen in many other national contexts, was the worry expressed by the UJC. In 2008 Julio Martínez, First Secretary of the UJC, made the point that the UJC was not doing enough to prevent or resolve *desvinculación*: 'La responsabilidad de la UJC es con todos los jóvenes. [. . .] Si [los desvinculados] no aceptan las opciones que les damos tenemos que insistir, mantenernos en contacto con ellos, convencerlos' (The UJC has responsibility for all young people. [. . .] If [the *desvinculados*] don't accept the options we give them, we must persist, we must keep up our contact with them, we must persuade them) (Barrios, 2008). This hardening of attitude on the part of the UJC is related to the fact that the culture/discourse of youth (which will be explored in detail below), places an onus of unconditional success on the UJC, not least because the UJC had within its own ranks, according to Martínez, some 3,000 members who neither studied nor worked (Barrios, 2008).

The Symbolic Idealisation of Youth in the First Decade of the Revolution

The moral panic over young people who neither work nor study and, equally, the enduring belief that young people 'hold the key' to the con- tinued success and evolution of the Revolution both have their foundation in the first decade of the Revolution. The way in which youth came to be understood informed youth policy and culture, and thereby determined the circumstances and conditions which were experienced by young people.[3] The discourse of the Revolution built up an ideology of youth during the

---

3   In 1959 it was rare to have a youth policy in Latin America. As Balardini points out: 'the pre-1960s conservative approach [to policy-making] ignored the specific characteristics and needs of the youth in relation to adults and hardly produced any youth-specific policies. This has only recently begun to change, with the exception of Mexico, Venezuela, Costa Rica and Cuba who were the first to implement policies designed specifically for young people, although these were mostly restricted to sports and leisure programmes for urban students' (Balardini, 2000: 43).

1960s that survives largely intact today. Through speeches to and about youth, and through the construction of youth-hero/martyr figures, a dominant discourse of youth emerged with which young people were encouraged to identify. There was through this a stabilisation of meaning of the notion of youth, which became tied up with the discourse of rebirth of nationhood and a young revolution. The two central features of youth that emerge in this discourse are *purity* and *enthusiasm*. In August 1962, for example, Castro made one of several references to the connection between youth and enthusiasm, reflecting that, before the Revolution, young people were unable to express themselves, because '[no] era capaz aquel mundo de canalizar eso que todo joven lleva dentro, que es fuerza vital, que es entusiasmo, que es sed de futuro, sed de lucha, sed de vida' (that world was incapable of channelling that which every young person has within himself – vitality, enthusiasm, a yearning for the future, an urge to struggle, a thirst for life) (Castro, 1962b: 3).

Where Castro was empirical in his treatment of the concept, Guevara took a more philosophical approach to youth, through the use of the notion of purity.[4] He argued, in a speech to students in 1963, that age was more significant than social class because of the idealism of youth: 'Había olvidado yo que hay algo más importante que la clase social a que pertenezca el individuo: la juventud, la frescura de ideales, la cultura que en el momento en que se sale de la adolescencia se pone al servicio de los ideales más puros (I had forgotten that there was something more important than the social class to which the individual belongs: youth, fresh ideals, a culture which, at the point of leaving adolescence, is devoted to serving the purest of ideals) (Guevara, 1977d: 220).

Neither Guevara nor Castro, however, refer to purity in essentialist terms. Instead, they account for the purity of youth by the fact that young people born into the Revolution were pure by virtue of being untainted by Cuba's corrupt bourgeois past. This attitude is clear from the outset of the Revolution, when Castro referred to his hopes for the nascent youth organisation (referring in this case to training for young pilots) on this basis:

> ¡Esos jóvenes son el producto más puro de esta Revolución! (APLAU-SOS), ¡el orgullo más grande y más legítimo de esta Revolución! (APLAUSOS), la semilla de la patria nueva, los que constituirán una generación mejor preparada para seguir la obra revolucionaria. *Porque la Revolución debe garantizar su marcha ascendente, un futuro mejor todavía*

---

4   These ideas also contributed to his thesis of the *hombre nuevo* [*new man*] expounded in *Man and Socialism in Cuba* (Guevara, 1970: 367–384).

que el entusiasmo de hoy; y que un pueblo que se libera sea sustituido por el
entusiasmo de una generación que será por entero producto de la Revolución.

These young people are the purest product of this Revolution! The
most legitimate and awe-inspiring! They will be the seeds for the new
fatherland because they will build a generation that will be better
prepared for continuing our revolutionary effort. *The Revolution must*
guarantee our climb to an ever better future. The enthusiasm of the people today
must be replaced with the enthusiasm of a generation which will be entirely the
product of the Revolution. (Castro, 1960a, my emphasis)

This view is corroborated and expounded further by Guevara in 'El Socialismo
y el hombre en Cuba': 'En nuestra sociedad, juegan un gran papel la juventud
y el Partido. Particularmente importante es la primera, por ser la arcilla
maleable con que se puede construir al hombre nuevo *sin ninguna de las taras*
anteriores (In our society, youth and the Party play an important role. The
former is particularly important, as it is the pliable clay out of which the new
man, *with none of the earlier faults*, can be fashioned) (Guevara, 1970: 380; my
emphasis).[5]

The negative use of the past, that is the assumption of inherent flaws in
those Cubans 'tainted by' pre-1959 life, was complemented by an affirmative
use of the past. The definition of what youth *should be* (as opposed to what
youth inherently is) was supported in speeches by the reference to Cuba's
radical history, in particular through a canonisation of young martyrs of
the rebellion, in parallel with (and in a similar way to) a celebration of
young heroes of the rebellion. Miller points to the fact that the revolutionary
government 'embarked on a large-scale propaganda effort to represent itself
as the culmination of Cuban history' (Miller, 2003: 148). In this way, the
process began whereby 'history is a salient part of day-to-day life and of
Cubans' sense of their identity' (Miller, 2003: 161). With regard to youth (as
in other sectors), the uses of history and in particular the creation of heroes
and martyrs were a part of this general trend.

The two key heroes (including the key martyr) built into the discourse of
youth in the early years of the Revolution were, respectively, Joel Iglesias
and Conrado Benítez. The focus on those two was based on two elements.
First, it was based on the idea that these men (note that there was little focus
on female heroes or martyrs) represented all young Cubans. In a sense, they

---

5   The context makes it unclear whether Guevara is referring to youth or to the
    UJC specifically, but the implication of the comment remains the same whichever
    translation is used.

were Cuba's youth. Second, their rise to glory was connected to their youth; in other words, they were glorious *because* of their youth. They personified that pure, unsullied, enthusiastic character of youth that had been built up so carefully in the discourse.

Benítez – a volunteer teacher murdered by counter-revolutionaries in the Escambray mountains in January 1961 – took the role of martyr, where Iglesias – a *comandante* in the rebel army who became leader of the AJR and later the UJC after the victory of 1959 – was the hero, and yet the standing was the same, and the language with which they were described was similar.[6] Both were prime examples of the idealised incorruptible *obrero-campesino* (worker-peasant) revolutionary of the time.

The hero role was ascribed to Iglesias in two ways. First, he was represented as an ordinary young man, that is to say, a person whom any young person could emulate:

> [E]se comandante del Ejército Rebelde llegó a la Sierra con quince años, que apenas sabía leer y no sabía escribir nada; y que hoy puede dirigirse a toda la juventud, no porque se haya convertido ya en un filósofo, en un año y medio, sino porque puede hablar al pueblo porque es parte misma del pueblo y porque siente lo que todos ustedes sienten todos los días, y lo sabe expresar, sabe llegar hasta ustedes.

> [T]his Rebel Army commander came to the Sierra aged fifteen, barely able to read and completely unable to write; and yet today, he can speak to all the youth of the nation – not because he was transformed into a philosopher in the space of one and a half years, but because he can speak to the people, as a part of the people, and because he feels what all of you feel in your everyday lives, and knows how to put it into words, how to reach you. (Guevara, 1977a: 87)

Guevara built a proximity between Iglesias and the audience, encouraging the latter to believe that they, in a sense, *were* (or at the very least could follow

---

6   Guevara made clear the difference between heroes and martyrs in his speech of November 1961 where he referred to those young students who were executed by the Spanish authorities on 27th November 1871: 'aquellos jóvenes no eran culpables de nada, no se les puede llamar exactamente héroes, sino, más bien, mártires. Eran estudiantes acomodados porque en aquella época los estudiantes tenían que ser de familias acomodadas' (Those young people were guilty of nothing; they cannot be described as heroes exactly, but rather as martyrs. They were well-to-do students because, at that time, students had to come from wealthy families) (Guevara, 1977b: 604). The idea of a bourgeois hero was not possible within Guevara's world view.

the same path as) Iglesias. He did this in two ways: by bringing particular attention to Iglesias's semi-literacy at the time when Iglesias entered the Rebel Army and by making a virtue of his prior intellectual naivety and inexperience. The second way in which Guevara built the hero image for Iglesias came across in the speech that the former made when announcing that Iglesias was moving from the army to the youth movement. He outlined the heroic role Iglesias had played in the Ejército Rebelde, explaining such heroism as not in spite of, but *because of*, his youth:

> [E]l compañero Joel Iglesias, cuando ingresó en nuestro Ejército Rebelde [. . .] tenía apenas 15 años, y [. . .] 15 años es una edad donde ya el hombre sabe por qué va a dar la vida y no tiene miedo de darla cuando tiene naturalmente dentro de su pecho, un ideal que lo lleva a inmolarse.

> When our comrade Joel Iglesias joined our Rebel Army [. . .] he was only 15, and [. . .] 15 is an age at which a man already knows what he is prepared to die for, and is not afraid to die, when he has an ideal in his heart for which he is prepared to make this sacrifice. (Guevara, 1977b: 605)

There is no distinct phase of adolescence described here; rather at the age of fifteen the youth/man is considered able to act with an adult level of responsibility. This does not imply that the youth *is* adult (because, according to the discourse, he holds the ideals that are as yet uncorrupted by adult life) but that in the new definition a young person may be willing (and may have the opportunity) to die if necessary for his ideals.

The way in which Iglesias was described as a young hero has clear parallels with the way in which the other figure important to youth, Conrado Benítez, came to be understood as martyr through the leadership speeches:

> ¿Quién era este joven? [. . .] [E]ra un hombre joven de 18 años que sólo conocía del sudor honrado, que sólo conocía de la pobreza, que sólo conocía del sacrificio; era un joven humilde, y un joven negro, por lo cual conoció también de la discriminación cruel e injusta; era pobre, era negro y era maestro. He ahí las tres razones por las cuales los agentes del imperialismo lo asesinaron; era joven, era negro, era maestro.

> Who was this young man? [. . .] [H]e was a young man of 18 who had known nothing but honest sweat, poverty and sacrifice; he was a humble young man, a black man, and for this reason he was the victim of cruel and unjust discrimination. He was poor, he was black

and he was a teacher. These were the reasons that the agents of imperialism killed him: he was young, he was black, he was a teacher. (Castro, 1961a)

Castro then implored the volunteers (who it must be remembered were a young constituency) to embark on the struggle for literacy in memory of Benítez. The martyr became both inspirational symbol and motivational incentive.

The canonisation of heroes and martyrs was used repeatedly in discourse: Martí, Maceo, Mella, Camilo Cienfuegos and Echevarría and, after his death, Guevara, were constantly present in speeches of the leadership.[7] Benítez and Iglesias were particularly relevant in this case because of the intimate link with the discourse of youth; moreover the propagandist technique of using heroes, martyrs and anniversaries was one way in which the view of what an 'ideal' youth should be, and who (anyone) or how (sacrifice, commitment etc.) this ideal could be reached. This process, however, carried an unexpected disadvantage. The hazard of personifying the perfection of youth in these two young men, however, was that it made the ideal feel unattainable by young Cubans, because the myth that was created around those biographies did not account for real doubts or weaknesses (unless so attributed by the said myth) on the part of the heroes/martyrs. A disjuncture would inevitably open up, which will now be explored.

The Discourse of Youth in Practice: The Union of Young Communists

If the discourse of youth, discussed above, brought about a new ideology of youth, then responsible for the implementation of the policy implications of this ideology resided with the youth organisation (UJC). Given the importance that youth as a concept has to the Cuban Revolution it is very surprising that there was, and still is, no mass youth organisation.[8] This historical

---

7   A revolutionary slogan at the time of writing is 'Queremos que sean como el Ché' (We want you to be like Che), displayed on a large placard at the monument dedicated to Guevara in Santa Clara, quoting Castro's speech of 18 October 1967 following Che's death in Bolivia (Castro, 1967a). Kapcia examines how young Cubans in 2000 identified with the myth of Che, stating that 'to them, *Che* is the Revolution to which they would have adhered had they been alive in the 1960s, and identifying with him is thus a way of being committed and dissenting' (2000: 212).

8   The first unified mass youth organisation that emerged in the first two years of the Revolution was the Asociación de Jóvenes Rebeldes (AJR), originally the

anomaly meant that, since April 1962, only those young people who were termed 'vanguard' have had a role to play as members of the youth political organisation. The move from inclusive mass to selective vanguard meant that, while, in the early years of the Revolution, political activism had the potential to be a mass culture among young people, after 1962 a small body of young people who were accepted as members of the UJC claimed the authority to determine what constituted revolutionary youth activism. As soon as this was the case, there arose the possibility of a distance between members and non-members opening up.

Through looking at the UJC, it is possible to witness the meeting of revolutionary discourse and real-life experience. The use of the denomination 'communist' in 1962, some three years before the parent party was named as such, is a case in point. Much was made by Castro and Guevara about the new nomenclature, and the name seems to have been popular with the members: in Castro's speech to the Congress there was reportedly applause every time he mentioned the words *socialismo* and *comunismo* (Castro, 1962a). Guevara, in a crucial speech laying out what was to be expected of a young communist, placed young communists at the centre of the revolutionary project and emphasised the point that he expected young people in the organisation to live up to the name communist as a vanguard both for youth and for all society:

> Ustedes [...] deben ser la vanguardia de *todos los movimientos*. Los primeros en los sacrificios que la revolución demande, cualquiera que sea la índole de esos sacrificios. Los primeros en el trabajo. Los primeros en el estudio. Los primeros en la defensa del país.

> You [...] must be the vanguard of *all movements*. You must be the first in terms of the sacrifices demanded by the Revolution, irrespective of the nature of these sacrifices, the first in terms of work, the first in terms of study, the first in the defence of the country. (Guevara, 1967a: 357; my emphasis)

---

brain child of Guevara, and founded under the auspices of the Fuerzas Armadas with the aim of providing a framework of activity for those people who were neither working nor studying. Because of the literacy campaign, militias and general appeal of the organisation because of its guerrilla credentials, it enjoyed spectacular growth, but, in the context of a public auto-crítica (self-criticism), was re-launched in 1962 as the selective UJC (*Revolución*, 1962: 5). The statutes of the UJC stated that the UJC, while being structurally independent, would serve as the youth organisation of the United Party of the Socialist Revolution (PURS), which later became the Communist Party (PCC).

He expanded this point later in the speech saying that a young communist must 'ser un ejemplo vivo, ser el espejo donde se miren los compañeros que no pertenezcan a las juventudes comunistas, ser el ejemplo donde puedan mirarse los hombres y mujeres de edad más avanzada que han perdido cierto entusiasmo juvenil' ('be a living example, a mirror for friends who are not members of the young communists, an example for older men and women who have lost something of their youthful enthusiasm') (Guevara, 1967a: 364).

This created a dichotomy that continues to exist today for the UJC – on the one hand it claims to represent all young people, but on the other it is the training ground for membership of the PCC, so it has a highly limited membership and strict membership criteria. It functions under the strict criteria of what a young communist should be, and is the embodiment of the ethos of youth as pure and enthusiastic. Not all young people over the history of the Revolution, however, have been interested in joining the UJC, whereas they perhaps would have been interested in joining a mass organisation. The result is that large numbers of *quite* engaged youth do not have a specific organisation for themselves. Furthermore, because the UJC espouses the narrow doctrine of young people as the hope for the future, it finds it almost impossible to meet the demands on it. Its insecurities of itself feed into moral panic surrounding those *within* its ranks who may not be living up to the discourse, and those *outside* its ranks who are problematic (the *desvinculados*). Because of the limited membership, the successes claimed by the UJC exclude those who were in part responsible for making the successes, in other words, the masses. Young people in Cuba in the 1960s by and large did not conform to the idealised symbolic image of youth, and as a result of this, problems arose at both ends of the youth dichotomy, generating moral unease similar to that of the past decade.

Moral Panic: Discourse and Practice Collide

Young people were repeatedly found, by the revolutionary leadership and by the UJC, to be under-achieving in their attempts to attain the unattainable. This sense of under-achievement occurred at all levels, with the under-achievers ranging from the members of the youth organisation at one end of the spectrum through to the young people who were acting entirely outside the revolutionary youth identity at the other end. The *militantes* (members) of the youth organisation were chided by the revolutionary leadership over what could be described as moral weakness. Guevara's concerns in this respect lay, as we would expect given his philosophical dependence on the concept of a young vanguard, with the faults that he had identified in some revolutionary cadres:

> Así hemos ido encontrando multitud de nuevos cuadros que se han desarrollado en estos años; pero su desarrollo no ha sido parejo, puesto que los jóvenes compañeros se han visto frente a la realidad de la creación revolucionaria sin una adecuada orientación de partido. Algunos han triunfado plenamente, pero hay muchos que no pudieron hacerlo completamente y quedaron a mitad del camino, o que, simplemente, se perdieron en el laberinto burocrático o en las tentaciones que da el poder.

> So, we have seen many new cadres developing during this period; however, their development was different, because these young comrades found themselves facing the situation created by the Revolution without having received adequate guidance from the party. Some of them managed to achieve complete success, but there were many who were unable to make the grade and were left behind in mid-stream, or simply lost their way in the bureaucratic maze or amid the temptations of power. (Guevara 1977c: 157)

In early 1963, Castro added his unease with standards of behaviour in young people:[9]

> ¿Por qué esos errores? Porque también mucha gente jovenzuela no sabía ni lo que era una revolución, y creía que las cosas se hacían de a porqué sí, o por generación espontánea, o porque estaba escrito en un libro, o en virtud de una ley histórica.

> Why were these mistakes made? Because many young people at the younger end of the scale had no idea what a Revolution meant and believed things happened automatically or spontaneously, or because it was written in some book or because of some law of history. (Castro, 1963a: 4)

Both Castro and Guevara had been compelled to accept that young people were not living up to the idealised concept they had built up. Perhaps it is too strong to term this a moral panic, but it is certainly moral unease, as the

---

9 This speech was directed to medical students, and specific problems in that respect, but the point he made was a general one.

philosophical base of the revolutionary discourse of youth was challenged, as reality brought a different complexion to the youth issue.

A more severe (but no less enduring) unease regarding young people emerged in the 1960s that is much more recognisable as moral panic. It was partly fed by the youth organisation and partly fed by the leadership speeches and was a reaction to the reality that not all actions of young people fitted within the revolutionary youth identity.[10] The UJC fanned the flames of this moral panic through humour in the pages of *Mella*, the UJC's magazine. One cartoon strip, showing a young man dressed in a Western style, flanked by two girls in miniskirts, bore the caption: 'Lo hacen ídolo ciertos elementos ... a todas horas nos quiere empujar a los Beatles por la cabeza ... son los rebeldes sin causa ... ellos no lo saben, pero les dan cuerda' (Certain groups idolise him ... he wants to fill our heads with the Beatles all the time ... these groups are the rebels without a cause ... they don't know it, but someone else is pulling their strings), that last phrase describing the final frame showing the man as a wind-up doll, with Uncle Sam turning the key (Nuez, 1965: 11). This fear of capitalist decadence was problematic, as, with young people, the explanation of a bourgeois past did not hold the weight that it could in explaining a level of decadence in the older generation. Castro covered this worry at length in a speech given at the University of Havana on the anniversary of Echevarría's death in 1963, during which he attributed youth problems (as he saw them) to bourgeois *background* and external influence:

> Claro, por ahí anda un espécimen, otro subproducto que nosotros debemos combatir. Es ese joven que tiene dieciséis, diecisiete, quince, y ni estudia ni trabaja; entonces, andan de lumpen, en esquinas, en bares, van a algunos teatros, y se toman algunos libertades y realizan algunos libertinajes. Un joven que ni trabaje, ni estudie, ¿que piensa de la vida? ¿Piensa vivir de parásito? [...] Si los imperialistas no los reciben allá en su 'mundo libre', que se preparen también a trabajar. [...]
>
> Muchos de esos pepillos vagos, hijos de burgueses, andan por ahí con unos pantaloncitos demasiado estrechos (risas); algunos de ellos con

---

10   The issue of youth identity has also concerned the CESJ recently, who make the point that 'podemos abordar a la identidad juvenil como un proceso intersubjectivo de conformación de límites *no estáticos*' ('we can understand youth identity as a intersubjective process of conforming with boundaries which are *not static*') (Peñate Leiva and López Santos, 2008: 77; my emphasis). Part of the problem of the youth discourse is that it creates a static definition in an unstable set of circumstances, so what constitutes 'revolutionary' or 'vanguard' is contingent and changing in definition, in the 1960s in particular.

una guitarrita en actitudes 'elvispreyslianos', y que han llevado su libertinaje a extremos de querer ir a algunos sitios de concurrencia pública a organizar sus 'shows' feminoides 'por la libre'. [...] La sociedad socialista no puede permitir ese tipo de degeneraciones.

¿Jovencitos aspirantes a eso? ¿No! "Árbol que creció torcido . . .'. ya el remedio no es tan fácil. No voy a decir que vayamos a aplicar medidas drásticas contra esos 'árboles torcidos'; pero jovencitos aspirantes, no. (Castro, 1963b: 3)

Obviously here we have an example, another sub-product we have to oppose. These are young people, aged fifteen, sixteen or seventeen who neither study nor work; they hang around like disaffected 'lumpen' on street corners, in bars, they frequent certain theatres, behave badly and live in a profligate way. A young person who neither works nor studies – what's his general idea? Does he expect to be able to live like a parasite? [...] If there is no room for them in the imperialists' 'free world', they had better get ready to work.

Many of these idle and alienated individuals, the children of bourgeois families, roam the streets wearing trousers that are too tight (laughter); some of them carry a guitar, try to look like Elvis Presley, and have taken their licentious behaviour to the extremes of wanting to frequent certain public places to organise their effeminate shows just as the fancy takes them. [...] Socialist society cannot permit this type of degenerate behaviour.

Young people aspiring to that? No! 'A tree that grew twisted . . .'. – that's a difficult problem to solve. I'm not saying we plan to take extreme measures against these 'twisted trees'; but young people aspiring to imitate them . . . no.

The concept of youth deviance had entered the discourse as a reaction to ways of youth expression in Havana, and was felt particularly strongly because of the discursive power of the proverbial adage that 'el árbol que crece torcido, jamas su tronca endereza'.

The deviant groups, the young people neither working nor studying, or the *militantes* not doing well enough, featured as notable in the Cuban 1960s. Yet the young people who were none of the above were less evident. Castro did address this quiet majority in 1965, when he accepted the problem of identifying with the Revolution that young people who did not experience the rebellion (or pre-1959 life) might encounter, pointing out that 'ningún joven tendrá que sentir la nostalgia de no haber tenido más años cuando esta lucha comenzó ningún joven tendrá que sentir la nostalgia, ni albergar la idea que llegara tarde a esta lucha' (no young person will have to feel regret at having been too young when this struggle began; no young person should feel any regret or have the idea that he was too late to take part in this struggle) (Castro, 1965a: 10).[11] And yet the 1960s created a situation, which persists today, that could cause young people to feel such a regret, because young people were faced with a youth organisation that admitted only the vanguard, and an unrealistic – even unreachable – ideal of what a young person should be.

Where next for Cuban youth?

The ethos of youth created in the 1960s is now an embedded part of Cuban political culture, and the hopes for the future of the Revolution continue to be laid at the feet of young people. The dilemma that such an ethos has created, however, is that young people must meet a standard of behaviour, but, because this standard is unreachable, they by definition cannot. The politics surrounding that ethos led to the creation of a highly selective youth organisation at the same time that mass organisations for other groups were being founded. The two functions of the UJC clash with each other – it trains and supplies the membership of the PCC (79.2 per cent of new PCC members in 2007 came from the ranks of the UJC (Barrios, 2008)), but also it is *the* organisation of Cuban youth. The UJC's propagation of a vision of youth built into revolutionary discourse causes problems: on the one hand, the organisation's own *ni-ni* constituency renders the image of perfection unattainable; and, on the other, the militant urgency with which its vision is expressed undermines the effective actions of the normally quiet majority: those who attended dozens of meetings regarding Elián, those social workers, *instructores de Arte*, those trained in the Cursos de Superación who are successfully working and improving the situation of young people; indeed, the very endurance of the Revolution in often adverse conditions could be in part attributed to their actions. The fear of the 'árbol que crece torcido ...'. means that youth is deemed to be so important that the UJC is overburdened.

The burden of the revolutionary discourse on youth is carried heavily on the shoulders of a youth organisation that cannot be – but is desperately trying to act like – a mass organisation. The perception of youth as either

---

11 Interestingly there are parallels with the present day, with Raul Castro referring to the fact that the generation of 1959 is gradually dying off : he notes that the Communist Party will be of particular importance when: 'por ley natural de la vida, haya desaparecido la generacion fundadora y forjadora de la Revolucion' ('because of the laws of nature, the generation who founded and forged the Revolution, will be gone') (Raul Castro, 2008).

problem or saviour, renewed since 2000, cannot refer to the majority. It is a burden that the youth organisation, in spite of many successes, has failed to manage. So this in effect means that ironically the organisation itself has contributed to the cycle of elevation/moral panic. This moral panic over youth, particularly over young people neither working nor studying, coming from leadership, the older generation and from the UJC means that the idea of young people as neither problem nor solution is unthinkable. This means that the voices, lives and seemingly commonplace successes of the quiet majority continue to be obscured.

10

Afterword: Cuba and Latin America

ANTONI KAPCIA

University of Brighton, UK

In 1961, Che Guevara posed the question: was Cuba a historical excep-tion or a vanguard, of the anti-imperialist struggle (Guevara 1977e) His answer – that it was the latter, arguing the transferability of the Revolution's experience as a 'model' for revolutionaries in other Latin American countries and beyond – led to a sustained insurrectionary strategy in the region, to his personal cost, as his conclusion was thrown into doubt. However, it also coincided with, and helped to create, a long tradition – in academic literature and in political circles – of differing ways of viewing a phenomenon that had already challenged expectations and paradigms about the Latin American region, as well as about Cuba itself.

On the one hand, many from the outset considered the Revolution as representing something 'typical': this could either refer to Soviet-style Com-munism, Latin American *caudillismo* or patterns of personalism in politics, or, later on, of theories of social revolution. Others, meanwhile, suggested that the Revolution was unique, incapable of being imitated and quite different from earlier socialist models, something attributable either to the character of the leadership or to Cuba's unusual historical patterns and experiences. Whichever interpretation was (and has since been) followed, there was a tendency from the start to draw conclusions from Cuba's post-1961 isolation, which was seen either as preserving and confirming that uniqueness or, from Washington's point of view from 1962, as quarantining a 'typical' model, to be resisted, surrounded and eliminated. Hence, isolation and the Revolution's character were always seen as essentially interrelated.

Over the next decade, this pattern was seemingly confirmed, with Cuba's support for revolution in the region being sustained at cost but to little immediate effect. However, in the 1970s, the pattern was steadily reversed, as isolation gradually gave way to Cuba's integration into the Socialist Bloc and Comecon, and to the marginal disintegration of the US embargo, with more and more Latin American countries recognising and trading with Cuba. Then, in 1989–1991, the old pattern was suddenly resurrected by the collapse of global Communism, and with it, Cuba's comfortable carapace of material and ideological protection. In 1991, exactly 30 years after Guevara's original question, Cuba again faced isolation in the Americas, bereft of significant trading partners, and with the United States, triumphant after the end of the Cold War and determined to end the Cuban 'example', assuming either that its survival had depended on Soviet aid and protection, or that, being a 'typical' Communist dictatorship, the Revolution's days were numbered, an outcome to be accelerated with a tightened embargo and active support for the internal opposition.

Of course, what followed was a remarkable survival that upset the odds completely, raising once again the question of supposed uniqueness or typicality, strengthening the former (since Cuba did not prove to be 'the next domino' in 1989–1991). However, by then, another firm pattern in 'reading Cuba' had been cemented into the discourse: the highly polemical and politicised nature of debates on Cuba, even in academic circles, as the hegemonic interpretation inside the United States (invigorated by the growing Cuban-American community and the growing influence of its leadership) spilled over into political science, sociology and cultural studies, above all, affecting the nature of academic debate and even the evidence on which academic conclusions were drawn. While it would be wrong to suggest that this blighted all study of Cuba in US academia (indeed, the work of several well-known and serious US scholars has been consistently outstanding, subtle and able to get under the surface of preconceptions), the fact was that the greater difficulties that United States-based scholars and researchers have always faced in getting into Cuba and carrying out first-hand research there has inevitably meant that, over the decades, some areas of research have been easier for European or Latin American researchers to address than for US scholars, occasionally strengthening already differing patterns in the ways of understanding Cuba and the Revolution.

This collection of studies reflects that, perhaps helping to emphasise those differences, because all but one of the studies in the collection have been carried out by Europe-based researchers, whose familiarity with their subject and whose shared academic background have given the book a commonality that some 'compendium' studies might have lacked. While they do not necessarily adhere to the view that Cuba can only be understood as something unique, they do all tend to approach their subject as something that does not easily fit the paradigms that have largely dominated the literature on the Revolution, calling into question expectations and preconceptions that, they might argue, have sometimes clouded our vision of the Cuban reality.

In this respect, of course, they, like all Cuba scholars, run the risk of separating themselves from the general patterns of external approaches to the wider Latin American region. For Cuba as a subject does still suffer from something of an exclusion from mainstream Latin American studies, despite the fact that the impact of the Cuban Revolution has been fundamental to stimulating greater serious study of, and interest in, Latin America from the 1960s. Whilst there almost certainly would not have been a 'Latin American studies' in the UK in its current form and patterns without the shock of a revolution that stirred British policy-makers into the need to develop a greater awareness of a region hitherto neglected academically, most of the debates that have emerged in Latin American studies since the early 1960s have largely ignored Cuba. Greater study of, for example, the landless peasantry, the urban *informales* or *marginales*, the military's increasingly militarist propensity for intervention (and our subsequent interest in post-military democratisation), the domination of the economies by multi-national corporations, the notions of dependency and later ideas of globalisation – all were repeatedly assumed to have little or no relevance to Cuba, where either the problems identified were no longer an issue or where the social and political patterns had been changed so fundamentally as to be unrecognisable. The exception to this has perhaps been cultural studies, where wider paradigms of resistance and subalternity have, in the last two decades, tended to be applied to Cuba.

However, that marginalisation has also applied to political debates, even in Latin America itself. Despite the fact that, in the 1960s and early 1970s, Latin America's political Right, Left and 'centre' were all changed or shaped profoundly by the need to respond to Cuba (notably the new militarism, the 'New Left', and the more radical Christian Democracy), and that much of US policy after 1961 was influenced by the need to avoid a 'second Cuba' (for example, affecting actions in Brazil, the Dominican Republic, Central America, Grenada), the political and academic effect of the United States' quarantine of Cuba since 1963 has been to separate Cuba from readings of the rest of the continent. Only after the demise of the Soviet Union in 1991, and the end of the Cold War, which had shaped post-1948 US foreign policy, did Washington begin to assume that, because Cuba had always been 'typical' (of an alien Communism), it should now follow Latin American patterns of economic and political development (towards a free-market economy and multi-party democratisation). What began was a sustained drive to ensure that outcome.

However, it was of course precisely then that political forces emerging in the rest of Latin America began to move away from the Washington Consensus and to question, challenge and change the norms encouraged in the preceding two decades; the emergence of more radical, nationalist and popular governments and movements from the late 1990s generated a new way of thinking about social, economic and political development that not only meant a new inclusion for Cuba into the wider context, but also made those US prescriptions for Cuba seem anachronistic, and possibly imperialist in effect if not in purpose. In other words, just as Cuba was being encouraged to 'become Latin American', many Latin Americans were beginning to 'think

Cuban', changing the patterns of the debates between Cuba and the rest of the continent, and once again bringing into focus the original question of Cuba's 'exceptionality' or 'typicality'. Indeed, as several chapters have suggested, Cuba's new inclusion may simply confirm that its previous isolation and presumed exceptionality were always results of exogenous pressures rather than endogenous imperatives, and that 'the Revolution' was, and still is, always about creating, defining and defending a national identity that had been denied, marginalised or distorted by the same economic, political and ideological forces which affected the whole of Latin America.

11

References

Agencia de Información Nacional (2010) 'Cuba Has Trained over 8,000 Physicians from 54 Nations', 9 August. [WWW document]. URL http://www.granma.cubaweb.cu/2010/08/nacional/artic05.html [accessed 18 August 2010].

Agencia de Información Nacional (2011) 'Over 700 Haitian Physicians Graduated from Cuba's Caribbean School of Medicine', 7 July. [WWW document]. URL http://www.cubanews.ain.cu/2011/0707Over-Haitian-Physicians-Graduated-from-Cuba-Caribbean-School-of-Medicine.htm [accessed 7 October 2011].

Ali, T. and Watkins, S. (1998) *1968: Marching in the Streets*. Bloomsbury: London.

Altieri, C. (1983) 'An Idea and Ideal of a Literary Canon'. *Critical Inquiry* **10**(1): 41–64.

Álvarez, L. E. (2010) 'Leonid Kuchma: Unos mostraron lástima, pero Cuba nos ayudó'. Juventud Rebelde, 29 March. [WWW document]. URL http://www.juventudrebelde.cu/internacionales/2010-03-29/leonid-kuchma-unos-mostraron-lastima-pero-cuba-nos-ayudo/ [accessed 8 October 2011].

Alvelo Pérez, D. R. (2010) 'Estrategia para el desarrollo de competencias didácticas en profesores del Nuevo Programa de Formación de Médicos' *Revista Electrónica de Portales Médicos*, 27 March. [WWW document]. URL http://www.portalesmedicos.com/publicaciones.articles/2088/1/Estrategia-para-el-desarrollo-de-competencias-didacticas-en-profesores-del-Nuevo-Programa-de-Formacion-de-Medicos.html [accessed 15 September 2010].

American Association for World Health (1997) *Denial of Food and Medicine: The Impact of the US Embargo on Health and Nutrition in Cuba. American Association for World Health Report Summary of Findings*. American Association for World Health: Washington.

Amnesty International (2003) *Cuba: 'Essential Measures'? Human Rights Crackdown in the Name of Security*. Amnesty International: London.

Amnesty International (2009) *The US Embargo Against Cuba: Its Impact on Economic and Social Rights*. Amnesty International: London.

Anderson, T. (2010) 'Cuban Health Cooperation in Timor Leste and the South West Pacific'. In T. Anderson, *The Reality of Aid: Special Report on South-South Cooperation 2010*. IBON: Quezon City, Philippines, 77–86.

Annan, K. (2000) *Secretary-General, In Havana on Eve of First 'Group of 77' Summit Meeting, Evokes Promises and Pitfalls of Globalisation*. United Nations Press Release. [WWW document]. URL http://www.un.org/News/Press/docs/2000/20000412.sgsm7357.doc.html [accessed 25 January 2011].

Antón Carrillo, E. (2006) *Arqueología del discurso sobre razas de las élites cubanas durante el s.XX. Editoriales y artículos de opinión*. Unpublished doctoral dissertation. Universidad de Granada: Granada.

Appelbaum, N. P., Macpherson, A. S. and Rosemblat, K. A. (2003) 'Racial Nations' in N. P. Appelbaum, A. S. Macpherson, and K. A. Rosemblat (eds.) *Race and Nation in Modern Latin America*. University of North Carolina Press: Chapel Hill and London, 1–31.

Araújo, N. (2003) *Diálogos en el umbral*. Editorial Oriente: Santiago de Cuba.

Araújo, R. M. de (2009) 'A Snapshot of the Medical School, Faculty of Health Sciences, National University of Timor Lorosa'e, Democratic Republic of Timor-Leste'. Unpublished conference paper presented to the Expert Group on Finalization of Regional Guidelines on Institutional Quality Assurance Mechanism for Undergraduate Medical Education, WHO/SEARO, New Delhi, 8–9 October.

Arnedo, M. (2001) 'Arte Blanco con Motivos Negros: Fernando Ortiz's Concept of Cuban National Culture and Identity'. *Bulletin of Latin American Research* **20**(1): 88–101.

Arnedo-Gómez, M. (2006) *Writing Rumba: The Afrocubanist Movement in Poetry.* University of Virginia Press: Charlottesville and London.

Artaraz, K. (2009) *Cuba and Western Intellectuals since 1959.* Palgrave Macmillan: New York.

Artaraz, K. (2011) New Latin American networks of solidarity? ALBA's contribution to Bolivia's National Development Plan (2006–2010). *Global Social Policy* **11**(1): 88–105.

Asamblea Constituyente (2008) *Nueva Constitución Política del Estado. Versión Oficial.* Representación Presidencial para la Asamblea Constituyente (REPAC): La Paz.

Avalos Boitel, O. and Pérez Rojas, N. (2008) 'Inserción juvenil en Unidades Básicas de Producción Cooperativa'. *Estudio: Revista sobre juventud.* **6**: 44–55.

Azicri, M. (1988) *Cuba. Politics, Economics and Society.* Pinter Publishers: London and New York.

Balardini, S. (2000) 'Youth Policy in Latin America: From Past to Present' in J. Rollin (ed.) *Youth Between Political Participation, Exclusion and Instrumentalisation.* GTZ: Eschborn, 42–44. [WWW Document]. URL http://www2.gtz.de/dokumente/bib/00-0878.pdf [accessed 12 May 2006].

Baloyra, E. A. (1993) 'Socialist Transitions and Prospects for Change in Cuba' in E. A. Baloyra and J. A. Morris (eds.) *Conflict and Change in Cuba.* University of New Mexico Press: Albuquerque, 38–63.

Bardach, A. L. (2002) *Cuba Confidential: Love and Vengeance in Miami and Havana.* Random House: New York.

Barrios, M. (2008) 'Al debate hay que acudir sin perjuicios'. *Juventud Rebelde,* 26 March 2009. [WWW Document]. URL http://www.juventudrebelde.cu/cuba/2008-03-26/al-debate-hay-que-acudir-sin-prejuicios/ [accessed 25 August 2009].

Bauman, Z. (1993) *Postmodern Ethics.* Blackwell: Malden and Oxford.

Benner, T., Reinicke, W. and Witte, J. M. (2004) 'Multisectoral Networks in Global Governance: Towards a Pluralistic System of Accountability'. *Government and Opposition* **39**(2): 191–210.

Bhola, H. (1984) *The Cuban Mass Literacy Campaign, 1961.* UNESCO: Paris.

Birkenmaier, A. and González Echevarría, R. (eds.) (2004) *Cuba: un siglo de literatura (1902–2002).* Editorial Colibrí (Colección Literatura): Madrid.

Bolender, K. (2010) *Voices from the Other Side: An Oral History of Terrorism against Cuba.* Pluto Press: London.

Bossi, R. (2009) 'Qué es el ALBA? Construyendo el ALBA desde los pueblos'. [WWW document]. URL http://www.alianzabolivariana.org/modules.php?name=News&file=article&sid=470 [accessed March 2010].

Bowles, S. (1971) Cuban Education and the Revolutionary Ideology. *Harvard Educational Review* **41**(4): 472–500.

Brennan, B. and Olivet, C. (2007) 'Regionalisms Futures: The Challenges for Civil Society'. *Global Social Policy* **7**(3): 267–270.

Brice, A. (2009) 'OAS Lifts 47-year-old Suspension of Cuba'. *CNN World*. [WWW document]. URL http://articles.cnn.com/2009-06-03/world/cuba.oas_1_oas-organization-of-american-states-purposes-and-principles?_s=PM:WORLD [accessed 22 January 2011].

Briceño Ruiz, J. (2007) 'Strategic Regionalism and Regional Social Policy in the FTAA Process'. *Global Social Policy* 7(3): 294–315.

Brubaker, R. ([1996] 2003) *Nationalism Reframed. Nationhood and the National Question in the New Europe*. Cambridge University Press: Cambridge.

Caño Secade, M. C. (1996) 'Relaciones raciales, proceso de ajuste y política social'. *Temas* 7: 58–65.

Carbonell, W. (1961) 'Editorial' in *Cómo surgió la cultura nacional*. Yaka: Havana.

Carter, J. (2002) *President Carter's Cuba Trip Report*. The Carter Center: Atlanta GA.

Carter, J. (2011) *Trip Report by Former US President Jimmy Carter to Cuba*. The Carter Center: Atlanta.

Casal, L. (1971) 'Literature' in C. Mesa-Lago (ed.) *Revolutionary Change in Cuba*. Pittsburgh: University of Pittsburgh Press, 447–469.

Casamayor, O. (2009) 'Guanajerías post-soviéticas: Apuntes ético-estéticos en torno al humor en la narrativa de Ena Lucía Portela'. *La Gaceta de Cuba* 6: 3–7.

Casanova, P. (2004) *The World Republic of Letters* (trans. M. B Debevoise). Harvard University Press: Boston.

Castro Ruz, F. (1961) *La Historia me absolverá*. Ediciones Populares: Havana.

Castro, F. (1959) *Discurso pronunciado por el Presidente de la Republica de Cuba Fidel Castro Ruz, en Guines*, 29 Marzo 1959. [WWW document]. URL http://www.cuba.cu/gobierno/discursos/1959/esp/f290359e.html [accessed 10 December 2010].

Castro, F. (1960a) 'Discurso pronunciado en la Escalinata Universitaria', 27 November 1960. [WWW Document]. URL http://www.cuba.cu/gobierno/discursos/1960/esp/f271160e.html [accessed 27 May 2005].

Castro, F. (1960b) 'History Will Absolve Me'. *New Left Review* 1(5), pp. 50–58.

Castro, F. (1961a) 'Discurso pronunciado en el acto de graduación de los maestros voluntarios, efectuado en el Teatro de la CTC Revolucionaria', 23 January 1961. [WWW document]. URL http://www.cuba.cu/gobierno/discursos/1961/esp/f230161e.html [accessed 27 May 2005].

Castro, F. (1961b) 'Palabras a los intelectuales'. [WWW document]. URL http://www.min.cult.cu/historia/palabras.doc [accessed 24 March 2009].

Castro, F. (1962a) 'Discurso pronunciado en la clausura del Congreso de la Asociación de Jóvenes Rebeldes, en el Stadium Latinoamericano' (4 April 1962). *Revolución*, 5 April, 1, 5.

Castro, F. (1962b) 'Discurso pronunciado en la clausura del Primer Congreso Nacional de la Union de Estudiantes Secundarios, efectuada en la Plaza de la Revolución'. *Revolución*, 11 August, 3.

Castro, F. (1963a) 'Discurso pronunciado en la clausura del X Congreso Médico y Estomatológico Nacional' (24 February 1963). *Revolución*, 25 February 1963, 4.

Castro, F. (1963b) 'Discurso pronunciado en la clausura del acto para conmemorar el VI Aniversario del asalto al Palacio Presidencial, celebrado en la escalinata de la Universidad de La Habana' (13 March 1963). *Revolución*, 14 March 1963, 3.

Castro, F. (1965a) 'Discurso pronunciado en el acto celebrado en la escalinata de la Universidad de la Habana honrando a los mártires del 13 de marzo' (13 March 1965). *Verde Olivo* **VI**(11): 10, 61.

Castro, F. (1965b) *Declaraciones de La Habana y de Santiago*. Editora Política: Havana.

Castro, F. (1967a) 'Discurso pronunciado en la velada solemne en memoria del comandante Ernesto Che Guevara', 18 October 1967. [WWW document]. URL http://www.cuba.cu/gobierno/discursos/1967/esp/f181067e.html [accessed 27 May 2005].

Castro, F. (1967b) *Aniversarios del triunfo de la revolución cubana*. Editora Política: Havana.

Castro, F. (1980) 'Palabras a los Intelectuales', in Varios (eds) *Revolución, Letras, Arte*. Editorial Letras Cubanas: Havana, 7–30.

Castro, F. (2000) *Speech delivered by F. Castro Ruz at Cuban Solidarity Rally, Harbin, New York*, 8 September. [WWW document]. URL http://www.cuba.cu/gobierno/discursos/2000/ing/f080900i.html [accessed 6 June 2011].

Castro, F. (2002) 'Discurso pronunciado por el Presidente de la República de Cuba Fidel Castro Ruz, en el acto de inauguración oficial del curso escolar 2002–2003', 16 September 2002. [WWW document]. URL http://www.cuba.cu/gobierno/discursos/2002/esp/f160902e.html [accessed 22 December 2010].

Castro, R. (2008) 'Discurso pronunciado en las conclusiones de la session constitutive de la VII Legislatura de la Asamblea Nacional del Poder Popular', 24 February 2008. [WWW document]. URL http://www.cubadebate.cu/raul-castro-ruz/2008/02/24/discurso-en-la-sesion-constitutiva-de-la-vii-legislatura-de-la-asamblea-nacional-del-poder-popular/ [accessed 6 February 2011].

Castro, R. (2010a) 'Intervención del General de Ejército Raúl Castro Ruz, Presidente del Consejo de Estado y de Ministros en la sesión plenaria de la Cumbre de América Latina y el Caribe, el 23 de febrero de 2010'. [WWW document]. URL: http://cuba.cu/gobierno/rauldiscursos/2010/esp/r230210e.html [accessed 25 October 2010].

Castro, R. (2010b) 'Raúl Castro no teme a la mentira ni se arrodilla ante presiones'. Unpublished speech delivered at the closing of the IX Congress of the Unión de Jóvenes Comunistas de Cuba, 4 April. [WWW document]. URL http:www.cubadebate.cu/opinion/2010/04/04/cuba-no-teme-a-la-mentira-ni-se-arodilla-ante-pre [accessed 26 September 2010].

CEPAL–OIJ (2007) *La Juventud en iberoamerica: Tendencias y urgencia* (2nd edition). CEPAL/United Nations:Buenos Aires. [WWW document].URL www.oij.org/documentos/doc1202813603.pdf [accessed 1 February 2011].

CEPAL–SEGIB–OIJ (2008) *Juventud y cohesión social en iberoamerica: Un modelo para armar*. United Nations: Santiago de Chile. [WWW Document]. URL www.oij.org/documentos/Juventud_Cohesion_Social_CEPAL_OIJ.pdf [accessed 1 February 2011].

Chaple, S. (ed.) (2008a) *Historia de la literatura cubana*, Volume III. Editorial Letras Cubanas: Havana.

Chaple, S. (2008b) 'Introducción', in S. Chaple (ed.) *Historia de la literatura cubana*, Volume III. Editorial Letras Cubanas: Havana, 3–4.

Clemons, S. (2009) 'Cuba's Soft Power. Exporting Doctors rather than Revolution'. *HuffingtonPost.com*. [WWW document]. URL http://www.huffingtonpost.

com/steve-clemons/cubas-soft-power-exportin_b_355373.html [accessed 12 January 2011].

Cohen, S. (1987) *Folk Devils and Moral Panics. The Creation of the Mods and Rockers* (2nd edition). Basil Blackwell: Oxford.

Coltman, L. (2003) *The Real Fidel Castro*. Yale University Press: New Haven and London.

Commission for Assistance to a Free Cuba (2004) *Report to the President May 2004*. United States Department of State: Washington.

Commission for Assistance to a Free Cuba (2006a) *Report to the President July 2006*. United States Department of State: Washington.

Commission for Assistance to a Free Cuba (2006b) *Compact with the Cuban People*. United States Department of State: Washington.

Crow, J. (2010) 'Introduction: Intellectuals, Indigenous Ethnicity and the State in Latin America'. *Latin American and Caribbean Ethnic Studies* 2(2): 99–107.

Cubadebate (2010) *Lineamientos de la política económica y social*, November. [WWW document]. URL http://www.cubadebate.cu/wp-content/uploads/2010/11/proyecto-lineamientos-pcc.pdf.

De Araújo, R. M. (2009) 'A Snapshot of the Medical School, Faculty of Health Sciences, National University of Timor Lorosa'e, Democratic Republic of Timor-Leste'. Unpublished paper presented at the Export Group Meeting on Finalization of Regional Guidelines on Institutional Quality assurance mechanism for Undergraduate Medical Education, WHO/SEARO, New Delhi, October.

de la Barra, X. (2006) 'Who Owes and Who Pays? The Accumulated Debt of Neoliberalism'. *Critical Sociology* 32(1): 125–161.

de la Cadena, M. (2000) *Indigenous Mestizos. The Politics of Race and Culture in Cuzco, Perú, 1919–1991*. Duke University Press: Durham and London.

de la Cadena, M. (2005) 'Are *Mestizos* Hybrids? The Conceptual Politics of Andean Identities'. *Journal of Latin American Studies* 37: 259–284.

de La Fuente, A. (2001) *A Nation for All: Race, Inequality and Politics in Twentieth-Century Cuba*. University of North Carolina Press: Chapel Hill and London.

De la Nuez, I. (ed.) (2001) *Cuba y el día después. Doce ensayistas nacidos con la Revolución imaginan el futuro*. Mondadori: Barcelona.

Dello Buono, R. (2007) 'The redesign of Latin America: FTAA, MERCOSUR and ALBA'. *Critical Sociology* 33(4): 767–774.

Duno Gottberg, L. (2003) *Solventando las diferencias. La ideología del mestizaje en Cuba*. Iberoamericana: Madrid.

Eberstadt, N. (1988) 'Literacy and Health: The Cuban Model' in N. Eberstadt (ed.) *The Poverty of Communism*. Transaction: New Brunswick, 117–139.

Eckstein, S. E. (1994) *Back from the Future: Cuba under Castro*. Princeton University Press: Princeton.

Economic Commission for Latin America and the Caribbean (2010) *Economic Commission for Latin America and the Caribbean Annual Statistics 2010*. United Nations: Santiago de Cuba.

Economic Commission for Latin America and the Caribbean (2011) *Social Panorama of Latin America 2010*. United Nations: Santiago de Cuba.

Elizalde, R. M. and Báez, L. (2003) *'The Dissidents': Cuban State Security Agents Reveal the True Story*. La Habana: Editorial Política.

Elizalde, R. M. (2010) 'Fidel y la brigada "Moto Méndez": "La felicidad de hacer el bien". *Cubadebate*, 18 August. [WWW document]. URL http://www.cubadebate.cu/noticias/2010/8/18/fidel-y-la-felicidad-de-hacer [accessed 7 September 2011].

Elvy, J. C. (2005) *Notes from a Cuban Diary: Forty Women on Forty Years. An Inquiry into the 1961 Literacy Campaign Using Photographic, Video and Poetic Representation.* Canadian Association for the Study of Adult Education (CASAE): University of Western Ontario.

Espina Prieto, R. and Rodríguez Ruiz, P. (2006) 'Raza y desigualdad en la Cuba actual'. *Temas* **45**: 44–54

Espinosa, N. (2009) 'Punto de referencia: Entrevista a Ambrosio Fornet'. *Extramuros* **27**: 22–29.

European Union (1996) *Common Position of 2 December 1996 Defined by the Council on the basis of Article J.2 of the Treaty on European Union, on Cuba (96/697/CFSP).* European Union: Brussels.

Evenson, D. (1994) *Revolution in the Balance: Law and Society in Contemporary Society.* Westview Press: Boulder.

Fagen, R. R. (1969) *The Transformation of Political Culture in Cuba.* Hoover Institution Press: Stanford.

Federal Bureau of Investigation (1999) *Terrorism in the United States 1999: 30 Years of Terrorism, a Special Retrospective Edition.* United States Department of Justice: Washington.

Feinsilver, J. (1993) *Healing the Masses: Cuban Health Politics at Home and Abroad.* University of California Press: California.

Feinsilver, J. (2006) *Cuban Medical Diplomacy: When the Left Has Got It Right.* Council of Hemispheric Affairs, 30 October. [WWW document]. URL http://www.coha.org/2006/10/30/cuban-medical-diplomacy-when-the-left-has-got it-right [accessed 20 November 2009].

Feinsilver, J. (2010) *Cuba's Health Politics: At Home and Abroad.* Report prepared for the Council on Hemispheric Studies, March. [WWW document]. URL http://www.coha.org/cuba/%e2%80%99s-health-politics-at-home-and abroad [accessed 20 September 2010].

Fenton, S. and May, S. (2002) *Ethnonational Identities.* Palgrave Macmillan: New York.

Fernandes, S. (2003) 'Island Paradise, Revolutionary Utopia or Hustler's Haven? Consumerism and Socialism in Contemporary Cuban Rap. *Journal of Latin American Cultural Studies: travesía* **12**(3): 359–375.

Fernández, D. (2000) *Cuba and the Politics of Passion.* University of Texas Press: Austin.

Fernández Retamar, R. (1980 [1971]) 'Calibán', in Varios, *Revolución, Letras, Arte.* Editorial Letras Cubanas: Havana, 221–276.

Fornet, A. (2002) 'La crítica bicéfala: un nuevo desafío'. *La Gaceta de Cuba* **1**: 20–5.

Fornet, J. (2006) *Los nuevos paradigmas. Prólogo narrativo al siglo XXI.* Letras Cubanas: Havana.

Fowler, A. (1979) 'Genre and the literary canon'. *New Literary History* **11**(1): 97–119.

Freire, P. (1970) *Pedagogy of the Oppressed.* Nicholson: London.

Frow, J. (1995) *Cultural Studies and Cultural Value.* Clarendon Press: Oxford.

Fuguet, A. and Gómez, S. (1993) 'Urgentes, desechables y ambulantes' in A. Fuguet and S. Gómez (eds.) *Cuentos con walkman*. Planeta: Santiago de Chile, 11–16.

Fuguet, A. (2001) 'Magical Neoliberalism'. *Foreign Policy* Jul–Aug: 66–73.

Fuguet, A. and Gómez, S. (1996) 'Presentación del País McOndo' in A. Fuguet and S. Gómez (eds.) *McOndo*. Mondadori: Barcelona, 9–18.

García Canclini, N. (1990) *Culturas híbridas. Estrategias para entrar y salir de la modernidad.* Ed. Grijalbo: Mexico City.

García Márquez, G. (2006). *Cien años de soledad.* Cátedra: Madrid.

Gerassi, J. (1968) *Venceremos! The Speeches and Writings of Ernesto Che Guevara.* Weidenfeld and Nicholson: London.

Gleijeses, P. (2002) *Conflicting Missions: Havana, Washington and Africa, 1959–1976.* University of North Carolina Press: Chapel Hill and London.

Goldenberg, B. (1965) *The Cuban Revolution and Latin America.* Allen and Unwin: London.

Gómez, L. (2003) 'Cronología mínima de la Unión de Jóvenes Comunistas y el sistema de organizaciones juveniles e infantiles, 1959–2001'. Unpublished research document.

González Echevarría, R. (1985) 'Criticism and Literature in Revolutionary Cuba' in S. Halebsky and J. M. Kirk (eds.) *Cuba: Twenty-five Years of Revolution, 1959–1984.* Praeger: New York, 155–173.

González Echevarría, R. (2004) 'Oye mi son: El canon cubano' in A. Birkenmaier and R. González Echevarría (eds.) *Cuba: un siglo de literatura (1902–2002).* Editorial Colibrí (Colección Literatura): Madrid, 19–36.

Gorry, C. (2011) 'Haiti One Year later: Cuban Medical Team Draws on Experience and Partnerships'. *MEDICC Review* **13**(1): 52–55.

Gosse, V. (1993) *Where the Boys Are: Cuba, Cold War America and the Making of a New Left.* Verso: London and New York.

Graham, R. (1997) *The Idea of Race In Latin America (1870–1940).* University of Texas Press: Austin.

Granma (1971) '¡Adelante, cubanos, todos a los puestos de combate y de trabajo!'. *Granma* **7**(92) (17 April): 1.

Granma (2011) 'Destaca Evo Morales ejemplo solidario de Operación Milagro,' *Granma*, 3 September. [WWW document]. URL http://www.granma.cu/espanol/nuestra-america/3sept-Destaca%20Evo.html [accessed 8 October 2011].

Grogg, P. (2009) 'Chernobyl Kids Keep Arriving in Cuba'. *Inter Press Service*, 7 May.

Grogg, P. (2010) 'Biotecnología cubana toca las puertas del Norte'. *Inter Press Service*, 22 October.

Guanche, J. (1996a) *Componentes étnicos de la nación cubana.* Colección La Fuente Viva. Ediciones Unión: Havana.

Guanche, J. (1996b) 'Etnicidad y racialidad en la Cuba actual'. *Temas* **7**: 51–57.

Guerra, W. (2006) *Todos se van.* Bruguera: Barcelona.

Guevara, E. (1967a) '¿Qué debe ser un joven comunista?' (October 1962) in E. Guevara, *Obra Revolucionaria*. Ediciones Era: Mexico, 356–366.

Guevara, E. (1967b) 'Create Two, Three … Many Vietnams, That is the Watchword'. [WWW document]. *Tricontinental*. Available at: http://www.rcgfrfi.easynet.co.uk/ww/guevara/1967-mtt.htm [accessed 2 November 2011].

Guevara, E. (1977a) 'Despedida a las Brigadas Internacionales de Trabajo Voluntario' (30 September 1960) in E. Guevara, *Obras, 1957–1967, tomo II. La transformación política, económica y social*. (2nd edition). Casa de las Américas: Havana, 81–91.

Guevara, E. (1977b) '"El 27 de noviembre de 1871", Discurso en la Universidad de La Habana' (27 November 1961) in E Guevara *Obras, 1957–1967, tomo II. La transformación política, económica y social* (2nd edition). Casa de las Américas: Havana, 601–608.

Guevara, E. (1977c) 'El cuadro, columna vertebral de la Revolución' (September 1962) in E. Guevara *Obras, 1957–1967, tomo II. La transformación política, económica y social* (2nd edition). Casa de las Américas: Havana, 154–160.

Guevara, E. (1977d) 'En la clausura del Encuentro Internacional de Estudiantes de Arquitectura' (29 September 1963) in E. Guevara, *Obras, 1957–1967, tomo II. La transformación política, económica y social* (2nd edition). Casa de las Américas: Havana, 219–229.

Guevara, E. (1977e) 'El socialismo y el hombre en Cuba' (12 March 1965) in E. Guevara, *Obras, 1957–1967, tomo II. La transformación política, económica y social* (2nd edition). Casa de las Américas: Havana, 367–384.

Guevara, E. (1977f) 'Cuba, ¿excepción histórica o vanguardia en la lucha anticolonialista?' in E. Guevara, *Obras 1957–1967, tomo II. La transformación política, económica y social* (2nd edition). Casa de las Américas: Havana, 403–419.

Gugelberger, G. M. (1997) 'Decolonizing the Canon: Considerations of Third World Literature'. *New Literary History* **22**(3): 505–524.

Guillory, J. (1993) *Cultural Capital: The Problem of Literary Canon Formation*. University of Chicago Press: Chicago.

Hall, A. and Midgely, J. (2004) *Social Policy for Development*. Sage: London.

Harris, R. (2009) 'Cuban Internationalism, Che Guevara, and the Survival of Cuba's Socialist Regime'. *Latin American Perspectives* **36**(3): 27–42.

Hennessy, A. (1993) 'Cuba, Western Europe and the US: An Historical Overview' in A. Hennessy and G. Lambie (eds.) *The Fractured Blockade: West European–Cuban Relations during the Revolution*. Macmillan: Basingstoke and London, 11–63.

Hernández, R. (2002) '1912. Notas sobre raza y desigualdad'. *Catauro* **6**: 94–106.

Hernández-Reguant, A. (2009) 'Writing the Special Period: An Introduction' in A. Hernández-Reguant (ed.) *Cuba in the Special Period: Culture and Ideology in the 1990s*. Palgrave MacMillan: New York, 1–18.

Horowitz, I. L. (1977) 'Military outcomes of the Cuban Revolution' in I. L. Horowitz (ed.) *Cuban Communism. Third Edition*. Transaction Publishers: New Brunswick, NJ, 88–105.

Horowitz, I. L. (1991) 'New beginnings and familiar endings' (lecture, June 1991) in I. L. Horowitz, *The Long Night of Dark Intent: A Half-century of Cuban Communism*. Transaction Publishers: New Brunswick and London, 297–305.

Horowitz, I. L. (2008) *The Long Night of Dark Intent: A Half-century of Cuban Communism*. Transaction: New Brunswick, NJ.

Human Rights Watch (1993) *Freedom of Expression in Miami's Cuban Exile Community*. Human Rights Watch: New York.

Human Rights Watch (2009) *New Castro, Same Cuba: Political Prisoners in the Post-Fidel Era*. Human Rights Watch: New York.

Instituto de Literatura y Lingüística de la Academia de Ciencias de Cuba (1980) *Diccionario de la literatura cubana*. Havana: Editorial Letras Cubanas.

Inter-American Commission on Human Rights (2009) *Annual Report 2009*. Inter-American Commission on Human Rights: Washington.

Jameson, F. (1991) *Postmodernism, or The cultural Logic of Late Capitalism*. Duke University Press: Durham.

Jameson, F. (1994) *The Seeds of Time*. Columbia University Press: New York.

Jameson, F. (2005) *Archeologies of the Future. The Desire Called Utopia and Other Science Fictions*. Verso: London and New York.

Jolly, R. (1964) 'Education' in D. Seers, A. Bianchi, R. Jolly and M. Nolff (eds.) *Cuba: The Economic and Social Revolution*. University of North Carolina Press: Chapel Hill, 161–282.

Kapcia, A. (2000) *Cuba: Island of Dreams*. Berg Publishers: Oxford.

Kapcia, A. (2005) 'Educational Revolution and Revolutionary Morality in Cuba: The "New Man", Youth and the New "Battle of Ideas"'. *Journal of Moral Education* 34(4): 399–412.

Kapcia, A. (2005) *Havana: The Making of Cuban Culture*. Berg Publishers: Oxford.

Kapcia, A. (2008) *Cuba in Revolution: A History since the Fifties*. Reaktion Books: London.

Kapcia, A. (2009) 'Lessons of the Special Period: Learning to March Again'. *Latin American Perspectives* 36/164(1): 30–41.

Katz, C. (2006) *The Redesign of Latin America: FTAA, MERCOSUR and ALBA*. Ediciones Luxemburgo: Buenos Aires.

Kenner, M. and Petras, J. (1972) *Fidel Castro Speaks*. Pelican: Harmondsworth.

King, J. (1990) 'Cuban Cinema: A Reel Revolution?' in R. Gillespie (ed.) *Cuba After Thirty Years*. Frank Cass: London, 140–160.

Kirk, E. and Kirk, J. M. (2010) 'Uno de los secretos mejor guardados del mundo: La cooperación médica cubana en Haití' *Cubadebate*, 7 April. [WWW document]. URL http://www.cubadebate.cu/especiales/2010/04/07/la-cooperacion-medica-cubana-en-haiti [accessed 2 February 2011].

Kirk, J. and Erisman, M. (2009) *Cuban Medical Internationalism: Origins, Evolution and Goals*. Palgrave MacMillan: New York.

Klepak, H. (2005) *Cuba's military, 1990–2005*. Palgrave Macmillan: New York.

Kozol, J. (1978) 'A New Look at the Literacy Campaign in Cuba'. *Harvard Educational Review* 48(3): 341–377.

Kumaraswami, P. (2009) 'Cultural Policy and Cultural Politics in Revolutionary Cuba: Re-reading the *Palabras a los Intelectuales*'. *Bulletin of Latin American Research* 28(4): 527–541.

Kumaraswami, P. and Kapcia, A. (forthcoming) *Literary Culture in Cuba: Revolution, Nation-Building and the Book*. Manchester University Press: Manchester.

La política cultural (2008) *La política cultural del período revolucionario: memoria y reflexión. Ciclo de conferencias organizado por el Centro teórico-Cultural Criterios. La Habana, 2007. Primera parte*. Colección Criterios: Havana.

Lamrani, S. (2007) 'The Deceit of Reporters Without Borders'. [WWW document]. URL http://www.zmag.org/znet/viewArticle/15873 [accessed 16 June 2009].

Lamrani, S. (2008) *Double Morale: Cuba, l'Union Européenne et les Droits de l'Homme*. Éditions Estrella: Paris.

Leclercq, C. (2004) *El lagarto en busca de una identidad. Cuba: identidad nacional y mestizaje*. Iberoamericana: Madrid.

Leiner, M. (1985) 'Cuba's Schools 25 Years Later' in S. Halebsky and J. Kirk (eds.) *Cuba, Twenty-Five Years of Revolution, 1959–1984*. Prager: London, 27–44.

Leiner, M. (1987) 'The 1961 Cuban Literacy Campaign' in R. F. Arnove and H. J. Graff (eds.) *National Literacy Campaigns*. Plenum Press: New York, 173–196.

Leogrande, W. (1982) 'Foreign Policy: The Limits of Success' in J. Dominguez (ed.) *Cuba: Internal and International Affairs*. Sage: Beverly Hills, 167–192.

Levine, R. M. (2001) *Secret Missions to Cuba: Fidel Castro, Bernardo Benes, and Cuban Miami*. Palgrave Macmillan: New York.

Lievesley, G. and Ludlam, S. (eds.) (2009) *Reclaiming Latin America: Experiments in Radical Social Democracy*. Zed Books: London.

Lipovetsky, G. (1993) *L'Ère du vide. Essais sur l'individualisme contemporain*. Gallimard: Paris.

Lomas, L. (2008), *Translating Empire: José Martí, Migrant Latino Subjects and American Modernities*. Duke University Press: Durham.

Lorenzetto, A. and Neys, K. (1965) *Methods and Means Utilized in Cuba to Eliminate Illiteracy*. UNESCO Report: Paris.

Loss, J. (2007) 'Amateurs and Professionals in Ena Lucía Portela's Lexicon of Crisis' in A. Lambright and E. Guerrero (eds.) *Unfolding the City in Latin America*. Minnesota University Press: Minneapolis, 251–267.

Loss, J. (2009) 'Wandering in Russian' in A. Hernández-Reguant (ed.) *Cuba in the Special Period: Culture and Ideology in the 1990s*. Palgrave: New York, 105–123.

Ludlam, S. (2009) 'Cuban Labour at 50: What About the Workers?' *Bulletin of Latin American Research*. 28(4): 542–557.

Ludlam, S. (2011) 'Right-Wing Opposition as Counter-Revolution: the Cuban Case' in F. Dominguez, G. Lievesley and S. Ludlam (eds.) *Reaction and Revolt: the Right-Wing in the New Politics of Latin America*. Zed Books: London, 148–164.

Luis Luis, M. (2008a) 'Trabajo y juventud: algunas reflexiones en torno a la realidad cubana'. *Estudio: Revista sobre juventud* (special issue): 62–73.

Luis Luis, M. (2008b) 'Reflexiones en torno a la desvinculación juvenil en Cuba'. *Estudio: Revista sobre juventud*. **6**: 30-43.

Luis Luis, M. (2010) 'Socialización laboral de la juventud cubana (I parte). La preparación de los adolescentes para la inserción laboral'. *Estudio: Revista sobre juventud* **8**: 55–62.

Lutjens, S. (1998) 'Education and the Cuban Revolution: A Selected Bibliography'. *Comparative Education Review* **42**(2): 197–224.

Manke, A. (2011) 'Neue Aspekte der Gründung und Organisation der Revolutionären Nationalmilizen Kubas, 1959–1961' in C. Esser, M. Göttsch, J. Hartmann, M. Loschky, S. Wendle and J. Wöhrle (eds.) *Kuba. 50 Jahre zwischen Revolution, Reform – und Stillstand?* Wissenschaftlicher: Berlin, 91–120.

Medin, T. (1990) *Cuba. The Shaping of Revolutionary Consciousness*. Lynne Rienner Publishers; Boulder and London.

Mencía, M. (1971) 'La generación del Centenario'. *Bohemia* **63**(3) (July): 32–39.

Miller, N. (2003) 'The Absolution of History: Uses of the Past in Castro's Cuba'. *Journal of Contemporary History* **38**(1): 147–162.

Ministerio de Educación y Culturas (2006) *Ya puedo leer. Yo sí puedo más. Cartilla de lectura*. Ministerio de Educación y Culturas: La Paz.

Ministerio de Educación y Culturas (2008) *Bolivia se declara libre de analfabetismo este sábado en la ciudad de Cochabamba.* [WWW document]. URL http://www.minedu.gov.bo/minedu/showNews.do?newsId=1203 [accessed 30 March 2010].

Montaner, C. A. (1976) 'Los intelectuales extranjeros: Declaración del Primer Congreso Nacional de Educación y Cultura, 30 de abril de 1971' in C. A. Montaner, *Informe secreto sobre la Revolución cubana.* Ediciones Sedmay: Madrid, 147–153.

Moore, R. (1997) *Nationalizing Blackness: Afrocubanismo and the Artistic Revolution in Havana.* University of Pittsburgh Press: Pittsburgh.

Morales Agüero, J. (2009) 'Cómo vincularse a los desvinculados'. *Juventud Rebelde.* 10 January 2009. [WWW document]. URL http://www.juventudrebelde.cu/UserFiles/File/impreso/icontraportada-2009-01-10.pdf [accessed 20 January 2011].

Morales Domínguez, E. (2002) 'Un modelo para el análisis de la problemática racial cubana contemporánea' *Catauro* **6**: 52-93

Morales Domínguez, E. (2007) *Desafíos de la problemática racial en Cuba.* Ed. La Fuente Viva: Havana.

Morales Domínguez, E. (2008) 'Desafíos de la problemática racial en Cuba'. *Temas* **56**: 95–99.

Morejón, N. (1982) *Nación y mestizaje en Nicolás Guillén.* Ediciones Unión: Havana.

Morejón, N. (1988) *Fundación de la imagen.* Letras Cubanas: Havana.

Muhr, T. (2010) 'Counter Hegemonic Regionalism and Higher Education for All: Venezuela and the ALBA'. *Globalisation, Societies and Education* **8**(1): 1–27. [WWW document]. URL http://www.bris.ac.uk/education/research/centres/ges/post-doc-fellows/thomas-muhr/011.pdf [accessed 25 January 2011].

Murayama, C. (2010) 'Juventud y crisis: ¿hacia una generación perdida?'. *Economía UNAM* **7**(20): 71–78. [WWW document]. URL http://www.revistas.unam.mx/index.php/ecu/article/view/18125/17246 [accessed 30 August 2010].

Nuez (1965) (Cartoon) 18 January. *Mella* **307**: 11.

Nye, J. (2004) *Soft Power: The Means to Success in World Politics.* Public Affairs: New York.

O'Connor, J. (1970) *The Origins of Socialism in Cuba.* Cornell University Press: Ithaca and London.

OIE (2008) 'XVIII Cumbre Iberoamericana de Jefes de Estado y de Gobierno'. [WWW document]. URL http://www.oei.es/xviiicumbre.htm [accessed 20 January 2011].

Ortiz, F. (1991[1949]) *Estudios etnosociológicos.* Ed. Ciencias socials: Havana.

'Otra vez raza y racismo'. (2008) *Caminos (Revista Cubana de Pensamiento Socio-teológico)* 47.

Pardo Lazo, O. L. (2009) *Boring Home.* Bibliotecas Independientes de Cuba and Garamond: Praga.

Peñate Leiva, A. and López Santos, D. (2008) 'Acercamiento al tema de identidades: Identidad Juvenil'. *Estudio: Revista sobre juventud* **6**: 64–81.

Pérez, E. and Lueiro, M. (compilers) (2009) *Raza y racismo. Antología de caminos.* Editorial Caminos: Havana.

Pérez, E. C. (2010) 'Reconocen Gobierno y pueblo ucranianos atención cubana a niños de Chernóbil'. *Granma*, 4 March. [WWW document]. URL http://articulos.sld.cu/chernobil/archives/tag/tarara/page/3 [accessed 7 September 2011].

Pérez Cino, W. (2002) 'Sentido y práfrasis'. *La Gaceta de Cuba* 6: 23–28.

Portela, E. L. (1998) *El pájaro: pincel y tinta china*. Unión: Havana.

Portela, E. L. (2003) *Cien botellas en una pared*. Unión: Havana.

Portela, E. L. (2010) *One Hundred Bottles* (trans. A. Obejas). Texas University Press: Austin.

Republic of Cuba (1992) *Constitution of the Republic of Cuba*. Republic of Cuba: Havana.

Republic of Cuba (2006) *Cuba, Humans with Rights*. Republic of Cuba: Havana.

Republic of Cuba (2008) *National Report of the Republic of Cuba to the Universal Periodic Review of the Human Rights Council*. Republic of Cuba: Havana.

República Bolivariana de Venezuela (2011) 'Escuela Latinoamericana de Medicina ha formado a 10,000 Galenos', 29 July. [WWW document]. URL http://www.rbv.info/es/noticias-de-venezuela/nacionales/internacionales/4057-internacional-escuela-latinoamericana-de-medicina-ha-formado-a-10000-galenos-de-60-paises/ [accessed 8 October 2011].

Resumen Estadístico (2009) *Resumen Estadístico 2009*. Instituto Cubano del Libro: Havana.

Reuters (2010) *Cuba Says its Trade Figures Improving*. 1 November.

Revolución (1961) 'Reacción nacional ante la agresión'. *Revolución* 4(726) (14 April): 2–3.

Revolución (1962) 'Comité nacional: informe', *Revolución* 2 April, 1, 5.

Rivera Zvezdina, E. (2010) 'Universidad cubana gradúa médicos haitianos'. *Granma*, 5 August. [WWW document]. URL http://www.radionuevitas.icrt.cu/ultimas-noticias/noticias-internacionales/2496-universidad-cubana-gradua-medicos-haitianos.html [accessed 8 October 2011].

Robbins, J. (2003), 'Globalization, Publishing and the Marketing of "Hispanic" Identities'. *Iberoamericana* III(9): 89–101.

Rodríguez, R. (1997) *Génesis y desarrollo del instituto cubano del libro*. Unpublished Conference paper, University of Havana, Havana.

Rodríguez, R. (2001) 'Génesis y desarrollo del Instituto Cubano del Libro (1965–1980): Memoria y reflexión', *Debates Americanos* 11: 65-80.

Romero, C. (2010) 'South–South Cooperation between Venezuela and Cuba' in C. Romero, *South–South Cooperation: A Challenge to the Aid System* (special report of the Reality of Aid Network). IBON Books: Quezon City, 107–114.

Rondón Velazquez, A. (2009) 'No más sermones con los zánganos' (letter). *Granma* 16 January. [WWW document] URL http://granma.co.cu/secciones/cartas-direccion/cart-043.html [accessed 25 August 2009].

Rosales, G. (1987) *Boarding Home*. Salvat Editores: Barcelona.

Santos, B. (2009) 'Why has Cuba Become a Difficult Problem for the Left?' *Latin American Perspectives* 36(3): 43–53.

Santos, B. (2010) *Refundación del Estado en América Latina*. Plural: La Paz.

Sartre, J-P. (1961) *Sartre on Cuba*. Ballantyne Books: New York.

Sawyer, M. Q. (2006) *Racial Politics in Post-Revolutionary Cuba*. Cambridge University Press: Cambridge.

Serviat, P. (1986) *El problema negro en Cuba y su solución definitiva*. Editorial Política: Havana.

Shabbir, N. (2009) 'Seville: Cuba, Communists and Anticapitalists for the Elections'. *Cafebabel.com, the European magazine*. [WWW document]. URL http://www.cafebabel.co.uk/article/29976/seville-cuba-communism-eu-election-anticapitalism.html [accessed 21 January 2011].

Smith, J. (2009) 'Solidarity Networks: What Are They and Why Should We Care'. *The Learning Organisation* 16(6): 460–468.

Smith, W. S. (2006) *New Cuba Commission Report: Formula for Continued Failure*. Center for International Policy: Washington.

Smith, W. S. Harrison, S. and Adams, S. (2006). *Sanctuary for Terrorists: US Tolerance of anti-Cuban Terrorism*. Center for International Policy: Washington.

Somarriba López, L. (2011) 'Cuba ha salvado miles de vidas haitianas y seguiremos haciéndolo'. *Cubadebate*, 16 January. [WWW document]. URL http://www.cubadebate.cu/opinion/2011/01/16/cuba-ha-salvado-miles-de-vidas-haitinas [accessed 4 February 2011].

Spronk, S. (2008) 'Pink tide? Neoliberalism and its Alternatives in Latin America'. *Canadian Journal of Latin American and Caribbean Studies* 33(65): 175–189.

Stock, A. M. (2008) 'Tradition Meets Technology: Cuban Film Animation Enters the Global Marketplace'. *Cuban Studies* 39: 1–24.

Suchlicki, J. (1969) *University Students and Revolution in Cuba 1920–1968*. University of Miami Press: Coral Gables.

United Nations (1948) *The Universal Declaration of Human Rights*. United Nations: New York.

United Nations (1966) *International Covenant on Economic, Social and Cultural Rights*. United Nations: New York.

United Nations (1992) *Report on the Situation of Human Rights in Cuba Submitted by the Special Rapporteur, Mr. Carl-Johan Groth, in Accordance with Commission Resolution 1992/61, A/47/625*. United Nations: New York.

United Nations (2006) *Resolution Adopted by the General Assembly 60/251. Human Rights Council*. United Nations: New York.

United Nations (2008) *Necessity of Ending the Economic, Commercial and Financial Embargo Imposed by the United States of America against Cuba*. United Nations: New York.

United Nations (n.d.) 'A United Nations Priority: Universal Declaration of Human Rights'. [WWW document]. URL http://www.un.org/rights/HRToday/declar.htm [accessed 11 October 2011].

United Nations Committee on Social, Economic and Cultural Rights (1993) *Statement to the World Conference on Human Rights on Behalf of the Committee*. United Nations: New York.

United Nations Human Rights Council (2008) *Compilation Prepared by the High Commissioner for Human Rights – Cuba*. United Nations: New York.

United States Department of State (2011) *2010 Human Rights Report: Cuba*. United States Department of State: Washington.

United States Government Accounting Office (2007) *Economic Sanctions: Agencies Face Competing Priorities in Enforcing the US Embargo on Cuba*. United States Government Accounting Office: Washington.

van Dijk, T. (1993) *Elite Discourse and Racism*. Sage Publications: London.

van Dijk, T. (1998) *Ideology: A Multidisciplinary Approach*. Sage Publications: London.
Van Gelder, S. (2007) 'Por qué Cuba exporta asistencia médica a los pobres del mundo?' ALBA. [WWW document]. URL http://www.alternativaboli variana.org/modules.php?name=News&file=article&sid=2041 [accessed October 2007].
Volpi, J., Urroz, P. and Chávez, P. (2000) 'Manifiesto Crack'. *Lateral. Revista de Cultur* 70. [WWW document]. URL http://www.circulolateral.com/revista/tema/070manifiestocrack.htm [accessed 2 November 2011].
Wade, P. (1997) *Race and Ethnicity in Latin America*. Pluto Press: London and Chicago.
Wade, P. (2000) *Music, Race and Nation*. University of Chicago Press: Chicago.
Wade, P. (2002) *Race, Nature, Culture. An Anthropological Perspective*. Pluto Press: London.
Weinglass, L. (2005) 'The Trial of the Cuban Five' in S. Lamrani (ed.) *Superpower Principles: US Terrorism against Cuba*. Common Courage Press: Monroe, 114–124.
Whitfield, E. (2008) *Cuban Currency. The Dollar and 'Special Period' Fiction*. Minnesota University Press: Minneapolis and London.
Whitfield, E. (2009) 'Truths and Fictions: The Economics of Writing, 1994–1999' in A. Hernández-Reguant (ed.) *Cuba in the Special Period: Culture and Ideology in the 1990s*. Palgrave: New York, 21–36.

Newspaper Articles

Arce, L. M. (1976) El apartheid, sus padres y sus padrinos. *Granma*, 8 March, p. 2.
Barbeito, J. (1959) *Diario de la Marina*, 2 April, p. 4a.
Benítez, J. A. (1976a) Darwin, Marx, y la discriminación racial en Estados Unidos. *Granma*, 23 January, p. 2.
Benítez, J. A. (1976b) Apartheid, un invento norteamericano. *Granma*, 23 March, p. 2.
Benítez, J. A. (1976c) La lucha histórica del negro norteamericano. *Granma*, 1 April, p. 2.
Berges, J. (1976a) Los negros mercancía humana para el imperialismo. *Granma*, 1 June, p. 2.
Berges, J. (1976b) La desnaturalización forzosa de los chicanos. *Granma*, 2 June, p. 2.
Berges, J. (1976c) Los indios, destrucción de una raza. *Granma*, 4 June, p. 2.
Carrasco, J. (1976a) A once años del asesinato de Malcolm X. *Granma*, 21 February, p. 2.
Carrasco, J. (1976b) La crisis educacional en EE.UU. Reflejo del sistema. *Granma*, 27 February, p. 2.
Díaz, N. (1976) USA: Racismo con capucha y sin capucha. *Granma*, 12 June, p. 2.
Despestre, R. (1959) Astucias de la ideología racista. *Revolución*, 16 September, p. 2.
Fernández López, O. (Comisionado de Santa Clara) (1959) Hermano negro. *Revolución*, 21 August, p. 2.

García Pons, C. (1959) El DR. Castro y la discriminación racial. *Diario de la Marina*, 29 March, p. 4a.

Granma (1976a) Fidel: 'La sociedad clasista, la sociedad capitalista no podrá resolver jamás el problema ni de las minorías ni de las mayorías'. *Granma*, 26 June, p. 2.

Granma (1976b) Minorías nacionales: ciudadanos de segunda clase en Estados Unidos. *Granma*, 19 August, p. 2.

Granma (1976c) 'EE.UU.: Una 'democracia' que predica el racismo, *Granma*, 21 August, p. 2.

J. G. S. (1939) *'Onda Corta'. El Mundo,* **12 October, p. 4**.

Moreno Fraginals, M. (1976) Manuel de Angola. *Granma,* 12 March, p. 2.

Valdés, K. (1976) Las sublevaciones esclavas: primer signo de rebelión contra los explotadores. *Granma*, 9 March, p. 2.

Vázquez Candela, E. (1959) Zona rebelde. Concentración campesina y reforma psicológica. *Revolución*, 28 July, pp. 1, 19.

Yglesia Martínez, T. (1976) Gómez: 'Yo creo en una raza: la humanidad …'. *Granma*, 17 June, p. 2.

Interviews

Avila, A. (2009) Cuban Head Adviser to the literacy campaign, 16 June, La Paz.

Ayma, B. (2009) Bolivian Director of the literacy campaign, 1 August, La Paz.

Index